CHAGALL AND THE ARTISTS OF THE RUSSIAN JEWISH THEATER

CHAGALL AND THE ARTISTS OF THE RUSSIAN JEWISH THEATER

Edited by

Susan Tumarkin Goodman

Essays by

Zvi Gitelman

Susan Tumarkin Goodman

Benjamin Harshav

Vladislav Ivanov

Jeffrey Veidlinger

The Jewish Museum, New York

Under the auspices of the Jewish Theological Seminary of America

Yale University Press

New Haven and London

This book has been published in conjunction with the exhibition *Chagall and the Artists of the Russian Jewish Theater, 1919–1949,* organized by The Jewish Museum.

The Jewish Museum, New York
November 9, 2008–March 22, 2009

Contemporary Jewish Museum, San Francisco
April 19–September 7, 2009

The Jewish Museum
Director of Publications: Michael Sittenfeld
Curatorial Publications Coordinator: Jenny Werbell
Curatorial Program Associate: Afshaan Rahman
Manuscript Editor: Anna Jardine

Yale University Press
Publisher, Art and Architecture: Patricia Fidler
Editor, Art and Architecture: Michelle Komie
Manuscript Editor: Jeff Schier
Production Manager: Mary Mayer
Photo Editor: John Long

Designed by Rita Jules, Miko McGinty, Inc.
Set in Kepler and Knockout
Printed in Singapore by CS Graphics Pte Ltd.

The Jewish Museum
1109 Fifth Avenue
New York, New York 10128
thejewishmuseum.org

Yale University Press
P.O. Box 209040
New Haven, Connecticut 06520–9040
yalebooks.com

Library of Congress Cataloging-in-Publication Data

Chagall and the artists of the Russian Jewish theater / edited by
    Susan Tumarkin Goodman; essays by Zvi Gitelman . . . [et al.].
p. cm.
Published in conjunction with an exhibition held at the Jewish
    Museum, N.Y., Nov. 9, 2008–Mar. 22, 2009, and at the Contem-
    porary Jewish Museum, San Francisco, Apr. 19–Sept. 7, 2009.
Includes bibliographic references and index.
ISBN-13: 978-0-300-11155-2 (hardcover : alk. paper)
ISBN-10: 0-300-11155-x (hardcover : alk. paper)
ISBN-13: 978-0-87334-202-5 (pbk. : alk. paper)
ISBN-10: 0-87334-202-x (pbk. : alk. paper)
1. Jewish theater—Soviet Union—History. 2. Theater, Yiddish—
    Soviet Union—History. 3. Chagall, Marc, 1887–1985. I. Goodman,
    Susan Tumarkin. II. Gitelman, Zvi Y. III. Jewish Museum
    (New York, N.Y.) IV. Contemporary Jewish Museum (San
    Francisco, Calif.)
PN3035.C43 2008
792.089'924047—dc22
2008021042

A catalogue record for this book is available from the
British Library.

This paper meets the requirements of ANSI/NISO z39.48-1992
(Permanence of Paper).
It contains 30 percent postconsumer waste (PCW) and is certified
by the Forest Stewardship Council (FSC).

10 9 8 7 6 5 4 3 2 1

Cover illustration: Marc Chagall, *Introduction to the Jewish Theater* (detail), 1920. The State Tretyakov Gallery, Moscow. © 2007 Artists Rights Society (ARS), New York/ADAGP, Paris
Frontispiece: Natan Altman, *Portrait of Mikhoels*, 1927. Oil on canvas, 41⅜ × 28⅜ in. (105 × 72 cm). A. A. Bakhrushin State Central Theater Museum, Moscow. Art © Estate of Natan Altman/RAO, Moscow/VAGA, New York

CONTENTS

DONORS TO THE EXHIBITION

Chagall and the Artists of the Russian Jewish Theater, 1919–1949,
was made possible by a leadership gift from
Sammy and Aviva Ofer.

Major funding was provided by
the David Berg Foundation,
the Andrea & Charles Bronfman Philanthropies,
the Blanche and Irving Laurie Foundation,
the Lucius N. Littauer Foundation,
the Skirball Foundation,
the Kanbar Charitable Trust,
and The Blavatnik Family Foundation.

Generous support was also provided by
the S. H. and Helen R. Scheuer Family Foundation,
the Leo and Julia Forchheimer Foundation,
the Trust for Mutual Understanding,
and other donors.

The catalogue was funded through
the Dorot Foundation publications endowment.

In San Francisco, the Contemporary Jewish Museum's presentation of
Chagall and the Artists of the Russian Jewish Theater, 1919–1949,
was made possible by the lead support of
the Koret and Taube Foundations
and the Helen Diller Family Foundation.

Austrian Theater Museum, Vienna

A. A. Bakhrushin State Central Theater Museum, Moscow

The Merrill C. Berman Collection, Rye, New York

Beth Hatefutsoth, The Nahum Goldmann Museum of the Jewish Diaspora, Tel Aviv

The Blavatnik Archive Foundation, New York

Eretz Israel Museum, Tel Aviv

Musée National d'Art Moderne, Centre Georges Pompidou, Paris

Habimah National Theater of Israel, Tel Aviv

Israel Goor Theater Archive and Museum, Jerusalem

Vladislav Ivanov, Moscow

The Lotte Jacobi Collection, University of New Hampshire, Durham

The Jewish Theological Seminary of America, New York

Natalia Vovsi-Mikhoels and Nina Mikhoels, Tel Aviv

The Museum of Modern Art, New York

The National Center for Jewish Film at Brandeis University, Waltham, Massachusetts

Private collection, Paris

Russian State Archive of Literature and Art (RGALI), Moscow

Russian State Documentary Films and Photographs Archive, Krasnogorsk

State Tretyakov Gallery, Moscow

Tel Aviv Museum of Art

YIVO Institute for Jewish Research, New York

Ala Zuskin-Perelman, Tel Aviv

FOREWORD

In its examination of the momentous period from 1919 to 1949, *Chagall and the Artists of the Russian Jewish Theater* evokes a history marked by contradiction and tensions. It was an era that began with hope and new possibilities for Russian Jews and ended with fear and tragedy. The early days of the Russian Revolution saw an efflorescence of experimentation in art. Those innovations, combined with a new openness for Jewish cultural expression, found fertile ground in the Jewish theater, which was popular among Jews and non-Jews from its inception through the 1920s and 1930s. This exhibition provides a window into this complex period through a body of groundbreaking theater arts presented in its historical context.

Susan Tumarkin Goodman, Senior Curator at The Jewish Museum, has done a magnificent job organizing and interpreting a vast body of material on the Russian Jewish theater. Her abiding interest in the intersection of Russian art and Jewish culture was reflected in her earlier Jewish Museum exhibitions *Russian Jewish Artists in a Century of Change* (1995), which surveyed the works of Jewish artists from 1890 to 1990, and *Marc Chagall: Early Works from Russian Collections* (2001), which brought together paintings and works on paper by one of the twentieth century's greatest Russian artists. *Chagall and the Artists of the Russian Jewish Theater* focuses on an aspect of the Soviet period—the Jewish theater—that to some degree was represented in the two prior exhibitions, yet here is greatly expanded and illuminated. The extraordinary Chagall murals of 1920 are shown

in the context of the history of the theater for which they were made, and the art of Natan Altman, Robert Falk, Ignaty Nivinsky, and others is seen through drawings, paintings, costume designs, photographs, and maquettes, as well as the film *Jewish Luck*. Many of these items were borrowed from international institutions—including the A. A. Bakhrushin State Central Theater Museum and the Russian State Archive of Literature and Art (RGALI), both in Moscow, and the Israel Goor Theater Archive and Museum in Jerusalem—and have never been seen before by the public.

The exhibition is amplified by this fine publication. Susan Goodman provides an overview of the subject with an introduction to those directors, writers, artists, and actors who participated in the two most important Russian Jewish theater companies—Habima, which performed in Hebrew, and the Moscow State Yiddish Theater (GOSET), which presented plays in the more commonly spoken Yiddish. Essays by Vladimir Ivanov and Jeffrey Veidlinger delve into the histories of Habima and GOSET. Their discussions are complemented by Benjamin Harshav's analysis of Chagall's role in the early years of GOSET and Zvi Gitelman's examination of twentieth-century Soviet Jewry.

Thanks to the work of Susan Goodman and her colleagues, in *Chagall and the Artists of the Russian Jewish Theater* we can imagine rather extraordinary achievements: the theater as a vital and innovative force in spite of the imposition of conformity by the Bolsheviks and by Stalin; and stage productions that provoked tears or uproarious laughter even though much of their audience did not understand the language in which they were presented. The exhibition and book thus raise a curtain on a time and place whose history is like a play in three acts: the Revolution allowed innovation and cultural identity to flourish; political change brought paranoia, repression, and the demise of Jewish theater and culture in Russia; and, in the end, the art of the Russian Jewish theater had a lasting influence on European, Israeli, and American culture, an influence that present-day Jewish society continues to document and discuss.

The Jewish Museum's ability to present this ambitious project has depended on the cooperation and enthusiastic participation of staff, consultants, lenders, and donors. On preceding pages we acknowledge the donors whose financial support enabled the museum to realize its dreams in bringing this subject to public view, and those institutions and individuals who lent works to the exhibition. We thank both groups for their tremendous generosity. We are also grateful for the commitment of The Jewish Museum's Board of Trustees to the mission of exploring the intersection of art and Jewish culture through new scholarship and visual presentations. Their continuing dedication to the museum has enabled it to grow and thrive, and to enrich the experience of our audience immeasurably.

Joan Rosenbaum
Helen Goldsmith Menschel Director
The Jewish Museum

ACKNOWLEDGMENTS

In the newfound artistic freedom of the years following the 1917 Bolshevik Revolution, the Jewish theaters Habima and the Moscow State Yiddish Theater became catalysts for modernist experimentation, revolutionizing acting methods and theater design. Some of the most innovative artists of the time, including Marc Chagall, Natan Altman, Robert Falk, and Ignaty Nivinsky, joined forces with leading Russian Jewish authors, actors, and producers to create a theater experience that would enthrall audiences for decades to come.

I first encountered the artworks created for these theaters over a decade ago, while organizing an exhibition at The Jewish Museum focusing on Russian Jewish artists. Hidden from public view since 1949, these artworks had been largely forgotten. They became available to scholars only when the Soviet Union initiated a new policy of openness (*glasnost*) in 1985. These materials revealed a vibrant theatrical world and, beyond that, served as a window into the Jewish experience under Soviet rule.

Most of the works in the current exhibition and in this volume have never been exhibited or published in Russia or anywhere else. Furthermore, the murals made by Chagall for the Moscow State Yiddish Theater have not previously been shown in the context of materials designed expressly for that theater.

The primary lender to the exhibition is the A. A. Bakhrushin State Central Theater Museum, which has been instrumental in bringing to light the story of the Jewish theater in the Soviet Union. A repository of all forms of Russian theater art since its founding in 1894 in a mansion in central Moscow, the museum was once the home of Alexei Alexandrovich Bakhrushin (1865–1929) and is now a place esteemed by all Russian theater lovers. We wish to thank the administration of the A. A. Bakhrushin State Central Theater Museum, Dmitriy Viktorovich Rodionov, Director; Andrey A. Vorobiev, former Deputy Director for External Affairs and Exhibitions; Tatiana Egorova, Head of the Foreign Relations Department; and Ekaterina Kartamysheva, Scientific Worker, Scenery Department, for having made available works from the museum's remarkable collection. Their commitment was essential to this project, and I am grateful for their involvement.

The drawings in the Bakhrushin collection were for many years kept by Irena Duksina. Her intimate knowledge of this material was greatly valued and extremely important for our research. We are deeply appreciative of her willingness to share her expertise with us.

The Russian State Archive of Literature and Art (RGALI) also made available its extensive archive. Its involvement in this project cannot be overestimated, and I greatly appreciate RGALI's willingness to lend materials to the exhibition. My sincere thanks to the Director Tatiana Mikhailovna Gorjaeva and Ksenia Yakovleva, Exhibition Curator.

We are exceedingly thankful to the State Tretyakov Gallery for agreeing to share the murals made by Chagall for the Moscow State Yiddish Theater. We thank Lydia Iovleva, First Deputy Director, Tatiana Gubanova, Head of International Relations and Overseas Exhibition Department, and Ekaterina L. Selezneva, Chief of Conservation.

The majority of artworks documenting the achievements of Habima as well as a number of artifacts from the Moscow State Yiddish Theater are in the collection of The Israel Goor Theatre Archive and Museum in Jerusalem. We are grateful to Director Luba Yuniverg for making available works from their remarkable collection. The Habima National Theater of Israel in Tel Aviv kindly agreed to share original costumes brought to Israel from Russia by the troupe. Our gratitude also goes to Ruth Tonn Mendelson, Head of the Artistic Department at Habima; Conservator Sigal Benzoor for her efforts in the preservation of these costumes; Zippi Rosenne, Director of the

Visual Documentation Center at Beth Hatefutsoth— The Nahum Goldmann Museum of the Jewish Diaspora; and Nitza Behrouzi, Curator of the Ethnography Pavilion at Eretz Israel Museum.

At the Musée National d'Art Moderne at the Centre Georges Pompidou in Paris, Curator Didier Schulmann was a gracious colleague, showing me less-known but essential works by Chagall and generously agreeing to lend them to the exhibition. Other lenders, listed on page vi, played a vital part in the success of this project, and I am thankful for their participation.

Descendants of some of the important figures in the Moscow State Yiddish Theater played important roles in the exhibition. The daughters of Solomon Mikhoels, Natalia Mikhoels-Vovsi and Nina Mikhoels, have provided invaluable insights. Victoria and Katia Bishofs, Mikhoels's granddaughter and great granddaughter, respectively, have graciously made themselves available, providing information and assistance during the planning phases. Ala Zuskin-Perelman, the daughter of actors Benjamin Zuskin and Eda Berkovskaia, has been extraordinarily helpful in sharing her extensive knowledge, and in lending us documents and photographs.

I am grateful as well to Bella Meyer and Meret Meyer Graber, granddaughters of Marc Chagall, for their support of this exhibition.

There are many individuals whose involvement was indispensable to this exhibition. Professor Alexander M. Shedrinsky helped enormously with advice and logistical suggestions, and we are deeply grateful for his assistance in navigating the Russian loan process. My sincere gratitude to the art professionals, scholars, critics, and art dealers in Russia, Israel, France, and the United States who have given generously of their time: Faina Balakovskaya; Sonya Bekkerman, Head of the Russian Art Department at Sotheby's New York; Faina Burko; Julie Chervinsky,

Access Industries, New York; Jesse Aaron Cohen, Photo and Film Archivist, YIVO Institute for Jewish Research; Daniel Dratwa, Curator, Jewish Museum, Belgium; Marina Drozdova; Olga Gershenson, Assistant Professor, University of Massachusetts, Amherst; Meira Geyra, Artistic Director, American-Israel Cultural Foundation, Inc., Tel Aviv; Mel Gordon, Professor, University of California, Berkeley; Marat and Julia Guelman; Aleksandr Hochinsky; Sherry Hyman, Director of the Archives and Records Department, American Jewish Joint Distribution Committee; Mikhail Kamensky; Sharon Levy, Dovetail Productions, Inc., New York; Michelle Margolis, Special Collections Assistant, Jewish Theological Seminary Library, New York; Robert Marx, Vice President, The Fan Fox and Leslie R. Samuels Foundation, Inc.; Natalia Metelitsa, Director, St. Petersburg State Museum of Theater and Music; Mikhail Mitsel, Archivist, American Jewish Joint Distribution Committee; Maria Oleneva; Beátrice Picon-Vallin, Director of the CNRS Performing Arts Research Laboratory, Paris; Mila Razuvanova; Alan Rosenfeld; Dr. Aleksandra Shatskikh; Eve Sicular, Metropolitan Klezmer; Kris Stone; Jacob Baal Teshuva; Zelfira Tregulova, Deputy Director, Exhibitions, Moscow Kremlin Museums; Vladimir Tsarenkov; Alla Verlotsky, President, Seagull Films, New York; and Fred Wasserman, Deputy Director for Programs, Contemporary Jewish Museum, San Francisco.

We deeply appreciate the assistance of Nicolas Iljine, whose professionalism and insight have been important to this project and to The Jewish Museum.

Joan Rosenbaum, Helen Goldsmith Menschel Director at The Jewish Museum, has given her wholehearted support to the exhibition from the outset. Her recognition of the project's importance was a constant source of encouragement. Ruth Beesch, the Deputy Director for Program, provided shrewd advice and creative solutions to the numerous administrative and artistic issues. Norman L. Kleeblatt, Susan and Elihu Rose Chief Curator, gave me sage counsel on many aspects of the exhibition and, as always, has been a valued colleague.

This project is profoundly indebted to Jeffrey Veidlinger for his groundbreaking book on the Moscow State Yiddish Theater. His involvement in the organizational phases of our exhibition was invaluable. We have also closely consulted the work of Benjamin Harshav, particularly his recent book *The Moscow Yiddish Theater: Art on Stage in the Time of Revolution*. Professors Harshav and Veidlinger have kindly offered counsel and answered many queries as we worked on this project. It is a pleasure to include their essays in this volume along with the contributions of our other distinguished scholars, Zvi Gitelman and Vladislav Ivanov. My thanks to Galya Korovina for her translation of Mr. Ivanov's text, and to Terry Taffer for her work on the glossary and timeline.

Michael Sittenfeld, Director of Publications at The Jewish Museum, approached this project with his usual insight and alacrity as he oversaw the editing and production of this volume. I am grateful as well to Jenny Werbell, Curatorial Publications Coordinator, who played a central role at every stage of creating this book, and Anna Jardine, whose exacting eye improved the manuscript in countless ways. We are indebted to Miko McGinty and Rita Jules, who conceived the attractive design of this publication as well as the exhibition graphics. Our copublisher, Yale University Press, embraced this project from its inception and ensured the high quality of this volume. I thank Patricia Fidler, Publisher, Art and Architecture; Michelle Komie, Editor, Art and Architecture; Jeff Schier, Manuscript Editor; Mary Mayer, Production Manager; and John Long, Photo Editor. Also of great help at Yale was Jonathan Brent, Editorial Director, who took an avid interest in this book at an early stage and shared his considerable wisdom with us.

Adam Rolston, assisted by Hilary Fulmer, created an effective exhibition design that thoughtfully integrates the works of art with archival objects and other materials. I extend my thanks to two individuals who brought their expertise at various points to the media component of the exhibition: Sam Ball, Director, and Kate Stilley Steiner, Editor, of Citizen Film, San Francisco; and Robin White Owen of MediaCombo, New York.

Many other colleagues at The Jewish Museum were essential to the realization of this project. My deep appreciation goes to Afshaan Rahman, Curatorial Program Associate, for her tireless and efficient efforts throughout the preparation of this exhibition. She was preceded in her role by former Jewish Museum staff members Jessica Williams and Alyssa Phoebus, who both made countless contributions to this project. Sally Lindenbaum performed many invaluable tasks with grace and good humor, and Yocheved Muffs graciously and skillfully assisted me with research and catalogue-related details. I offer heartfelt thanks to the many interns who have worked with me on Soviet Jewish theater in the last few years: Elana Bensoul, Alec Burko, Adam Eaker, Amanda Elbogen, Oksana Fedorko, Katherine Gulick, Andrew Lee, Yael Levy, Lauren Pollock, Rebecca Pristoop, Ekaterina Prokopenko, Chana Prus, Liba Rubenstein, Tamar Rubin, and Patricia Tuori.

Jane Rubin, Director of Collections and Exhibitions, and Amanda Thompson, Assistant Registrar, handled the multitude of arrangements necessary for the gathering, shipping, and insuring of the artworks. Dolores Pukki, Coordinator of Exhibitions, provided much-appreciated help with the budget and other logistical matters. Anne Scher, Director of Communications, and Alex Wittenberg, Communications Coordinator, deftly managed the publicity for the exhibition. Sarah Himmelfarb, Associate Director of Development, Institutional Giving, and Susan Wyatt, Senior Grants Officer, did a remarkable job in helping to secure funds for the exhibition.

I am grateful as well to other Jewish Museum colleagues for their many contributions to this project: Sabina Avanesova, Executive Assistant to the Director; Nelly Silagy Benedek, Director of Education; Andrew Ingall, Assistant Curator; Al Lazarte, Director of Operations; Karen Levitov, Associate Curator; Elisabeth Manzi, Collections Manager; Niger Miles, Audiovisual Coordinator; Jennifer Mock, Public Programs Coordinator; Valeriy Ognev, Building Engineer; Frank Sargenti, Storeroom Coordinator; Nikolay Silenko, Building Engineer; Katharine Staelin, Assistant Curator, Web Projects; and Aviva Weintraub, Associate Curator.

Throughout the lengthy process of planning and completing this project, the one constant has been the encouragement and support of my husband, Jerry Goodman, to whom I extend my deepest thanks.

Susan Tumarkin Goodman
Senior Curator
The Jewish Museum

A vexed issue in the English rendering of the Russian language is the translation of individuals' names. For example, the name of the director of the Moscow State Yiddish Theater is given here as Aleksei Granovsky. While authoritative scholars refer to him alternately as Aleksandr, we have used the first name accepted by most native Russian speakers. We have applied the same principle to other names in this book.

In Russian and in Yiddish the same word signifies both "Yiddish" and "Jewish." Therefore, in Russian and Yiddish texts the term "Yiddish theater" also means "Jewish theater." This explains inconsistencies in scholarly references to Habima and the Moscow State Yiddish Theater (GOSET). In this volume, "Jewish theaters" denotes both Habima and GOSET.

Because there were a number of State Yiddish Theaters throughout the Soviet Union in the 1920s and 1930s, in this book GOSET is the designation for the Moscow State Yiddish Theater. The name of GOSET evolved as follows:

1919   The theater was established in Petrograd as the Yiddish Chamber Theater (*Evreysky kamerny teatr* in Russian, and *Yidisher kamer teater* in Yiddish)

1920   With its move to Moscow, the theater was brought under the auspices of the Theatrical Department of the Commissariat of Enlightenment and was renamed the State Yiddish Chamber Theater (*Gosudarstvenny evreysky kamerny teatr* in Russian, and *Melukhisher yidisher kamer teater* in Yiddish), commonly referred to in both Russian and Yiddish by the acronym GOSEKT.

1922   GOSEKT relocated to its permanent home, a larger theater on Malaia Bronnaia in Moscow.

1924   The word "chamber" was dropped, and the theater was renamed the State Yiddish Theater (*Gosudarstvenny evreysky teatr* in Russian, and *Melukhisher yidisher teater* in Yiddish) and became known in Russian and Yiddish by the acronym GOSET.

Other State Yiddish Theaters included BelGOSET (Belorussian State Yiddish Theater), UkrGOSET (Ukrainian State Yiddish Theater), and later BirGOSET (Birobidzhaner State Yiddish Theater). In order to distinguish GOSET from the regional theaters, it was sometimes referred to with the acronym MGET (Moscow State Yiddish Theater).

Marc Chagall's works in this volume were sometimes not dated at the time they were created. In a number of instances, the artist ascribed earlier dates to his works. This fact accounts for some of the discrepancies between the dates on the works and the actual dates of execution. A few of the drawings in this exhibition are dated 1919, but Chagall spent that entire year in Vitebsk and was not to begin working with GOSEKT until 1920.

SOVIET JEWISH THEATER IN A WORLD OF MORAL COMPROMISE

Susan Tumarkin Goodman

> In a totalitarian state the theater is not merely a place for entertainment, but . . . a place in which a message can be sent out in veiled language that one would not dare to write on paper or to speak out loud, for fear of the authorities.
>
> —Ala Zuskin-Perelman, daughter of the GOSET actor Benjamin Zuskin

The 1948 murder of Solomon Mikhoels, the most gifted actor on the Soviet Yiddish stage, by Joseph Stalin's secret police not only meant the death of a great performer—it also sounded the death knell of Jewish theater in the Soviet Union. That Stalin ordered Mikhoels's assassination demonstrates the growth in importance of the Jewish cultural institutions that the October 1917 Bolshevik Revolution had encouraged and that Soviet authorities later sought to suppress.

The ultimate clash between the political aspirations of the Soviet regime, and the art and culture created during the first decade after the Revolution, cannot be better represented than in the singed edges of a drawing for a costume design for the play *God of*

Vengeance, presented by the Moscow State Yiddish Theater, or GOSET (fig. 1). This was one of many documents and artworks burned in a 1953 fire of suspicious origin in Moscow's Bakhrushin State Central Theater Museum, and it serves as evidence of an attempt to eradicate the legacy of the Jewish theater.

At a time when traditional Jewish identities in the former Pale of Settlement were disintegrating, and the future of a secular Jewish society was in flux, the artists, actors, and directors of the Jewish theater assumed great significance as key constituents of a changing Jewish community. During the years in which they flourished, two theater companies, the Hebrew-language Habima ("the stage") and the Yiddish-language GOSET, represented the foremost expression of Jewish culture and identity in the Soviet Union.

The theater was able to retain a collective Jewish consciousness by recalling old folk legends or examining past and contemporary writings, and turning them into stylized theater productions. According to the art historian Avram Kampf, "If there was a theater,

FIG. 1 Isaac Rabinovich, *Shloyme (Costume Design for Mikhail Shteiman in God of Vengeance),* 1921. Pencil on paper, 12¾ × 8 in. (32.5 × 20.5 cm). A. A. Bakhrushin State Central Theater Museum, Moscow.
Shloyme is Yankel Tshaptshovitsh's pimp, a handsome, arrogant man whom playwright Sholem Asch characterized thus: "He is dressed like a good-for-nothing—high boots and a short jacket—and he acts like one."

МОСКОВСКИЙ ГОСУДАРСТВЕННЫЙ ЕВРЕЙСКИЙ КАМЕРНЫЙ ТЕАТР

FIG. 2 Members of GOSET in front of their theater on Malaia Bronnaia, Moscow, 1924. Photograph, 6¾ × 8¼ in. (17 × 21 cm). The Russian State Archive of Literature and Art, Moscow

there had to be a community; and if there was a community there had to be a theater. The existence of one was proof of the existence of the other" in the Soviet Union.[1] Natalia Vovsi-Mikhoels, daughter of Solomon Mikhoels, remembered the vibrant spirit of the Jewish theater: "Jews regarded [GOSET] as their home, their club, their synagogue, a place to [gather] and reminisce, a place to meet their friends . . . a place where they could talk Yiddish freely and without lowering their voices" (fig. 2).[2]

For a time, these two companies vied for preeminence as the national Jewish theater, reaching their apex in the years after the Revolution. Performing in Hebrew, a language largely unfamiliar to the majority of the approximately 2.5 million Russian Jews, Habima

finally felt compelled to leave the country in 1926—a reflection of shifting state policies (fig. 3). The other company, the Moscow State Yiddish Chamber Theater (GOSEKT; it became GOSET in 1924), drew upon the latest theatrical techniques. It performed in Yiddish, the primary language of most Eastern European Jews, but was forced to disband in 1949. Both companies captivated Russian and European audiences with their innovative performances.

As a modern, secular institution, the Jewish theater had its roots in Purim plays, which during the festival season dramatized the life of Esther and other biblical figures. There was also a tradition of performing songs and comical skits in provincial locales. In the mid-1870s Avrom Goldfadn, a Romanian Jewish folk dramatist, was the first to succeed in forming a lasting professional theater for the Jewish masses. His success spurred the creation of wandering troupes in Eastern Europe, and writers began to meet the growing demand for a Yiddish repertory.[3] These performances were often melodramas, comedies, and farces set in a Jewish context. However, the growth of Jewish theater throughout the Pale of Settlement was halted in 1883, when the tsarist government squelched the culture of ethnic minorities in Russia, including a ban on Yiddish performances.[4] Despite this ban, in the years leading up to the Revolution the Jewish theater continued to survive underground, and in 1912 there were sixteen Yiddish companies in Russia.

A loosening of the restrictions against the Jews started with the great displacements of World War I. The Bolsheviks, who took power in October 1917, supported the efforts of various minorities to form organizations defined by their national identities. In January 1918 the concept of "Jewish nationality" in the Soviet Union was approved, and Jews were granted legal status by the regime. Moscow, which until the Revolution had been closed to Jews, except for those with special permits, now opened to an influx of Jewish intelligentsia.[5]

The results of abolishing the restrictive and repressive tsarist anti-Jewish laws were almost immediate, resulting in an unprecedented outburst of cultural activity. Jewish actors, musicians, and other theater artists were encouraged to respond to the immense changes brought about by the Revolution, and they sought to distinguish themselves from the earlier traditional Jewish theater, known for its farcical style of acting. Bolshevik theoreticians in the 1920s envisioned the theater as an ideal medium to communicate what they viewed as "revolutionary culture." They believed theatrical performances could influence and enlighten the populace more readily than could lectures or books, particularly when the overwhelming majority was still illiterate.

In the years following the Revolution, the regime saw no contradiction between an expression of national culture and a devotion to revolutionary ideals. However, it failed to produce a proletarian ethos dedicated to its own network of state-controlled institutions. Thus the government actually encouraged the establishment of theaters among all nationalities and permitted a variety of artistic forms, without promoting any specific ideological or aesthetic direction. However, to demonstrate the involvement of Soviet national minorities in building the new state,

FIG. 3 Members of Habima in the theater lobby, Lower Kislovka, Moscow, 1926. Photograph, 10⅜ × 14 in. (26.3 × 35.4 cm). Courtesy of Vladislav Ivanov, Moscow

FIG. 4 Alexandra Exter, *Maquette, Famira Kafared*, 1987, reconstruction after 1916 original. Wood, cardboard, fabric, gouache, 23⅛ × 33½ × 19⅜ in. (58.7 × 85 × 49.3 cm). A. A. Bakhrushin State Central Theater Museum, Moscow

FIG. 5 Members of GOSET, left to right: Boris Ingster, Alexander Budeysky, Michail Steiman, Aleksei Granovsky, Lev Pulver, Benjamin Zuskin, Helena Menes, Solomon Mikhoels, Moscow, 1925

the authorities supported an ambivalent policy as far as the Jewish minority was concerned. It gave Habima as well as GOSEKT the moral and financial support they required from the newly instituted Commissariat of Enlightenment.[6] Thus both Jewish companies were encouraged to develop a national theater based in Moscow, the center of the nation's cultural life.[7]

To a large degree the Jewish theater was influenced by the mass pageants, street performances, Russian circus, cabaret, and music-hall burlesque of the early twentieth century. Acrobatic acting, movable sets, and innovative production techniques and stage ideas were evident in the work of such leading figures of the Russian theater as Konstantin Stanislavsky, Aleksandr Tairov, Vsevolod Meyerhold, and Evgeny Vakhtangov (fig. 4). Jewish artists absorbed the language of revolutionary art movements in Europe and Russia, notably Cubism, Futurism, and Constructivism, which came to be identified with their initial bold theatrical experiments.

The first years of both Habima and GOSEKT were fraught with difficulties. Even in Moscow, capital of a regime that ostensibly had created a "new order" following tsarist oppression, the theater companies were afflicted by economic deprivation as well as political uncertainty, which were of course common for all Soviet citizens. The postrevolutionary hardships faced by members of the Jewish theater illuminate the delicate social and political conditions under which they worked, especially the constantly shifting attitudes toward Jews. Compounding their problems

was the fact that members of both companies had only recently become part of the mainstream; they were theatrical novices, ignorant of Russian as well as broader European culture, and lacked funds, training, and experience. It seemed remarkable that they could succeed in an artistic climate where avant-garde theater flourished.

While Habima and GOSEKT excelled in Expressionist staging and were suffused with Jewish consciousness, their message and approach differed. Nevertheless, both troupes believed that it was their mission to create a Jewish national theater, and that through their language they would enrich the lives of former victims of tsarist oppression and pogroms. Despite the difficulties the leadership of the companies had to overcome, including work with a language and a cultural heritage not entirely familiar to them, the opportunities were tremendous (fig. 5). In a period of optimism and apparent promise, the possibility of founding an entirely new theatrical undertaking was irresistible, and directors of both theaters had the chance to mold their companies out of a group of raw, inexperienced young actors.

The two companies reflected opposite ends of the ideological-aesthetic spectrum. Because its founder, Naum Tsemakh, demonstrated fierce passion and zeal, Habima initially received official permission to organize.[8] But within a few years some Soviet officials viewed the company as too esoteric to reach the Jewish proletariat. Nevertheless, Habima flourished against all predictions, and its productions of Jewish mystical and folkloric plays gained attention for their rich visual effects (fig. 6). In contrast, GOSET mirrored everyday reality in its dramas, drew upon the language of the Jewish working class, and was intrinsically valuable as a means to reach the Jewish masses.

The Habima troupe was committed to the renewal of Jewish national life and the realization of the Zionist dream. They identified with the tragedy of the Jews' shared national experience. Employing Expressionistic means for theatrical purposes, Habima sought to serve as a vehicle for the revival of the Hebrew language, and as a significant voice in a general Jewish cultural renaissance. Paradoxically, this eventually alienated many of those to whom it was most intended to appeal; Hebrew was unfamiliar to the majority of Russian Jews, who considered it a language meant for prayer (fig. 7). Furthermore, modern Hebrew was linked to the Land of Israel, which was

FIG. 6 *(above)* Naum Tsemakh, founder of Habima, in his study with costume designs for *The Dybbuk,* Moscow, 1923. Courtesy of Vladislav Ivanov, Moscow

FIG. 7 *(below)* Natan Altman, *Synagogue Interior (Set Model for The Dybbuk),* 1922 (reconstructed later). Wood, metal, and cloth, 11½ × 22½ × 15½ in. (29.2 × 57.2 × 39.4 cm). Israel Goor Theater Archive and Museum, Jerusalem.

The first act of *The Dybbuk* takes place in a synagogue, where a white background formed by Cubo-Futurist overlapping planes accentuates the centrality of the ark. The Hebrew text hanging from the ceiling reads, "Hear, oh Israel," which is the beginning of the *Shm'a* prayer, and is the most fundamental statement of faith in Jewish tradition.

FIG. 8 Natan Altman, *Design for the Stock Exchange, Petrograd, for the Second Congress of the Comintern*, 1920. Pencil and watercolor on cardboard, 16 x 26⅛ in. (40.6 x 66.3 cm). © St. Petersburg State Museum of Theater and Music

geographically and conceptually remote. Habima was, in reality, a theater without a public.

The power of its art allowed Habima to survive intense ideological attacks, while it yielded profound theatrical experiences. The productions delighted Jewish and non-Jewish audiences alike. For those who understood the language, the sound of Hebrew on the stage was an emotional experience. For those who did not, spoken Hebrew was now introduced—and came to be expected—in a new and secular setting. Without comprehending the language, audiences were won over by the strength of a performance, the scenic design, or the actors' emotional intensity.

Tsemakh's determination to create a Hebrew theater convinced Stanislavsky, the director of the Moscow Art Theater, to appoint his Russian-Armenian protégé Evgeny Vakhtangov to serve as Habima's director. After joining the company in 1917, Vakhtangov remained with it until his death in 1922. He was responsible for Habima's most acclaimed production, S. An-sky's *The Dybbuk*. In order to adapt the play to the spirit of the times, Vakhtangov emphasized its social meaning, showing compassion for the wretched life of the shtetl inhabitants. As a student of Stanislavsky and a devoted adherent of his acting method, Vakhtangov searched for new theatrical forms to convey deeply moving psychological portrayals.[9] Without veering from faithfulness to real life, he brought tragic, grotesque, and even comedic qualities to the performance. He shortened certain sections of An-sky's original text, and elaborated on

the choreography of the section known as the "Beggars' Dance," which represented the abject conditions of the poverty-stricken shtetl. Natan Altman's sets and costumes combined traditional Jewish folk-art motifs with a stylized Cubo-Futurist ambience to conjure an intense, oppressive atmosphere (fig. 8).

Ultimately, Habima's preoccupation with mysticism and national rebirth alienated the Jewish public, while the Soviet regime feared that it endangered the embrace of Soviet ideology by Jews. Despite Stanislavsky's and Vakhtangov's efforts, there seemed to be no place in postrevolutionary Moscow for a "reactionary and Zionist" theater, since such a "bourgeois nationalist" institution was viewed as subversive. Habima was given permission to tour Europe and left the country in January 1926, never to return. This was a propitious move because its Zionist message was in conflict with the new Soviet dogma. And indeed, the following year all publications in Hebrew were halted.

Habima's departure left only the barest of traces on the Jewish community although its productions, notably *The Dybbuk* and *The Golem*, with their stylized performances, earned a reputation far beyond the Soviet Union.

Maintaining that Yiddish was the mother tongue, or the true language of all Eastern European Jewish communities, the Yiddish theater company assumed that Jewish audiences would respond to its productions with a sense of national pride and cultural identity. Founded by Aleksei Granovsky as the Yiddish Chamber Theater in Petrograd (St. Petersburg) in 1918, the company moved to a ninety-seat theater in Moscow. In 1921 the theater fell under the control of the Soviet government, which renamed it the State Yiddish Chamber Theater, or GOSEKT. Two years after its 1922 relocation to a larger, five-hundred-seat theater, it was given a new name: State Yiddish Theater, or GOSET.

The members of GOSET aspired to reject religion and replace it with a secular Jewish culture. This is evident in one of its first plays, *God of Vengeance*, a tale of a Jew who runs a brothel while trying to raise a perfectly respectable daughter in the same house.

Granovsky, who was as passionate about his company as Tsemakh and Vakhtangov were about Habima, was an acculturated Jew from an affluent, Russian-speaking family and relatively unfamiliar with Yiddish and Jewish cultural lore. He founded the Yiddish theater after working with, and coming under the strong influence of, the director Max Reinhardt in Germany. Granovsky was moved by the spirit of experimentation of the Russian theater and wished to capture it in his own productions. Greatly affected by trends in Europe, he aspired to remove any hint of the old Jewish ghetto theater from performances, and to build an institution equal to other Soviet avant-garde troupes. As he saw it, the Yiddish theater was "a temple of shining art, of joyous creation, where the prayer is sung in the Yiddish language."[10]

The approach of the actors and the style of future Yiddish theater productions derived largely from the work of Marc Chagall. In 1920, Granovsky sought a designer who would represent a Jewish viewpoint and also be willing to experiment. He asked Chagall, who was already famous in Russia, to design the sets and costumes for the troupe's inaugural production in Moscow, *An Evening of Sholem Aleichem*, which consisted of three one-act plays. Chagall, who had previously worked on theater projects—most of which had not been realized—was delighted with the opportunity to execute some of his theatrical ideas. Abram Efros, GOSEKT's artistic director, was particularly excited to engage Chagall. He was convinced that the young man from Vitebsk could combine the new ideas of the Western European avant-garde with a deep love for everyday Russian Jewish life. Chagall's antinaturalistic, Expressionist style would, Efros believed, fuel the radical changes that he and Granovsky wanted for the Yiddish theater, and thus the artist was given wide latitude. Chagall went far beyond traditional concepts and united all aspects of theatrical presentation in an integrated whole, creating murals that covered the entirety of the interior space.

He needed little more than a month to complete not only the walls of the small theater but also the ceiling and the stage curtain. Solomon Mikhoels, the company's principal actor, understood fully the unique character and energy of Chagall's line and color, and learned how to translate them into his acting style onstage.

Natan Altman, like Chagall, threw himself into the Soviet Union's new artistic climate, accepting nontheatrical political commissions while designing sets for Karl Gutzkow's *Uriel Acosta* at GOSEKT and, as mentioned, for *The Dybbuk* at Habima (fig. 9). The Cubo-Futurist sets in these productions suggest Aleksandra Exter's design motifs as well as elements from traditional Jewish folk art.[11]

If Habima was eventually considered by the authorities a "bourgeois nationalist" enterprise, the Yiddish Theater, performing in the everyday language of Jewish workers, was seen as the theater that could cast light on the worst aspects of capitalism and emphasize the death of the old shtetl lifestyle. As a result, it had the support of the Yevsektsia, the Jewish Section of the Communist Party.

Both Vakhtangov and Granovsky used avant-garde strategies to rework traditional Jewish sources, transforming familiar ethnic material—words, gestures, melodies—into an engaging and effective theatrical experience.[12] What were considered gesticulations typical of the shtetl were restaged as overtly artistic gestures, and by 1922, with the theatrical successes of Habima's *The Dybbuk* and GOSEKT's *The Sorceress: An Eccentric Jewish Play*, both theaters proved themselves fully supportive of the avant-garde.[13]

It is impossible to view the costumes and set designs for the two theaters by Chagall, Altman, Isaac Rabinovich, Robert Falk, and other painters without considering the influences of Russian avant-garde art. In the early 1920s the relationship between the avant-garde and the traditional systems of acting was still antagonistic. Habima tended to reflect Expressionist forms of theater grounded in Stanislavsky's method taught at the Moscow Art Theater. Granovsky's mentors for GOSET were the avant-garde director Vsevolod Meyerhold, as well as the most advanced stage designers and fine artists of the era, including Kazimir Malevich, Aleksandra Exter, Liubov Popova, and Varvara Stepanova. Granovsky found greater inspiration in Meyerhold's nonrealistic experiments, and he was attracted specifically by the concept of "biomechanics," which saw the human body as a trained machine to which the

FIG. 9 Left to right: Aleksei Granovsky, Natan Altman, and Isaac Rabinovich, Moscow, c. 1922. Photograph, 4⅜ × 6⅛ in. (11 × 15.5 cm). A. A. Bakhrushin State Central Theater Museum, Moscow

actor would apply stylized units of movement to gestures and expressions.[14]

While GOSET and Habima received the highest acclaim for their ethnic theatricality, the Berlin critic Alfred Kerr singled out the GOSET performers' extraordinarily expressive style. The actors, he observed, "talk not only with their hands but almost with their hair, their soles, their calves, their toes."[15] As if the companies were in a competition, the prominent author Maxim Gorky, an enthusiastic supporter of Habima, wrote of its 1919 performance of David Pinsky's *The Eternal Jew:* "As the curtain rose, the sheer power of the set penetrated my heart and transferred me through two thousand years back to a small town in Judea. As the play progressed, I found myself living the day of the disaster, the destruction of Jerusalem."[16]

In fact, their respective languages, one sacred and one secular, created a sharp divide between the two ensembles. Conscious of its spiritual and national roles, Habima was known for the aura of tragedy that imbued its performances, while GOSET emphasized the comedic, joyful aspects of its productions. Later GOSET performances were tinged with a sense of

the grotesque and the fantastic in the depiction of ghetto types and their environment. Granovsky employed mass crowd scenes, choral music, and group dances, situated on multilevel Constructivist sets with ladders, ropes, slanted planes, and steps so the actors could address one another and the audience simultaneously. He combined classic Yiddish texts, Constructivist-inspired set designs, and an exaggerated acting style, thus transforming "ordinary" shtetl scenes into unreal phantasmagoric tales.

Drawing from Avrom Goldfadn, and such writers as Sholem Aleichem, I. L. Peretz, and Mendele Mocher Seforim, Granovsky eliminated anything that might appear ideologically questionable or improper for a Soviet audience. But he also "took advantage of the censors' lack of familiarity with the Yiddish language and Jewish culture to insert symbolic protests into his plays, cryptically paying tribute to the Zionists and to those who believed that Jews had no future in the Soviet Union."[17] These theatrical satires scoffed openly at Jewish religious traditions as well as at entrepreneurs of the nascent Soviet New Economic Plan, a limited postrevolutionary initiative intended to allow private commerce in the wake of widespread hunger. GOSET's most virulent "attack on the old shtetl culture came in 1925, in a dramatic version of Peretz' surrealistic and controversial play [*At Night in the Old Marketplace: A Tragic Carnival*]."[18] According to one audience member, the Ukrainian-born American artist Louis Lozowick, "It revealed a poignant scenario, creating a strong indictment of the old and decrepit Jewish world. . . . The exaggerated make-up, the near frenzied movement, the acrobatics, grotesquerie, and the background music held one spellbound, and well nigh obliterated whatever message the play meant to convey."[19] In contrast, the German Jewish critic and essayist Walter Benjamin, who visited Moscow in late 1926, noted in his diaries that Granovsky had "created a farcical, anti-religious, and, from outward appearances, fairly anti-Semitic form of satirical comedy."[20]

Other productions followed, to great acclaim. But like so many other innovative individuals of his time, Granovsky overestimated official Soviet tolerance for experimental work. As Stalinist repression intensified, the director was charged with "right-wing deviation" and "bourgeois formalism." Even Yiddish-speaking audiences grew uncomfortable with GOSET's distortion of naturalistic dramaturgy. When Granovsky was allowed to take the company on what would be a triumphant tour of Western Europe in 1928, he defected and the company returned to Moscow without him (fig. 10). It is not surprising that Granovsky, an independent, artistic spirit, found the increasingly rigid political constraints of the post-Lenin period intolerable.[21] His name was officially excised from GOSET publicity, and the company was compelled to perform under heavy censorship and new ideological strictures.

After serving as a major player in the administration of GOSET alongside Granovsky, the lead actor, Solomon Mikhoels, assumed the directorship. In this new position, he became the most visible Jewish personality in what was the most visible Jewish institution in the Soviet Union.

Visitors to Moscow were advised to see GOSET's latest, state-approved productions, which, despite financial and political problems, drew hundreds of people each night. This helped transform the capital into one of the most dynamic centers of Jewish culture in the world. As with Habima, Jews and non-Jews alike attended GOSET's Yiddish productions.[22] Because the performances were dominated by song, dance, and elaborate sets and costumes, they could be appreciated even with little understanding of the dialogue. Mikhoels and fellow actor Benjamin Zuskin became

FIG. 10 Chagall (standing in second row, far right) with GOSET company at his villa near Paris, June 1928. Courtesy of Ala Zuskin-Perelman, Or-Yehuda, Israel

reigning stars in Moscow's theater world (fig. 11). Their ironic and original characterizations, their artistic sensibility and timing, together with their expressive acting, were widely praised in international journals, and Granovsky was considered to be "the impresario of Yiddish modernism."[23] The vast majority of GOSET's audiences came for the theatrical rather than the linguistic experience; a Russian-language synopsis of the Yiddish was sold each night to as many as two-thirds of the theatergoers.[24] For the government organizations that "sought to use the theater as a showpiece to demonstrate for foreigners the thriving culture of Soviet national minorities, the ethnic composition of the in-house audience made little difference."[25]

By the time GOSET staged *King Lear* in 1935, the political climate had become increasingly restrictive, following the launching, in the previous year, of Stalin's purges of Communist Party leaders and functionaries, a time known as the Great Terror (fig. 12). As requirements for an acceptable repertory became more rigid, the original avant-garde principles were

replaced by the doctrine of Socialist Realism. This was officially codified in 1934 at the First Writers' Congress, which glorified Soviet achievement and celebrated an idealized heroic proletariat.[26] Politics now shaped the direction of all theaters.[27] This new climate took a toll on GOSET, which had already suffered through a protracted transitional crisis after Granovsky's departure.

As artistic and political concerns came into further conflict, Mikhoels, Zuskin, and fellow company members "feared for their lives," as did other Jewish intellectuals in the Soviet Union.[28] To avoid problems

FIG. 11 *(left)* Solomon Mikhoels as Benjamin and Benjamin Zuskin as Senderl di Yidene (Senderl the Jewish Woman) in *The Travels of Benjamin the Third,* 1927. Photograph, 7 × 4½ in. (17.8 × 11.4 cm). Courtesy of Ala Zuskin-Perelman, Or-Yehuda, Israel

FIG. 12 *(above)* Solomon Mikhoels as King Lear, 1935. Photograph, 6⅛ × 4¾ in. (15.6 × 12.1 cm). Beth Hatefutsoth, Photo Archive, Tel Aviv, courtesy of Zuskin Collection

FIG. 13 Aleksandr Tyshler, *Costume Design for Boytre the Bandit*, 1936. Watercolor and pencil on paper, 16⅛ × 11¾ in. (41.1 × 29.8 cm). A. A. Bakhrushin State Central Theater Museum, Moscow. Art © Estate of Aleksandr Tyshler/RAO, Moscow/VAGA, New York

with authorities, GOSET began to present plays from an international repertory, including Shakespeare. By now deemed one of the nation's greatest actors, Mikhoels garnered high praise for his performance as Lear, and audiences attended the play in record numbers.[29] Some observers maintained that his was one of the greatest renditions of the tragic figure. The British actor, director, and Shakespearean scholar Gordon Craig wrote: "Since the time of my teacher, the great [Sir Henry] Irving, I can recall no such acting performance to move me so deeply, as Mikhoels' playing King Lear."[30]

Despite the constraints on the company, and the terror under which many members lived, GOSET continued to flourish, performing Socialist Realist plays into the 1930s. During those years its members had to carefully negotiate the obstacles of the Stalinist cultural revolution. By and large the plays performed under the leadership of Mikhoels—such as *Do Not Grieve!, Family Ovadis,* and *The Deaf*—represented celebrations of revolutionary heroism, patriotism, and socialist work ideals (fig. 13). The burst of creative activity, however, subsided after the onset of the Great Terror.

The theater's activity in the 1940s was overshadowed by World War II. As Soviet Jewry's most prominent personality, Mikhoels was appointed the head of the Jewish Anti-Fascist Committee, formed in 1942 to engage world Jewish support for the Soviet war effort against Nazi Germany. As the designated representative of Soviet Jews, in 1943 he spent several months in Canada, Mexico, the United States, and England, where he was received with great enthusiasm (fig. 14).

Once the war ended, and the Jewish Anti-Fascist Committee was no longer deemed necessary, Stalin turned against its leaders. This left Mikhoels hopelessly exposed. Government accusations of his being a "cosmopolitan"—a term suggesting disloyalty to the Soviet Motherland—coupled with his newly expressed support for a Jewish State in Palestine, placed Mikhoels in danger.[31] In 1948, while on a spurious mission to Minsk to review a play that was nominated for the Stalin Prize, the actor was murdered at Stalin's direction, his brutal death staged as a truck accident. The popular outpouring at Mikhoels's state funeral was remarkable, but his murder signaled a frightful period for the members of the Jewish Anti-Fascist Committee, ending only with Stalin's death in 1953 (fig. 15).[32] In 1948 and 1949, Committee members had been arrested and subjected to show trials.[33] On the night of August 12, 1952—dubbed the "Night of the Murdered Poets"— Benjamin Zuskin and twelve leading Jewish writers, scientists, and intellectuals were executed in the basement of Moscow's Lubyanka Prison.[34] These were not

FIG. 14 *(left)* Solomon Mikhoels at Sholem Aleichem's Grave, Mt. Carmel Cemetery, Brooklyn, 1943. Photograph, 10 × 8 in. (25.4 × 20.3 cm). Archives of the YIVO Institute for Jewish Research, New York.

During his tour of the United States, Solomon Mikhoels visited the grave of Sholem Aleichem in the Workmen's Circle Section of Mt. Carmel Cemetery, paying tribute to the author whose work had provided material for so many of GOSET's productions.

FIG. 15 *(below)* Bier for Solomon Mikhoels's coffin, Belorussian Railroad Station, Moscow, 1948. Photographic diptych, 5½ × 14¾ in. (14 × 37.5 cm). Israel Goor Theater Archive and Museum, Jerusalem.

After Solomon Mikhoels's murder in Minsk, his body was returned to Moscow, where it lay in state for two days in the GOSET theater on Malaia Bronnaia. Over ten thousand mourners came to view the body in a massive outpouring of emotion from the Soviet Jewish population.

random executions, but the culmination of a calculated campaign to eradicate Jewish institutional life.

Gradually many theaters disappeared, and in 1949 GOSET was liquidated. In the years that followed, the Soviet government effectively demolished the remnants of the Jewish community. The demise of the theater, which had survived under pressure since the 1930s, reflected the Soviet Union's expanding campaign to curtail Jewish culture. The fire set at the Bakhrushin State Central Theater Museum, where the GOSET archive was stored, damaged artwork and records, and was seen as an effort to further weaken Jewish communal life.

Despite its early support of the Soviet government, GOSET was unable to forge a lasting Yiddish secular culture. Soviet reality eventually created a climate where Jewish history and religion became taboo, relations with Jews in other countries were virtually severed, and pro-Jewish sentiments could at any time be denounced as antisocialist, bourgeois nationalist, or formalist. Furthermore, any institutional evidence of Jewish cultural awareness could not survive for long in an atmosphere of growing anti-Semitism, which Stalin himself nurtured.[35]

At the end of an exhilarating and painful era in Soviet Jewish theatrical history, it was difficult to remember the initial optimism that the 1917 Bolshevik Revolution had inspired among Soviet Jewish artists. In the 1930s Mikhoels looked back wistfully to the beginning: "In the era when worlds perished and new worlds took their place, a miracle occurred, a tiny miracle perhaps, but for us Jews it was big: the Jewish theater was born."[36] He could not know that in just over a decade the light from that "miracle" would be extinguished.

THE POLITICAL CONTEXT OF JEWISH THEATER AND CULTURE IN THE SOVIET UNION

Zvi Gitelman

Culture is conditioned by the political and social environment in which it is created, and never more so than in the Soviet Union. In that state, culture was viewed not as an end in itself but as a means to achieve a political goal. According to Soviet ideologists, the arts must be imbued with "party-mindedness" (*parti-inost*), ideological consciousness, and awareness of the "needs of the masses." Thus, abstract art, dissonant music, and literature that was deemed inaccessible to the average citizen were not to be supported by the state, and during the rule of Joseph Stalin they were absolutely prohibited (fig. 1). A book, one writer declared, should "address itself to our whole society and in principle, ideally, can be read by the whole society." It should "in equal measure stir a citizen with higher education, a university professor and one who has only completed a seven-year school, a machinist in a factory.... The ability to create such a book [is] not only a political and an ideological achievement, but an aesthetic achievement as well."[1] For Stalin, music that was not accessible to the simple

peasant was not considered "socialist." Moreover, from the 1930s on, music, like the other arts, had to carry a positive, uplifting, and socially useful message. Even great composers such as Dmitri Shostakovich ran afoul of the state when their music was deemed inappropriate for Soviet audiences.

Soviet conceptions of ethnicity paralleled ideas of accessibility to the arts and their political purposefulness. In contrast to the policy of the tsars, who favored the Russian people and discriminated against many others, the Soviets were committed to equal treatment of all peoples and "friendship of the peoples" (*druzhba narodov*), and to instilling all with the common ideals of Soviet-style socialism. Soviet policy toward the many nationalities inhabiting the

(opposite) Natan Altman, *Poster for Jewish Luck*, 1925 (see pl. 64)

FIG. 1 *(right)* Stalin's men, Russian politicians, left to right: Vyacheslave Molotov, Anastas Mikoyan, Communist Party Leader Josef Stalin, People's Commissar of Defense Marshal Kliment Efremovich Voroshilov, and Mikhail Ivanovich Kalinin, head of the Soviet central executive committee, Moscow, 1937. Photograph by Laski Diffusion

territories inherited from the Russian empire derived initially from the theories of Karl Marx. He and his followers looked forward to a "world without nations." Postulating that ethnicity and religion were inventions of the bourgeoisie that served to keep the working class divided against itself, they believed that social class was the fundamental cleavage in any society. Culture, politics, and the economy were shaped by the ruling class. Once the proletariat seized power from the middle class, distinctions among ethnic groups and nations would disappear. Social relations and culture would be shaped by the newly ascendant working class. Therefore, in 1903, Vladimir Lenin, leader of the Bolshevik faction of the Russian Social Democratic Labor Party (RSDLP), vigorously opposed the proposal by the Marxist Jewish Labor Bund that, given the strength of ethnic feelings and the desire by many peoples to determine their own cultural lives, Marxists should at least in the short run make some concession to national sentiments. This could take the form of "national-cultural autonomy," an idea the Bund borrowed from Marxists in the Austro-Hungarian Empire, where there were also many peoples as intent on ethnic self-determination as they might have been on economic and political emancipation. "National-cultural autonomy" meant that while all ethnic groups would be committed to the same political and economic goals, they would be able to determine for themselves the content and form of their cultural institutions.

Lenin, however, held that such autonomy would divert the proletariat's interests and energies from the formidable challenge of making a successful revolution and would perpetuate the division of society along ethnic lines. His Bolshevik faction joined with the Menshevik faction of the RSDLP in 1903 to expel the Bund from its ranks. Yet within a decade, Lenin, ever the pragmatic politician, realized that national resentments and aspirations could be harnessed to the revolutionary cause. By 1913 he expressed willingness to grant some form of autonomy to compactly settled ethnic groups—or "nationalities," in Russian and Soviet parlance—after a successful socialist revolution. This would not meet the national aspirations of Jews and other territorially scattered peoples, because geographic concentration was a sine qua non for autonomy. Lenin and Stalin—who, perhaps because he was not a Russian himself, had become the RSDLP's expert on ethnic matters—decisively rejected the idea that Jews were a nation. They lacked their own territory, a common language, and a common economy,

attributes that, in Stalin's view, were necessary for nationhood.

Nevertheless, after the 1917 revolution, the victorious Bolsheviks categorized Jews as a *natsionalnost,* or ethnic group, one of more than a hundred such "nationalities" who would be citizens of the emerging Soviet Russia, which by 1924 would become a federal state whose constituent parts were based on geographically concentrated "nationalities" (fig. 2).

ENCOURAGING ETHNIC CULTURES

Although the Bolsheviks anticipated the mutual assimilation of all the peoples of the world, Lenin developed a dialectical rationale for encouraging the flowering of ethnic cultures temporarily. He reasoned that, having been deprived of civil rights and the ability to develop their own cultures under tsarism, the non-Russian peoples should be given both. As they exercised their cultural rights, they would come to realize that class rather than ethnicity was their most important social "marker," and would turn their energies to the transnational cause of building socialism. Paradoxically, the best way to dampen ethnic demands and aspirations in the long run was to accommodate them in the short run, with the expectation that growing class consciousness would relegate these aspirations to a much lower priority once they had been partly satisfied. The Soviets called the campaigns to encourage national cultures *korenizatsia*—literally, "rooting"— which meant the "nativization" of Bolshevism, that is, bringing the Bolshevik message to the masses in their own languages. Thus, schools in nationality languages—Ukrainian, Belorussian, Tajik, Georgian, Armenian, for example—would be supported by the state, though Russian-language instruction would be mandatory. For Jews, *korenizatsia* meant the establishment of Yiddish as an officially recognized language.

There had long been a rivalry between the advocates of Yiddish and those of Hebrew, and the conference called in 1908 in Czernowitz (then in the Austro-Hungarian Empire; today Chernivtsi is in Ukraine) to establish the "Jewish national language" had failed to come to a resolution, each camp clinging to its own position. Generally, Jewish socialists favored Yiddish, while Zionists promoted Hebrew, with significant exceptions. After the revolution, Jewish communists persuaded Soviet authorities that Hebrew was the language of "clericals, Zionists, bourgeoisie, enemies of socialism," and consequently

FIG. 2 At the militia station, Belorussia, c. 1920s

Yiddish was ensconced as the language of Soviet Jewry. Indeed, in the 1897 census, 97 percent of Jews had given Yiddish as their "mother tongue," and 70 percent of them still did so in the 1926 census. Nevertheless, modern Hebrew culture had developed in the territories of the former Russian empire, beginning with the Haskala (Enlightenment) in the mid-nineteenth century. By the time of the revolution, leading lights of Hebrew literature such as Chaim Nachman Bialik, "the Hebrew national poet," the poet Shaul Tshernikhovsky, the journalist Moshe Kleinman, and the historian Ben-Zion Dinaburg (later Dinur) resided in Soviet Russia. Habima was the most inventive Hebrew-language theater of its time. The Communist Party's Jewish Section, or Yevsektsia, tried to suppress the activities of writers, theater groups, and other adherents of Hebrew language and literature. Some writers left the country in 1921, and Habima did not return from a 1926 foreign tour, making its way to Palestine. A few writers continued to produce Hebrew poetry and prose, but they could not publish in the USSR; the last Hebrew anthology, which was actually printed in Berlin, appeared as a Soviet publication in 1926. Writers became isolated and despaired of finding an audience. As one put it, "You write something in Hebrew, you come up with a new idea—there is no one to whom you can show it, there is no 'learned man' [*yodaia sefer*] in Berdichev."[2]

Even after winning the linguistic-cultural battle, the Yevsektsia activists differentiated between "bourgeois

Yiddish culture" and their own purportedly Soviet Yiddish culture. They "Sovietized" one of Kiev's famed Yiddish cultural associations, the Kultur-Lige, and derided the Yiddish culture of neighboring Poland and the distant United States, though for some time they maintained contacts with leading figures and institutions in both.

"Yiddishization" became a hallmark of Soviet policy toward Jews from about 1919 to the mid-1930s. This entailed the construction of a Soviet, socialist, secular culture and the institutions to support it. First, however, traditional Jewish culture had to be extirpated. It was deemed hopelessly reactionary because it was intimately bound up with Jewish religion. Synagogues and traditional schools were closed, ostensibly at the behest of the "toiling masses," and turned into workshops, gymnasiums, or workers' clubs. One Yevsektsia activist called it "a Jewish civil war" that implemented "the dictatorship of the proletariat on the Jewish street." Religion was vigorously criticized, and religious functionaries were deprived of various rights. Plays mocking Judaism were performed for Jewish audiences; posters, pamphlets, and newspapers featured satirical critiques of religion; and lecturers were dispatched to "enlighten the masses" about the evils of religion (fig. 3). Zionism, considered a "bourgeois reactionary nationalist movement," was suppressed, and individual Zionists were imprisoned or exiled—the fortunate ones to Palestine. Even though the Zionist-socialist group Hekhalutz (The Pioneer) was legalized in 1923, and was permitted to run its

FIG. 3 *Kheyder,* an anti-religious play, performed at the Belorussian State Yiddish Theater, M. F. Rafalsky, director. Archives of the YIVO Institute for Jewish Research, New York. The letters on the actors' trousers spell kosher.

FIG. 4 Lectures in the anatomy room at Polytechnic College in Birobidzhan, c. 1930s

collective farms originally designed to prepare young people for agricultural labor in Palestine, as soon as the Jewish Sections started their own campaign to settle the Jews in the Soviet Union, Hekhalutz was disbanded and many of its leaders arrested for being Zionists. By 1928, even those Zionist groups that had managed to continue functioning, mostly in small towns in the old Pale of Settlement (Belorussia and Ukraine), were suppressed. Zionist activity was considered anti-Soviet and punishable under the law.

With the destruction of traditional Jewish culture, sincere efforts were made to replace it with a new, Soviet Jewish culture. By 1931, about 1,100 Yiddish-language schools were operating in the USSR, all funded by the government (fig. 4). The USSR was the only state in history to support a network of Yiddish schools. There were numerous Yiddish daily newspapers, literary magazines, theaters, and musical ensembles. The Soviets also established Yiddish research institutes. A few trade unions and even Communist Party cells operated in Yiddish. State publishing houses turned out as many as five hundred Yiddish books a year. Most of these institutions were in the old Pale of Settlement, where the bulk of the Jewish population continued to live. With the industrialization of the 1930s, many Jews, along with millions of non-Jews, were drawn out of the Pale areas to factories, plants, and mines in the Russian Republic. Jewish cultural institutions usually did not follow them there. Jews, especially younger people, who moved out of the Pale regions tended to abandon Yiddish, acculturate to Russian, and, increasingly, marry non-Jews. By the last Soviet census, taken in 1989, only about 10 percent of Jews listed a Jewish language as their mother tongue.

Soviet Yiddish culture was not embraced eagerly by the "masses." They understood that their newfound access to higher positions, including hierarchies from which Jews had been barred in tsarist times, could be acted on only if they mastered the Russian language. Why send a child to a Yiddish elementary school (there were few Yiddish schools above the elementary level) when he or she would be at a disadvantage when competing to advance in education and in the vocations that operated in Russian? If Yiddish schools taught no Judaism—in fact, railed against it—and no Hebrew, and if Jewish history was limited to the "class struggle" among Jews in the Russian empire, traditional and Zionist parents saw no reason to prefer them to Russian, Ukrainian, or Belorussian schools, unless the Yiddish school was better overall or was the only school available in an old shtetl. Why read a Yiddish newspaper when, in many cases, it merely reported yesterday's news from a Russian paper and, of course, served as a vehicle for antireligious, anti-Zionist propaganda?

Among those who embraced state-sponsored Yiddish culture enthusiastically were secular Yiddish writers, artists, and musicians, most of whom had begun their creative activity before the revolution. Unlike their counterparts in the West, who had to struggle in market economies, these artists, writers, and musicians were supported by the Soviet state and honored in Soviet society—as long as they hewed to the party line. Poets such as Itzik Fefer were happy to do so. Writers and poets such as David Bergelson and David Hofstein, and scholars such as Nochum Shtif, immigrated to the Soviet Union from abroad in order to take advantage of the opportunities to publish without worrying about the market. Younger writers such as Zelik Akselrod, Izi Kharik, and Shmuel Halkin found their voices—and readers—in the new culture that was emerging. State-sponsored Yiddish theaters in the Russian, Belorussian, Ukrainian, and, later, Uzbek republics allowed dramatists, actors, producers, and directors to present older works, as long as they could be reconciled with Soviet ideology, and newer ones as well. Artists including El Lissitzky, Marc Chagall, Issachar Ryback, and Solomon Yudovin were able to experiment with new forms of Jewish art and to work in Russian culture (fig. 5).

Yiddishization was the cultural dimension of Soviet policy toward Jews. The economic dimension

FIG. 5 Marc Chagall (front row, first on the right) with author Der Nister (second row, second from right), the literary critic Yekhezkel Dobrushin (second row, third from right), and teachers and children, children's colony Malakhovka, near Moscow, 1923

FIG. 6 On a Jewish collective farm, c. 1930s

FIG. 7 The New Region Center, Birobidzhan, c. 1930s

included encouraging Jewish craftsmen to form cooperatives as a socialist form of economic organization, and turning Jews into peasants (fig. 6). Many craftsmen, and certainly their children, became factory workers, technicians, and engineers. The Soviet government developed plans to settle hundreds of thousands of Jews in agricultural colonies. Since the shtetls had been ruined by World War I, revolution, and civil war, and were losing their economically active populations, Jewish farming communities were established, mostly in the Crimea, Ukraine, and Belorussia, to rehabilitate the former shtetl dwellers economically. Some Soviet officials believed or hoped that, by virtue of their concentration in compact settlements, these Jews would also preserve their Yiddish language and ethnic Jewish identities better than city-dwellers would. The culmination of the agricultural settlement program was the announcement in 1928 that an entire region, or oblast, would be set aside in the Soviet Far East for a Jewish Autonomous Region, should enough Jews migrate there (fig. 7). The idea appealed to some Soviet Jews, and even to some Jews who immigrated to the region from abroad to help "build socialism"; yet despite the fact that the Jewish Autonomous Region was formally established in 1934, it never attracted a stable migration. Harsh economic and climatic conditions, as well as the great distance from the historic areas of Jewish settlement, worked against the project. It was further undermined by the purges of the late 1930s, which weakened its political and cultural leadership.

STALIN AND THE TURN TO RUSSIAN HEGEMONY

When Stalin gained firm control of the Communist Party leadership in the late 1920s, he formulated a plan for the extremely rapid industrialization of the Soviet state. It would be accomplished by the collectivization of agriculture, which would solidify political and economic control of the countryside and also create surplus peasant labor to be channeled into industry. This newly arrived labor force would build factories and plants across the vast expanses of the USSR. All human and natural resources were to be harnessed to this vastly ambitious plan, which was designed to overcome "capitalist encirclement" and secure the only country where socialism prevailed at the time (fig. 8). Therefore, efforts at developing ethnic cultures were to be decelerated or dropped altogether, as all the peoples of the USSR were to devote themselves to the gargantuan common tasks that would unite them. The mobilization of the Soviet population was accomplished by two complementary means: a "Great Terror," launched in 1934, which made the slightest deviation or the most hesitant demurral from the Stalinist plan tantamount to treason, punishable by imprisonment, hard labor, or death; and agitation and propaganda, which succeeded in rallying the support of many Soviet citizens, especially the young, for "laying the foundations of socialism."

The total, disciplined mobilization of Soviet society had contradictory consequences for Jews.

Yiddish cultural institutions rapidly fell into disuse in response to the signals from above that they, and all other non-Russian ethnic institutions, were no longer valued. The political leadership of Yiddish institutions, the elite and foot soldiers of the Jewish Sections of the Communist Party, had lost their raisons d'être, and by the end of the 1930s many were charged with "petit-bourgeois nationalism" for activities that had been entirely legitimate, indeed party-sponsored, a few short years earlier. Like many of their counterparts among Ukrainians, Belorussians, Central Asians, and Caucasian nationalities, Yevsektsia leaders were imprisoned, shot, or sentenced to "corrective labor." In February 1930, the Jewish Sections were dissolved. By the end of the decade, nearly all Yiddish schools had closed, probably as a result of both mass indifference and political pressure. The circulation of Yiddish periodicals fell, and many Jewish cultural institutions were purged of their staffs and closed. Except in Birobidzhan, the Jewish Autonomous Region, Jewish collective farms were merged with those of other nationalities in a process designated as "internationalization." Religious and Zionist Jews were increasingly pressured, as were other religions and nationally minded groups and individuals.

Yet individual Jews took part in the general repression. Though the proportion and perhaps number of Jews in the top party and government leadership declined in the 1930s from their levels in the decade after the revolution, there still were Jews in prominent posts. Leon Trotsky, the first commissar of foreign affairs and first leader of the Red Army, had been politically defeated and exiled, but his fellow Ukrainian Jew, Lazar Moiseevich Kaganovich, was secretary of the Communist Party of Ukraine, supervisor of the Moscow subway construction project, and a member of the Politburo, the top party body. Until their purge in 1937–38, Jewish military figures such as Yona Yakir, Yan Gamarnik, Yakov Smushkevich (1941), and Grigory Shtern were in the uppermost echelons of the armed forces. Between 1934 and 1941, Jews made up 19 percent of all NKVD (secret police) personnel. (In 1939, Jews represented 1.8 percent of the total Soviet population and 4.7 percent of its urban population.) They were more than a third of the "central apparatus" of the secret police. However, in the NKVD central apparatus of more than 2,600

FIG. 8 Workers at a machine-tractor station preparing for the harvest, Soviet Union, c. 1920s

people, by the end of the 1930s the proportion of Jews was pretty much in line with the proportion of Jews in the urban population. There were parallel trends in the NKVD in Ukraine. In 1936, "60 of 90 ranking officers (captain and above) of the NKVD in Soviet Ukraine had declared themselves to be of Jewish nationality."[3] Jews made up two-thirds of the "highest leadership of the NKVD in [the] Ukrainian SSR," whereas Russians were 14 percent and Ukrainians 7 percent. (In the 1926 census, Ukrainians were three-quarters of the population, Russians were 8 percent, and Jews were 7 percent.) The heads of the entire gulag (labor camp) administration included Naftali Frenkel and Matvei Berman, both Jews. From 1934 to his purging in 1936, Genrikh [Henoch Gershonevich] Yagoda, also a Jew, was commissar of internal affairs (and thus, effective head of the secret police).

These men were not acting as Jews, nor were they involved in any form of Jewish culture, but their presence in such high and politically sensitive positions testifies to the rapid rise of individual Jews to positions of prominence in the Soviet system. Most of them eventually were devoured by the very system they had helped create or administer. Yet they remained symbols of state oppression to those who resented the ascension of Jews to power. When the Nazis invaded the USSR in 1941, their propaganda stressed that they had come to liberate the masses from the "yoke of the Judeo-Bolshevik regime." After the war, party policy turned against Jews, who were now considered potentially disloyal, second-class citizens. By the 1960s, there were very few Jews in the repressive organs of the state, almost none in the higher echelons of party and government, and only

older officers of Jewish origin in the upper ranks of the armed forces.

The regimentation of the arts accompanied political repression. If society was to be directed toward a common political and economic goal, culture would have to play its part. By 1934, artistic experimentation, seen by many of the creative intelligentsia as a logical outcome of the political revolution, was being curbed. Where once Soviet poets, painters, and musicians used the freedoms the revolution had brought to experiment with new and radically different forms, and people debated what genuine "proletarian culture" should be, the state now insisted that "art for art's sake" was a useless bourgeois notion and that the arts' function was to inspire the "masses" to exert ever greater efforts toward the goals set by the political leadership. A doctrine of "Socialist Realism" was made the uniform aesthetic of Soviet culture. Literature and the arts were to be "positive," optimistic regarding the Soviet future. Trotsky had anticipated this in 1924, when he wrote that "the new art is incompatible with pessimism, with skepticism, and with all the other forms of spiritual collapse. It is realistic, active, vitally collectivist, and filled with a limitless creative faith in the Future."[4] The "good guys" would always prevail, and the "class enemies," no matter how clever and dedicated to their cause, would go down in ignominious defeat. Films and plays conveyed the same messages. Industrial and agricultural achievements were to be the stuff of human drama. Thus, novels with titles like *Cement* and *How the Steel Was Tempered* were lauded for their inspirational and politically directed characters. Art and music were to be representational, so that every Soviet citizen could

FIG. 9 *(left)* Actors and director of the State Jewish Theater of Birobidzhan, c. 1930s

FIG. 10 *(opposite)* At prayer in the home of a colonist, Tagancha, Krivoi, Rog district, Ukraine

understand the messages they conveyed—happy, smiling peasants bringing in the bountiful harvest, cheerful workers lustily singing songs of socialist construction, of young men and women falling in love as much with a tractor as with each other.

Of course, Yiddish literature, drama, and "folk" songs had to conform to this general line. Ordinary workers were encouraged to become newspaper correspondents; amateur Yiddish theater groups and choirs were organized, as were artists' clubs (fig. 9). No doubt most people joined in these activities simply because they enjoyed them. But as Anna Shternshis observes, "Although Jews attended Yiddish theater to express and affirm their Jewish identity, Jewish activists saw the theater as a useful tool for disseminating propaganda. . . . The state had a special interest in the development of stage productions in all the languages spoken in the USSR."[5] By the end of the 1930s, such efforts were deemed to have outlived their usefulness, as the younger generations had acquired facility in Russian, and ethnic cultural activity was increasingly seen as irrelevant to the common cause, or as even politically suspect.

REVIVAL AND REPRESSION OF JEWISH CULTURE

During World War II, realizing that many Soviet citizens were more motivated to fight for their homeland or their families than to preserve the Soviet system, Stalin relaxed restrictions on religions and, to some extent, ethnic cultures. About 2.5 million Soviet Jewish citizens in 1941 were murdered by the Nazis and their allies in the course of the war. But those who fled or were evacuated or deported to Central Asia, Siberia, and the Caucasus were able to practice religion and indulge in Jewish cultural pursuits to a greater extent than immediately before the war (fig. 10). But by war's end it was clear that Russians were the privileged nationality in the "Soviet family of peoples." On May 24, 1945, Stalin celebrated the Soviet victory over the Nazis: "I would like to raise this toast to the health of the Soviet people," he declared, "and first of all, of the Russian people. I drink first of all to the . . . Russian people because it is the most outstanding nation of all the nations who belong to the Soviet Union. . . . The trust of the Russian people in the Soviet Government turned out to be the decisive force that guaranteed the historic victory over the enemy of humanity—fascism. Thanks to the Russian people for that trust! To the health of the Russian people!"[6]

During the war, a Jewish Anti-Fascist Committee had been created to rally support of world Jewry for the Soviet war effort. After the war, Stalin dismantled it, probably because he was suspicious that its ties to foreign Jews could undermine the USSR, now engaged in the Cold War against the United States and its allies. First, he arranged to have Solomon Mikhoels, principal actor and director of GOSET, the State Yiddish Theater, killed in a staged "accident" in January 1948 (fig. 11). Later that year, the leading Yiddish newspaper and publishing house were closed, and many prominent Yiddish cultural figures arrested. A campaign against "rootless cosmopolitans," clearly directed against Jews, was launched shortly thereafter, and many were demoted, fired, or denied admission to institutions of higher education or positions of responsibility. In 1953, leading Jewish physicians serving in the Kremlin were accused of trying to poison and medically murder high Soviet officials; the allegations of the "doctors' plot" sent tremors of apprehension throughout the Jewish popu-

lation, which feared a massive purge and perhaps deportation. On August 12, 1952, thirteen prominent Jews, who had been arrested in 1948 and 1949, were shot. Only the death of Joseph Stalin in March 1953, and the ensuing repudiation of the "doctors' plot," brought a measure of relief to Soviet Jewry (fig. 12).

Nonetheless, Jewish culture, even in its desiccated Soviet form, was not revived. Not a single Yiddish school or state-sponsored theater was reopened. In subsequent years a few amateur theater groups were permitted to form in the Baltic republics and Birobidzhan, and in 1961, responding to Western pressures, a Yiddish periodical, *Sovetish haimland,* was launched. Effectively, even after Nikita Khrushchev's denunciation in 1956 of Stalin's crimes, no Jewish cultural revival was allowed, though a few Yiddish books were published. The Holocaust was ignored or played down, Jewish themes did not appear in literature, the arts, or music, except on rare occasions, and Jews were written out of histories, even of the ancient Near East.

The years 1964–82, when Leonid Brezhnev headed the Soviet Communist Party, came to be called the "era of stagnation." Unlike Khrushchev, who took the risk of denouncing Stalin and experimented, often disastrously, with economic and administrative schemes, Brezhnev and his colleagues seemed content

FIG. 11 Benjamin Zuskin speaking at the public viewing ceremony for the late Solomon Mikhoels, 1948. Photograph, 5½ × 9 in. (14 × 22.9 cm). Courtesy of Ala Zuskin-Perelman, Or-Yehuda, Israel

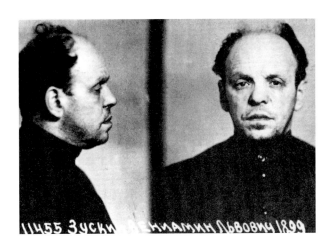

FIG. 12 Prison photograph of Benjamin Zuskin, 1949

with keeping the lid on Soviet society and maintaining the system rather than reforming it. The trial of the dissident writers Andrei Sinyavsky (who frequently wrote as Abram Tertz) and Yuli Daniel in 1966 signaled the unwillingness of the regime to countenance experimentation and innovation in culture and the arts. The Soviet-led invasion of communist but reformist Czechoslovakia in August 1968 showed that political reform, even within a socialist framework, would not be tolerated.

The Jewish movement that emerged after 1967, which began as a drive to gain cultural rights but quickly shifted its focus to emigration and "repatriation" to Israel, was hounded and monitored. By the 1980s there were an estimated 11,000 "refuseniks," meaning Jews who had applied for the right to emigrate—which was reluctantly and selectively granted starting in March 1971—but who had been refused permission to do so. Most were demoted or fired from their jobs, and dismissed from higher educational institutions. Some were imprisoned or sent to labor camps. They became the focus of a campaign in the United States, Israel, and Western Europe, to "let my people go." In 1987, Mikhail Gorbachev, an even more radical reformer than Khrushchev, launched a program aimed at uncovering and rectifying the economic and political ills of the Soviet system. Political and economic liberalization were complemented by attempts to improve ties with the West, and that entailed, among more ambitious

changes, permitting free emigration. Gorbachev's reforms allowed the revival of public, organized Jewish life as well as mass emigration. But many Jews feared that impending economic and political crises would lead to a breakdown of social order, perhaps anarchy; a "panic migration" ensued. When the Soviet Union was dissolved in late 1991, the uncertainties of life in newly independent republics spurred emigration further. From 1989 to 2002, some 1.6 million Jews and their non-Jewish first-degree relatives emigrated from the Soviet Union and its successor states. About 60 percent, or 962,000, went to Israel, joining about 175,000 who had gone on *aliyah* in the 1970s and 1980s.

Ironically, this massive emigration has undermined the reconstruction of unrestricted Jewish life. Today there are about 400,000 "core Jews"—those who consider themselves fully Jewish—in the former Soviet territory; some twenty years ago, according to the January 1989 census, there were 1,445,000. Understandably, Jewish arts and literature have taken a backseat to welfare services, the main focus of Jewish communal organizations. Curiously, it is in Israel that a Russian-language Jewish culture has flourished. A "Russian-Jewish culture" is developing as much outside the former Soviet Union as within it. From a larger historical perspective, it is another link in a long chain of East European Jewish culture that extends from the tenth century to the present, from the Baltic to the Sea of Japan to the renewed Jewish state—and to all parts of the Jewish world.

HABIMA AND "BIBLICAL THEATER"

Vladislav Ivanov

In early October 1917, shortly before the Bolshevik coup in Moscow, a convention of "Jewish Artists and Supporting Casts" was held in Kiev. Welcoming addresses were delivered by representatives of the provisional government and political and cultural associations, by theater people and prominent Jewish writers. Fiery inaugural speeches were followed by a performance featuring two orchestras; banners were held aloft, bearing such slogans as "Down with the Old Slapstick—Long Live High Art!" and "Theater, Like Education, Belongs to the State!" A procession affirming the glory of "high art" may have struck onlookers as comical. Yet the spectacle demonstrated that the idea of a Jewish art theater that could transcend the crude entertainment of the shtetl and elevate the public was no longer the dream of a select few.

While many of the appeals voiced at the convention were answered promptly, it was often in a distorted, unclear fashion. "High art" seems not to have caught on. In part this was due to the interference of Soviet authorities, and in part was the result of artistic ideals that were too broadly defined, or were too closely tied to nonaesthetic concerns.

The Jewish theater Habima and the Moscow State Jewish Theater (GOSET) came to symbolize two very different approaches to the destiny of the Jewish people, the future course of Jewish theater, and the nature of artistic universalism. Habima sought in the mytho-poeic tales of the Bible a universal language that everyone, not only Jews, could understand. GOSET, by contrast, was interested in precisely the disenfranchised shtetl existence that Habima was ashamed of and tried to forget.

Lacking a solid dramatic tradition of their own, Jewish companies took their first steps in Moscow in the late 1910s and early 1920s, when theatrical life was extraordinarily vibrant. Konstantin Stanislavsky (fig. 1), Evgeny Vakhtangov, Aleksandr Tairov, and Vsevolod Meyerhold were among the leading figures, each of their names standing for a theatrical movement, if not an entire system. It was in this environment that Naum Tsemakh and Aleksei Granovsky, founding members of Jewish theaters, had to decide their guiding principles.

For Habima, the decision was obvious. The members of the company regarded a fantastic messianic Hebrew theater with enthusiasm; for them, it could absorb the millennial Jewish experience and direct it toward the future (fig. 2). The practical aspects of the enterprise, however, were not nearly as obvious. The theatrical ideals were as fervent as they were aesthetically vague. Tsemakh had intended to gain knowledge and experience in Paris, but fate brought him to Moscow. There, by his own account, his first stop was the Moscow Art Theater—then widely regarded as one of the wonders of the world.

(opposite) Ignaty Nivinsky, *Golem*, 1925 (see pl. 20)

He considered Anton Chekhov's *The Seagull* and *The Three Sisters* and Maurice Maeterlinck's *The Blue Bird* not as classics but as "discoveries," in terms of their "staging and unique performance style."[1]

As Menachem Gnesin, another member of Habima, later recalled, the group experienced a keen "sense of nothingness."[2] Compared with the Moscow Art Theater, whatever they did seemed ordinary and accidental. Discontent was brewing in the company. Tsemakh and Gnesin concluded that "it made no sense to organize Habima if it couldn't make its presence felt in this city."[3] Such a presence was impossible "without a clearly defined artistic statement." The company sought help from Stanislavsky, founder of the Moscow Art Theater, whose authority was deemed unquestionable. His method, which called on actors to use their "emotional memory" as they responded to the onstage environment, was highly influential in the Soviet Union, as eventually it would be in the United States. At a meeting in late 1917, Stanislavsky recommended that his disciple Evgeny Vakhtangov serve as Habima's artistic director. Other teachers and directors who were directly or indirectly connected to the Art Theater followed Vakhtangov to Habima; they included Leonid Leonidov, Vakhtang Mchedelov, Boris Sushkevich, Boris Vershilov, and Sergei Volkonsky.

The ideological confrontation between Habima and GOSET might be described as that between reactionary religious art on the one hand and a progressive art that was close to the Jewish working masses on the other. From a theatrical perspective, the difference related to the debate between the Art Theater and Vsevolod Meyerhold. Drawn by the logic of GOSET's polemical self-determination, and led by his own artistic taste, Aleksei Granovsky gravitated to the leftist theatrical flank led by Meyerhold.

Habima's first Moscow production was *An Evening of Studio Works,* presented on October 12, 1918. It was in reviews of this production that the company's intention to stage *The Dybbuk* was first mentioned (fig. 3).

Chaim Nachman Bialik, the poet and translator of S. An-sky's play into Hebrew, remembered rehearsals under Vakhtangov: "Was this a dream, madness, or intoxication? Perhaps, because of all its reversals, Habima had drunk from an intoxicating vessel. I don't know whether Habima people will ever again . . . live through such inspiring times."[4]

The rehearsals did not begin in such an impassioned atmosphere. And they dragged on for more than three years. Vakhtangov, who initially was content with an ethnographic replication of Jewish life, reached an impasse (figs. 4, 5). A folkloric style

FIG. 1 *(left)* Konstantin Stanislavsky, c. 1930. Photograph, 9 × 6½ in. (22.9 × 16.5 cm). Archives of the YIVO Institute for Jewish Research, New York

FIG. 2 *(above)* The First Twelve, Habima. Standing, left to right: Shlomo Cohen, Miriam Elias, Starovinits, Reuben Persitz, Hanna Rovina, and Eliyahu Weiner; sitting, left to right: Chaya Grubel, Menachem Gnesin, Naum Tsemakh, David Vardi, Shoshana Avivit, and Moshe Halevi, Moscow, c. 1920s

FIG. 4 Natan Altman, *Third Batlan (Costume Design for Moshe Ha Levi in The Dybbuk),* 1922. Pencil and gouache on paper, 13⅞ × 6⅝ in. (35 × 17.5 cm). Israel Goor Theater Archive and Museum, Jerusalem. Art © Estate of Natan Altman/RAO, Moscow/VAGA, New York.
Batlan means idler. Traditionally an honorable role, *batlanim* (plural) are men who devote their time to communal affairs.

FIG. 5 Natan Altman, *Rabbi Azriel, the Tzaddik of Miropol (Costume Design for David Vardi in The Dybbuk),* 1922. Pencil on paper, 11¾ × 6⅞ in. (30 × 17.5 cm). Israel Goor Theater Archive and Museum, Jerusalem. Art © Estate of Natan Altman/RAO, Moscow/VAGA, New York

FIG. 6 *(opposite left)* Natan Altman, *Leah's Friend, Act 2 (Costume Design for Tamar Robbins in The Dybbuk),* 1922. Pencil and gouache on paper, 12⅜ × 7⅝ in. (31.5 × 19.5 cm). Israel Goor Theater Archive and Museum, Jerusalem. Art © Estate of Natan Altman/RAO, Moscow/VAGA, New York

suited neither his own goal of an "ultimate generalization of everything and treatment of every event as the embodiment of the universal order"[5] nor the biblical aspirations of Habima itself.

Tsemakh entered into discussions with Marc Chagall, hoping to involve him in the set design for the play, but these plans didn't work out. A meeting with Vakhtangov had left the artist bitter. The director had insisted that "the only true method was Stanislavsky's," while Chagall believed firmly that "this system was not suitable for the renaissance of the Jewish theater." He was convinced that his approach would ultimately prevail: "You'll stage the play as I see it, even without my participation," he told Vakhtangov. "There is no other way to stage it!"[6]

In one sense, at least, Chagall was correct: he was replaced by Natan Altman, who brought with him from Petrograd (St. Petersburg) sketches for scenery

and costumes (figs. 6, 7). Upon seeing a dry run of the first act, Altman was taken aback by the difference between his approach and Habima's. The people depicted in his sketches were "tragically distorted and twisted, like trees that grow on dry and barren soil. Their colors were those of tragedy. Movements and gestures were exaggerated."[7] And yet the members of the company were still performing in the composed manner that had been rejected by Chagall.

Nonetheless, over time, Vakhtangov seems to have realized that the old theatrical approaches had played themselves out. His director's intuition brought him to other shores. In the course of rehearsing *The Dybbuk*, he became interested in the Kabbalah as a sphere of magical, secret knowledge, capable of disclosing the mystical and esoteric. Vakhtangov had, as it were, seen the light, and work continued amid "a fabulous excitement, almost an ecstasy."[8]

FIG. 7 *(above)* Natan Altman, *The Tutor, The Groom, The Father-in-Law (Costume Design for The Dybbuk),* 1922. Pencil and gouache on paper, 8⅝ × 12¼ in. (22 × 31 cm). Israel Goor Theater Archive and Museum, Jerusalem. Art © Estate of Natan Altman/RAO, Moscow/VAGA, New York. Pictured left to right: Mendl (Menashe's teacher, played by Bana Schneider), Menashe (Leah's bridegroom, played by Zvi Rabinovitz Raphael), and Nachman (Menashe's father, played by Yehuda Rubinstein)

FIG. 8 Natan Altman, *In-Laws (Costume Design for The Dybbuk),* 1922. Pencil and gouache on paper, 13¾ × 8½ in. (35 × 21.5 cm). Israel Goor Theater Archive and Museum, Jerusalem. Art © Estate of Natan Altman/RAO, Moscow/VAGA, New York

The play opened on January 31, 1922. Even in the early 1920s, when powerful theatrical impressions abounded, Vakhtangov's staging had an incomparable aesthetic and emotional impact. In a note to the director Vladimir Nemirovich-Danchenko, inviting him to see *The Dybbuk* (which, Vakhtangov admitted, "cost me my health"), Vakhtangov referred to simple themes: "I had to find a way to present everyday life onstage in a theatrical yet contemporary manner"

(figs. 8–10).[9] In their reviews of the production, critics repeatedly touched on broader topics. Samuel Margolin, in a typical response, described it as "a modern tragedy, drenched in the blood of war and revolution."[10]

Vakhtangov imbued every detail with a vitality and an intensity utterly different from An-sky's original. In the second act of the play, the strong emotions of one group of characters, the beggars, were expressed by means of masks rendered in a Cubist style. Brightly colored circles, triangles, and rhombuses were darkly outlined for powerful clarity. The actors' makeup emphasized their cheekbones. Eyes were thickly bordered with concentric zones of white and red. Noses, painted white on one side and black on the other, were made to look asymmet-

FIG. 9 Natan Altman, *Poor Woman, Act 2 (Costume Design for Elisheva Sacktrovitch in The Dybbuk),* 1922. Pencil and gouache on paper, 13¾ × 5¾ in. (35 × 14.5 cm). Israel Goor Theater Archive and Museum, Jerusalem. Art © Estate of Natan Altman/RAO, Moscow/VAGA, New York

FIG. 10 Natan Altman, *The Frog, Act 2 (Costume Design for Hannah Hendler in The Dybbuk),* 1922. Pencil and gouache on paper, 12¾ × 7⅝ in. (32.5 × 19.5 cm). Israel Goor Theater Archive and Museum, Jerusalem. Art © Estate of Natan Altman/RAO, Moscow/VAGA, New York

rical. Vigorous zigzags accentuated every gesture, and the frozen features possessed "a supernatural, mystic brightness."[11]

In the second act, the curtain was "not yet opened when we heard some monotonous music and tramping."[12] So begins the traditional wedding feast for the beggars in the courtyard of Sender, the rich merchant father of the bride. Blind, armless, hunchbacked, and lame, the guests rejoice and glorify their generous host. Yet the joy is feverish, devoid of gaiety, and engenders a "feeling of unavoidable dread."[13]

Vakhtangov passed the Jewish ceremony through a fine theatrical filter, separating out the descriptive details and subordinating the ethnic motif to an overall concept. Life itself was presented "as a feast of beggars . . . an allegory of a chain of diseases, deformities, heinous greed, lewd antics, and abominable roars of laughter; the ringleader of this 'feast of life' turned out to be a blind man, monstrous and haughty, as if resurrected from the grave."[14]

By emphasizing contrasts, Vakhtangov transcended the limits of the human. For each beggar he searched for an appropriate animal character, which was then refined in studies of plastic improvisation: the mannerisms of an old, defeated fox; a bird of prey; a hyena; a hungry wolf; an enraged monkey. Disguised in human form, the animal character was revealed fully and distinctly only at the moment of the theatrical metamorphosis, when an animal "jumped out" of a frenzied person.

Vakhtangov's creative imagination for the varieties of ugliness was seemingly inexhaustible. For each character he achieved a lively balance between expressive monstrosity and unprecedented concentration. The drawings had sharp graphic outlines (figs. 11–12).

FIG. 11 Natan Altman, *Weeping Woman, Act 1 (Costume Design for Chaya Grover in The Dybbuk)*, 1922. Pencil and gouache on paper, 12¾ × 6⅝ in. (32.5 × 17.2 cm). Israel Goor Theater Archive and Museum, Jerusalem. Art © Estate of Natan Altman/RAO, Moscow/VAGA, New York

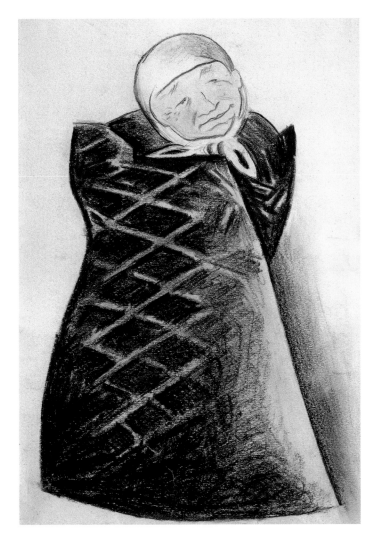

Each character was effectively distinguished from the others and infused with such emotional and physical tension that the audience was captivated as soon as any character appeared onstage.

At the same time, the crowd onstage formed a single, unified body, existing according to its own laws. Vakhtangov recognized the magical impact of a monotonous rhythm and the ritual repetitions of certain forms. Reviewers referred, disapprovingly, to "shamanism."[15]

In the story of *The Dybbuk*, every beggar has the right to dance with the bride, Leah (fig. 17). Thus, Leah meekly passes from the old shrew with the hanging lip to the hunchback to the blind man. But then a witch who "has not danced for forty years"

enters, picks Leah up, and draws her into a phantasmagoric dance. Frenzy engulfs the stage like a wildfire: "Each character joins the dance in his own manner, is distinguished from the crowd for a [moment], and once again blends into it in a whirlwind motion. This was Goya on the stage."[16]

The action leaps from narrative interpretation to imagination, in a rhythmic and tactile metamorphosis. Animal features betray themselves in humans, resulting in a detailed bestiary: "The ecstatic dance transforms the beggars into a . . . circle of monsters. . . . Vakhtangov does not respect purity: he soils it with toads' paws and monkeys' touches."[17] Then comes another leap, and the action is a nonfigurative, nonobjective "blind chaos, eternal dark dawn."

In the words of the German director Max Reinhardt: "The dance of the beggars with all its fantasies came across as the dance of the witches, that is, of creatures who do not belong to this world. Only absolute dedication to art can achieve such a level of execution."[18]

For the critic Andrei Levinson, the production was "a very strange amalgam of prophetic fury and discipline, of the spontaneous and the artificial, of fantasy and observation."[19] His favorable response contained, however, an insurmountable perplexity, despite the fact that he was able to see in Vakhtangov's artistry the same awareness, founded on the traditions of the sacral theater, that avant-garde directors were forever trying to instill (figs. 14–16). The director Jerzy Grotowski believed that "spontaneity and discipline mutually enhance each other . . . enrich each other, and bring a vibrancy to the actor's performance."[20] (Antonin Artaud, with his distinct approach, observed, "Cruelty is discipline and rigor.")[21]

The actor and director Yuri Zavadsky described the reaction of the audience: "It felt as though the power of art moved you beyond the limits of time and space. You forgot where you were and what was happening to you. And when you woke up, you realized that, yes, this was amazing theater."[22] It was, he continued, "as if you approached the mysteries of earthly existence, were elevated to spheres . . . that you had never known before, and encountered terrible demonic powers." Rather than depict reality, this art was concerned with introducing the audience to the endless universal transformation that destroys and creates all. Here, ritual functions like a window onto another dimension. In such a theater no finale can be definitive—a fact that moved the critic Pavel Markov to comment that there was an "overcoming of tragedy" in *The Dybbuk.*

Vakhtangov's cosmic ecstasies forestalled Artaud's cosmic trance. Vakhtangov's work had an indisput-

FIG. 15 Natan Altman, *Hasid (Costume Design for The Dybbuk),* 1922. Pencil and gouache on paper, 11⅜ × 6⅞ in. (29 × 17.5 cm). Israel Goor Theater Archive and Museum, Jerusalem. Art © Estate of Natan Altman/RAO, Moscow/VAGA, New York

FIG. 16 Hannah Hendler as a young Hasid in *The Dybbuk,* 1922. Photograph, 9¼ × 6¾ in. (23 × 17 cm)

קל חתן וקל כלה

FIG. 17 The Beggars' Dance (Scene from *The Dybbuk*), 1922. Photograph, 5⅞ × 8⅞ in. (15 × 22.5 cm). A. A. Bakhrushin State Central Theater Museum, Moscow.

This scene takes place in the prosperous house of Sender, decorated for the wedding of his daughter Leah. The Hebrew letters hanging from the ceiling read, *Kol Chatan v'kol Kalah* (the voice of the groom and the voice of the bride), part of the seven marriage blessings in the Jewish wedding ceremony. As part of the wedding festivities, Sender has invited the beggars of the village to the feast.

able advantage over the dreams and exorcisms of the French poet: his theater was presented armed with stage tools, realized in material art.

Only beauty that had passed through the most extreme stage of negation and through the phases of its destruction was acceptable for *The Dybbuk*. In the play, the ugly flared up with unexpected new beauty, and was all at once capable of transforming chaos. The actor Nikolai Volkov captured the essence of Vakhtangov's approach: the director had found, and managed to convey, "the beauty of the ugly" (fig. 17).

The Dybbuk satisfied various expectations, some of which seemed mutually exclusive. It delighted both traditionalists and innovators—proof of the universality of its synthesis, rather than of an eclectic

FIG. 18 Naum Tsemakh as the Prophet in *The Eternal Jew*, c. 1920

FIG. 19 Hanna Rovina as the Prophet's Mother in *The Eternal Jew*, c. 1920

compromise. Vakhtangov's grotesque staging linked creative destruction and destructive creation, and negated the visible world. His style encompassed dissimilar artistic trends to become the new art of the twentieth century.

In 1926, the play conquered *le tout Paris*. Marc Chagall was part of the enchanted audience. As a token of reconciliation he gave Tsemakh his self-portrait with the inscription "To my dear Naum Tsemakh, the director of the wonderful Habima, as a memento of myself . . ."

In the early 1920s, the members of Habima saw the future of their theater in tales and images from the Bible, which they thought would guarantee their universality. Their greatest success, however, *The Dybbuk*, was not directly related to the Bible. All the company's tours, even the shortest, opened and closed with An-sky's play. And its characters were those same disparaged shtetl Jews whom Habima longed to forget, in favor of mighty biblical heroes. Yet with his production of *The Dybbuk*, Vakhtangov demonstrated the primacy of artistic approach over plots or characters or motifs. His staging yielded a performance of biblical vision and pain rather than a simple reenactment of biblical subject matter. The play propelled Habima to the forefront of public interest.

The Eternal Jew was the theater's first production after Vakhtangov's death in 1922. Directed by Vakhtang Mchedelov, with Georgy Yakulov as artistic director, the play opened on June 5, 1923, in an atmosphere of high expectations. It was compared, inevitably, to

Vakhtangov's masterpiece, but critics voiced reservations about the production.

Vakhtangov's unity of irony and pathos was replaced with a style that held pathos at its center. *The Eternal Jew* was a "national Jewish tragedy about wandering and messianism" (fig. 18).[23] The "turmoil of the masses," which the members of Habima had discovered in *The Dybbuk*, now became a standard of their theatrical craft: "The Eternal Jew is all of Judea, rather than an individual character. The old and the young, men and women, mothers and whores, . . . beggars, workers and the rich—they were all . . . the voices of a single chorus."[24] The chorus was often jumbled, not only because of the differences in skill, but also, as Margolin remarked, because of the disparity "between those who carried in their bodies the spirit of Habima and those who carried in their bodies only the burden of their bodies."[25]

"The righteous" of *The Eternal Jew* were the characters close to God. Sometimes standing apart from the choir, sometimes blending with it, were two soloists: Naum Tsemakh, as the Prophet, and Hanna Rovina, as the Prophet's Mother (fig. 19).

Tsemakh, with the "unexpected turns of his insane head, his adamant fanaticism,"[26] projected an image of biblical power. Still, his interpretation was not universally praised. Andrei Levinson regarded his majesty as too deliberate, and his stern demeanor dispassionate.[27] Hanna Rovina, in what could be viewed as a supporting role, was singled out[28] for her "exceptional artistry": "Probably only Rovina sounded a genuinely tragic tune. . . . She clearly displayed the spiritual heritage that Vakhtangov left to Habima."[29]

"The unity of sound," supported by Aleksandr Krein's "excellent music," gathered the motley Oriental crowd into an integrated ensemble, prompting the Berlin critic Bernhard Diebold to characterize the play as an example of a collective drama, similar to Sergei Eisenstein's *The Battleship Potemkin,* the first and greatest example of the majestic "mass" film.[30]

While avoiding both folklore and pastiche, the creators of *The Eternal Jew* strove for authenticity—"a stone language that could have been used by the pyramids."[31] The Orient here was archaic, a wild desert. The dancing whore, who led a chain of people, was like a "human Tower of Babel who, unable to seduce the citizens of Babel, seduced the sons of the desert."[32]

The play culminated in the mass lamentation over the destruction of Jerusalem and the Temple, with the elders "downtrodden at the feet of the Prophet, near the last beggar despised by them."[33] It was almost "impossible to describe, monumental and psalmodic."[34] In this tragic biblical lamentation, didactic purpose merged with poetry to became theater.

Not quite two years later, on March 15, 1925, Habima presented *The Golem,* by H. Leivick (figs. 20, 21). The play was directed by Vakhtangov's disciple Boris Vershilov, whose connection to Vakhtangov was likely the only reason he had been invited to direct; he had done nothing of note before then. Ignaty Nivinsky, who had already collaborated with Vakhtangov, was chosen as art director. Vershilov and Nivinsky's collaboration showed how varied the fruits of Vakhtangov's legacy could be.

FIG. 20 *(right)* Ignaty Nivinsky, *Beggar (Costume Design for The Golem),* 1925. Pencil, gouache, and colored ink on cardboard, 19 × 13½ in. (48.3 × 34.2 cm). A. A. Bakhrushin State Central Theater Museum, Moscow

FIG. 21 *(left)* Ignaty Nivinsky, *Water Carrier (Costume Design for The Golem),* 1925. Pencil and gouache on cardboard, 19 × 13½ in. (48.3 × 34.1 cm). A. A. Bakhrushin State Central Theater Museum, Moscow

FIG. 22 Ignaty Nivinsky, *Gypsy Woman (Tzoanit) (Costume Design for The Golem)*, 1925. Pencil and watercolor on paper, 9⅛ × 5⅞ in. (23 × 15 cm). The Russian State Archive of Literature and Art, Moscow

FIG. 23 Ignaty Nivinsky, *Woman with Child (Costume Design for The Golem)*, 1925. Pencil and watercolor on paper, 9⅛ × 5⅞ in. (23 × 15 cm). The Russian State Archive of Literature and Art, Moscow

The A. A. Bakhrushin State Central Theater Museum and the Russian State Archive of Literature and Art (RGALI), both in Moscow, house large collections of Nivinsky's sketches for *The Golem* (figs. 22, 23). A brief look at those that Vershilov accepted suggests the director's approach. He rejected all fantastic proposals in favor of the most modest, those in line with the general theatrical perception of the "seventeenth-century style, slightly refracted through theatrical convention."[35]

The play passed the review of government censors, but not without difficulty. A "pronounced mystical and religious tendency" seems to have bothered Soviet officials. They also balked at the theme of an artificial human being, "a new Frankenstein," which cast a shadow on the notion of the "new man," conceived in the ideological test tube or as a result of the mass remaking of consciousness.

Vershilov's staging was considered solid. He delivered on his promise to use minimal special effects and to concentrate on directing the actors. Even the most demanding critics, who found that the production "displayed much more of the influence of the old

Moscow Art Theater than the school of Vakhtangov,"[36] admitted the development of the actors' craft. From the principal roles to the mass scenes, *The Golem* demonstrated "an original and assured culture of acting."[37]

Vakhtangov's ecstasy and Mchedelov's inspiration were replaced with Vershilov's mastery, on which all critics remarked. Expressive symbolism and burlesque deformations gave way to more straightforward performances and everyday speech.

Andrei Levinson described the director's "healthy fantasy" and pointed out how it differed from Vakhtangov's "fantastic realism": "In *The Dybbuk* we admired the transformation of earthly reality. In *The Golem* we [are] offered the realistic depiction of the imaginary. The myth [is] implanted in a true story (figs. 24, 25). In this case we watch not the soul rising to the empyrean, but rather the miraculous descent into the valley of tears. Here Jacob's ladder is used for descent rather than ascent."[38]

The drama of the magician who challenges God, who wants to continue creation, was overshadowed by the suffering of the monster whom the magician has created, who wants to become human.

FIG. 24 Ignaty Nivinsky, *Skeleton (Sheled) (Costume Design for The Golem)*, 1925. Pencil and watercolor on paper, 9⅛ × 5⅞ in. (23 × 15 cm). The Russian State Archive of Literature and Art, Moscow.

The Hebrew text at the top right says *met* (dead), and the word at center right is *sheled* (skeleton).

FIG. 25 Ignaty Nivinsky, *Master of Horns (Baal-Karnayim) (Costume Design for The Golem)*, 1924. Pencil, gouache, and tempera on cardboard, 18½ × 13 in. (47.1 × 32.9 cm). A. A. Bakhrushin State Central Theater Museum, Moscow

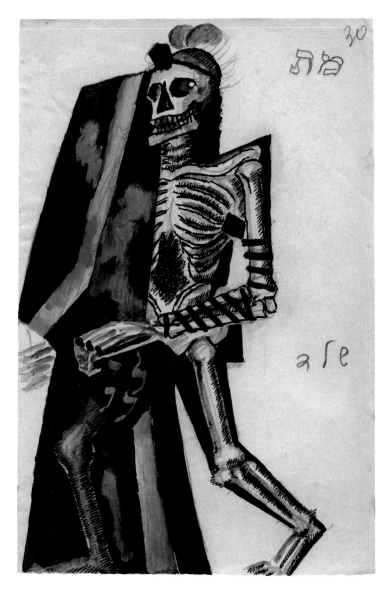

In one of Nivinsky's sketches, the Golem looks like something from the pages of a science fiction novel, a huge snow-white figure surrounded by electrical discharges. Although Vershilov rejected the sketch, he borrowed something of it to formulate the psychology of the character.

In an interview, Vershilov termed the Golem's creator "a great scientist" rather than a rabbi or magician. The actor A. Prudkin selected for his character's "excellent makeup that accentuated the deep eyes and fine face bones" and brought out "the plasticity of the somewhat delicate body."[39] The contrast between the character's spiritual might and his physical frailty heightened the expressionistic tension.

The Golem, as played by Aaron Meskin, appeared onstage as a regular "Jewish Caliban," with "a low forehead, hardly visible behind the shock of hair; rough features, as if modeled from clay; long and clumsy hands; and a blunt, bullish gaze of eyes that seemed made of glass."[40] His face was painted white, the eyes outlined with red circles. Everything in him was exaggerated. Meskin's powerful bass voice roared phenomenally low notes, evoking wild nature. And despite his slow movements, his character embodied nature. Repulsive in the first scenes, the Golem was reduced to dust in the end; he died like a human being. In him,

FIG. 26 *(left)* Ignaty Nivinsky, *Frog (Tsefardeya) (Costume Design for The Golem)*, 1925. Pencil and watercolor on paper, 9⅛ × 5⅞ in. (23 × 15 cm). The Russian State Archive of Literature and Art, Moscow

FIG. 27 *(right)* Ignaty Nivinsky, *Fever (Kadachat) (Costume Design for The Golem)*, 1925. Pencil and watercolor on paper, 9⅛ × 5⅞ in. (23 × 15 cm). The Russian State Archive of Literature and Art, Moscow

crying to live, was that very soul he had been refused. And his cry found an unexpected response in the audience: "We all are like poor golems," one viewer wrote. "The miracle that created us then destroys us. Nobody can escape this. Everything is again turned to dust."[41] The play, which was advertised as an illustration of "stages of liberation movement," ends with the bitterness of Ecclesiastes.

Richard Beer-Hofmann's play *Jacob's Dream* had to wait its turn to be staged by Habima. There was reason for the company's delay with the production, first mentioned in October 1922, just as there was reason for its haste when the group actually began working on it.

The members of Habima had proclaimed their ideals for a "biblical theater," then proceeded to debate the subject for several seasons. *The Eternal Jew, The Golem,* and *The Dybbuk* were only indirectly related to Scripture. In order to stage a production that involved the Bible more immediately, the company needed a playwright who could appreciate and help fulfill the actors' aspirations—someone the group had so far been unable to find. *Jacob's Dream* seemed to offer a solution.

It is possible that Beer-Hofmann turned to the Old Testament on the advice of his friend Theodor Herzl, the Viennese journalist (and playwright himself) and pioneer of the Zionist movement. *Jacob's Dream* was the first installment of an ambitious—and ultimately unfinished—biblical trilogy. In it, Beer-Hofmann depicted the dialectic of being the chosen and then the rejected, from its frightening apocalyptic side. Jewish existential catastrophism helped nourish the literary expressionism of the play. In the early 1920s, as the Hebrew Renaissance lingered, many people thought the worst experiences of the Jewish people lay in the past. The Habima enthusiasts and Beer-Hofmann operated on different planes.

As confirmed by the playbill and reviews, the official director of the production was Boris Sushkevich. The contemporary press, however, persistently associated the production with Stanislavsky. One of the few documents to offer a more or less coherent (albeit

FIG. 28 Ignaty Nivinsky, *Fish (Dag) (Costume Design for The Golem),* 1925. Pencil and watercolor on paper, 9⅛ × 5⅞ in. (23 × 15 cm). The Russian State Archive of Literature and Art, Moscow.
The Russian text reads, "siren with the head of a woman."

incomplete) account of the production is a transcript of a conversation with Robert Falk about his work with Stanislavsky.[42] Yet even this document should be consulted with caution. The conversation with Falk took place in January 1944—nearly twenty years after the first production of *Jacob's Dream*. By then, it seems, Habima had been deleted from the history of Soviet theater. This fact must have affected Falk, consciously or not, and he altered his account of what had actually happened. In addition, his version may reflect his personal feelings toward Habima, in particular his anger at the group's changes to his stage designs: "Everything [was] lost!" he recalled. "I terminated the contract and took my name off the playbill."[43]

Falk did discuss Stanislavsky's intense work on *Jacob's Dream:* "K.S. came there three times a week; he was supposed to have worked for three or four hours at a time, but he would end up staying for five or six. . . . He was carried away and did not spare himself. . . . For a month, a month and a half, two months, Stanislavsky continued his work with the company."[44] Whether Stanislavsky conducted rehearsals for four weeks or six or eight before passing the responsibility on to his assistant Sushkevich, the amount of work that he did on the play was considerable.

The joint reading of the great biblical tale of Jacob was difficult from several perspectives, among them the theatrical point of view (fig. 29). Perhaps equally important, the Bible for Stanislavsky was not the same as it was for Habima. But both director and theater company deemed their shared perceptions more

significant than their differences. Stanislavsky believed in Beer-Hofmann's work, deficiencies and all—as is confirmed by Falk: "He tried to make me accept the play, and to find some redeeming features in it."[45]

The director insisted that the archangels in the Habima production wear wings. Falk felt that the wings should be "symbolic . . . as if they extended the masses rather than the arms." He yielded on another matter related to the wings: "K.S. wanted the archangels' wings to move, to work." And so the artist had to design "a special mechanism that controlled the movement of the colossal wings, each of them four meters in length. The wings were colored, they sparkled and shined."

Stanislavsky and Falk designed technical contrivances that were put to good use in the most challenging scene of the play. As Falk recounted: "K.S. said, 'Look at these archangels. When they lower the wings, you should feel as if your hands are drawn to them, as if they are bound to the wings with invisible chains and links, and that your body is also drawn to them. They draw you with enormous force, with their words and movements, while you resist and hang back.' . . . This was very hard to produce—a struggle through space rather than a visible struggle."

In those years Stanislavsky conducted long rehearsals, often transforming them into lessons and deviating from his actual director's tasks. The pedagogy gradually took over the work on the play, and the production ceased to be the main goal. Under different circumstances, the members of Habima would have been glad to receive this education; but with a play in production, each new lesson put them under tighter time constraints. A tour was already planned and the

FIG. 29 Stage set at Habima for *Jacob's Dream*, c. 1920

FIG. 30 Naum Tsemakh as Esau in *Jacob's Dream*, c. 1920

departure date scheduled, but the prospect of the premiere looked hazy. Once again Habima was laboring in an atmosphere of high expectations; the actors were especially cautious.

The rehearsals, which had started out smoothly, began to disintegrate. By all appearances, neither Habima nor Stanislavsky was satisfied. Falk's feelings were probably justified: "As time passed, I felt more and more strongly that [Stanislavsky] was becoming very frustrated, and I was not surprised in the least when one day I learned that he could no longer continue."[46] In his memoirs, one member of the company, Raikin Ben-Ari, paints a picture of harmonious cooperation and gives Stanislavsky's illness as the reason for his departure.[47] This is supported by a brief item that appeared in the press in late October 1925: "K. S. Stanislavsky, the head of the Moscow Art Theater, has fallen ill."[48] It was probably then that he handed the position over to Boris Sushkevich.

Falk described Sushkevich's work bluntly: "At one point he was considered more 'progressive' than K. S. He completely destroyed my artistic design, and did not understand a thing about lighting."[49]

Falk's experience notwithstanding, *Jacob's Dream* was a critical and popular success. Habima's readiness for "Jewish opera" was manifested in the richness and beauty of the vocal arrangement, and in the synthesis of all aspects of the production (fig. 30).

Max Reinhardt's appraisal points to the company's accomplishments, and perhaps predicted its future: "During the first act of *Jacob's Dream* it seemed to me that *The Dybbuk* was the highest achievement of Habima and its most valuable legacy, but after the third act . . . I became convinced that in this production the members of Habima have also achieved extraordinary success."[50]

Jacob's Dream exemplifies the varied course of Habima's destiny. The members of the company had prepared themselves for failure as they worked on Beer-Hofmann's play. Within months, despite the vagaries of personnel and production, Habima had triumphed.

Habima left the Soviet Union in 1926 and toured internationally. After establishing itself in Tel Aviv in 1928, it was officially anointed Israel's national theater. Habima's "biblical theater" turned out to be a utopian dream, for the land of the Bible ultimately did not need biblical theater. Habima was ordained to adapt to Israel's desire for a different type of dramatic company.

Translated from Russian by Galya Korovina

YIDDISH CONSTRUCTIVISM: THE ART OF THE MOSCOW STATE YIDDISH THEATER

Jeffrey Veidlinger

The departure of Marc Chagall was a major blow for the Moscow State Yiddish Theater, whose earliest productions merged so seamlessly the folk-art fantasies of Chagall with the futuristic calisthenics of Aleksei Granovsky and the satirical tales of Sholem Aleichem. It was in part due to the success of Chagall's designs that the theater was transformed after his departure from an intimate chamber theater into a vital link in the Moscow cultural scene of the 1920s. In the spring of 1922, the theater opened in its new location, a newly renovated five-hundred-seat auditorium on Malaia Bronnaia, in the heart of Moscow's theater district. The theater had outgrown the intimate space into which Chagall had installed his famous murals, and instead had been thrust into the vibrant and exciting world of the Soviet avant-garde. The chamber-theater style so admired by modernist theater directors, who, like Bertolt Brecht, sought to break down the fourth wall between the audience in the gallery and the actors on the stage, was much more difficult to achieve in this larger space. The theater therefore had to find new artistic directions, while simultaneously retaining the dynamism that infused its first productions.

Natan Altman, who joined GOSET as set designer, was in many ways the perfect successor to Chagall. Indeed, a curious synchronicity could be observed between the two artists' careers. The two had been working in parallel for at least a decade: both lived and worked among the Russian émigré community in Paris in 1910–1911; both returned to their respective hometowns in Russia after departing Paris; both had moved to St. Petersburg by 1914; both were members of the Jewish Society for the Encouragement of the Arts and exhibited their work in the society's 1916 exhibition; both exhibited in the 1916 Jack of Diamonds exhibition in Moscow; and both found their way to Moscow and Jewish theater in the aftermath of the 1917 Bolshevik Revolution (fig. 1). Both were also heralded as the future of Jewish art and frequently compared with each other. At this early stage of their careers, however, many critics would have wagered that Altman rather than Chagall would emerge as the Jewish artist par excellence. Altman's designs for the 1922 production of *The Dybbuk* at the Hebrew-language Habima theater resonated internationally, propelling the theater to the heights of modern stage design. Chagall's sets for GOSET's first Moscow production, on the other hand, were well received but failed to evoke the excitement and enthusiasm that Altman's would garner. In fact, at the time of his involvement with the Jewish theaters, Altman was one of the Soviet Union's most celebrated artists: he had been appointed Vladimir Lenin's first portraitist, commissioned to design the first Soviet postage stamp, and commissioned to design the celebration for the first anniversary of the October Revolution. Chagall, on the other hand, despite his apparent initial

(opposite) The Marketplace in *The Sorceress*, 1922 (see pl. 56)

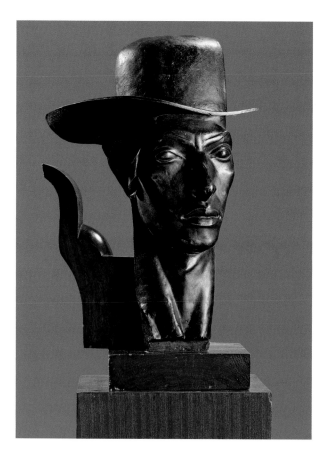

FIG. 1 *(left)* Natan Altman, *Head of a Young Jew*, 1916. The State Tretyakov Gallery, Moscow. Art © Estate of Natan Altman/ RAO, Moscow/VAGA, New York

FIG. 2 *(opposite)* Alexandra Exter, *Salome* (*Costume Design for Two Jews*), 1917. Pencil and gouache on cardboard, 26¾ × 20⅝ in. (68 × 52.4 cm). A. A. Bakhrushin State Central Theater Museum, Moscow

enthusiasm for the Revolution, never seemed to find a place for himself among the elite group of artists anointed by the Bolshevik leadership. He had even lost the reins of artistic leadership in his native Vitebsk to his artistic nemesis, Kazimir Malevich.[1] Chagall could only watch helplessly as Altman, his most important competitor at the helm of Jewish art, soared in reputation and official acclaim. But it is characteristic of the vicissitudes of revolution that within a decade these positions would be sensationally and perpetually reversed.

Like Chagall, Altman painted schematic figures of geometric shapes and patterns modeled on those commonly employed in Russian folk art, and infused these images with a sense of motion. His designs for Vakhtangov's production of *The Dybbuk*, for instance, had been influenced by many of the same folkish and modernist trends that reached apotheosis with Chagall. He was influenced by the same Cubo-Futurist trends that inspired Chagall and shared Chagall's desire to remake Jewish folklore in a Cubo-Futurist mold. Cubo-Futurism sought to combine the aesthetics of French Cubism with the transnational linguistic experiments of the Russian Futurist poets, who consciously broke conventional writing rules in order to create neologisms and invent new rhythms

and meters without the constraints of formal grammatical and syntactical limitations. Many leading Cubo-Futurist artists, like Aleksandra Exter and Kazimir Malevich, eventually came to reject all depictions of figurative and representational images, preferring instead complete abstractions and nonobjective art. Both Malevich's Suprematism and Exter's Constructivism in general represented an adherence to geometric form and abstraction that came to dominate the Russian avant-garde of the 1920s and the designs of GOSET.

For its first production in its new theater hall, GOSET merged modern Constructivist aesthetics with enlightenment rationalism in its rendition of Karl Gutzkow's *Uriel Acosta*. This play, which the theater had earlier performed in St. Petersburg, was a reworked Yiddish translation of the classic 1846 Enlightenment play. The play is based on the true story of Uriel Acosta, a seventeenth-century converso (Jew forcibly converted to Catholicism) who fled the religious persecution of Portugal to Amsterdam in order to return to Judaism. He found, however, that the thriving Portuguese Jewish community of Amsterdam was less tolerant of religious diversity than he had imagined. After publishing a treatise questioning the biblical basis for belief in the immortality of the soul, Acosta was excommunicated by the rabbinical leadership. He was later readmitted into the community but continued to express heretical beliefs based on rationalist readings of Judaism. After being excommunicated and publicly humiliated a second time, Acosta took his own life.

GOSET's staging of *Uriel Acosta* was as much Altman's vision as it was Granovsky's. Like Aleksandr Tairov at Moscow's Chamber Theater, and Vsevolod Meyerhold at the Meyerhold Theater, Granovsky sought to create a synthetic theater that would combine visual art, music, and performance on one stage. The stage was intended to surround the actor, to serve

as an extension of the actor's three-dimensionality, thereby emphasizing the kinetics of the theatrical production as a supplement to the dramatic narrative. To achieve this goal, directors sought to attract the leading artists of the generation to the theater, converting the entire performance space into a dynamic canvas. The aspirations of theatrical directors coincided neatly with those of many noted artists who wished to construct grand architectural projects and reformulate large-scale landscapes, but who lacked the resources to realize their fantasies in concrete and mortar. It is for this reason that the stage attracted not only many prominent Russian artists of the revolutionary period, like Exter, Malevich, Aleksandr Rodchenko, and Vladimir Tatlin, but also

many important Jewish artists, who contributed to the Russian avant-garde in general and participated in parochial Jewish artistic ventures as well (fig. 2). Chagall, Altman, Isaac Rabinovich, and Robert Falk, for instance, all contributed to the Jewish stage in the 1920s, whereas other important Jewish artists of the Russian avant-garde, like El Lissitzky and Issachar Ryback, pursued various additional Jewish projects, primarily in the field of graphic arts.

These artists brought the aesthetics of the Russian avant-garde to Jewish art and Jewish artistic motifs to the Russian avant-garde. Altman was perhaps most famous for his design for the mass festival in St. Petersburg's Palace Square celebrating the first anniversary of the Russian Revolution and for his portraits of Vladimir Lenin and of Anna Akhmatova, but his work for the Hebrew and Yiddish theaters was also an important part of his artistic oeuvre. His sets for *Uriel Acosta* were firmly within the Cubo-Futurist framework popular within contemporary avant-garde Russian theater. He painted the walls of the theater black and left the stage empty except for several geometric shapes suggesting furniture. The backdrop was set against a stairway, representing motion and ascension. To further provide the impression of movement, the sets were slanted, giving the entire stage a kinetic and somewhat disorienting appearance. The costume design for the title character, played by the lead actor Solomon Mikhoels, mirrored the set as a whole, with its sharp angles and geometric patterning. The design was intended to evoke in the audience the feelings of anguish and emptiness felt by the play's protagonist as he is led to despair and suicide.

These abstract montages of geometric shapes and color suggested the urbanized and industrialized future. At the same time, Altman borrowed again from the simplicity of folk art, but here his influences were barely discernible as he maintained only the sharp lines and geometric patterns he observed in the art of the countryside, emancipating the form from any semblance of the material objects or human figures from which they were derived. In this manner, Altman's creative path has a close parallel with that of Malevich. Like Altman, Malevich's early works, portraying peasants in the field through simple geometric shapes, were derived from folk art. Malevich's set designs for the 1913 production of the Futurist spectacle *Victory over the Sun* at St. Petersburg's Luna Park theater, though, represented a move toward abstraction that heavily influenced Altman and came to define Cubo-Futurist theater. For this spectacle, Malevich constructed a black and white set of freestanding shapes, and costumes composed of brightly colored geometric forms. Similar techniques were also used by Exter in her famous set design for Innokenty Annensky's *Famira Kifared,* which played at Tairov's Chamber Theater in 1916. Exter set the play against a sparse background of cones and cubes of various sizes set at intersecting angles along a stairway, initiating what came to be known as volumetric stage design.

After *Uriel Acosta,* GOSET continued its aesthetic explorations and embrace of kinetic energy, while moving away from the abstractions of Altman's Cubo-Futurism toward a more Constructivist style. Constructivist theater design had reached its apogee on the Moscow stage with Meyerhold's 1922 production of *The Magnanimous Cuckold,* designed by Liubov Popova. Rather than paint sets on a two-dimensional canvas, Popova built a multileveled architectural construction of wooden scaffolding, stairs, trellises, platforms, and mobile shapes on which the actors moved and glided (fig. 3). The set resembled both a construction site and a fairground, uniting popular theater with industrial progress. Meyerhold's innovative rhythmic biomechanics precisely matched the architectural decor of Constructivism. Inspired by Taylorism and the Soviet drive toward bodily perfection, biomechanical exercises were designed to train the individual to move in conjunction with the collective down to the smallest gesture, in emulation of machinery. The calisthenics and acrobatics of biomechanics forced the body to coordinate itself with the elaborate stage platform while maintaining its own equilibrium and balance. The Constructivist set, with its multilayered stages for action, was also well suited to the type of mass action and mass spectacle very much in vogue in revolutionary Russia. Meyerhold employed similar Constructivist sets and acting techniques in his 1923 production of Aleksei Faiko's *Lake Lyul.* The style quickly caught on with Constructivist productions in place at the Chamber Theater (G. K. Chesterton's *The Man Who Was Thursday,* 1923), the Bolshoi Dramatic Theater (Aleksei Tolstoy's *Mutiny of the Machines,* 1924), and the Moscow Theater of the Revolution (Vladimir Bill-Belotserkovsky's *Echo,* 1924), to name but a few examples. It was Granovsky's innovation, however, to combine this precise, linear, coordinated motion on multiple planes of a Constructivist set with the folkish and comedic melodrama of Yiddish theater.

On GOSET's stage, Constructivism was most evident in Isaac Rabinovich's sets for Avrom Goldfadn's *The Sorceress: An Eccentric Jewish Play* (1922) as well as Aleksandr Stepanov's set designs and Isaac Rabichev's costumes for *200,000: A Musical Comedy* (1923), based on a story by Sholem Aleichem. Both these plays took popular stories by well-known Yiddish writers and transformed them into revolutionary spectacles. Both also could be interpreted as portending revolution through their critical exploration of bourgeois sensibilities and their portrayals of the disastrous potential of the capitalist profit motive.

The Sorceress, about a young woman who is robbed of her inheritance by her wicked stepmother, was originally a typical nineteenth-century melodrama, full of harrowing adventures, disastrous mishaps, narrow

FIG. 3 *The Magnanimous Cuckold*, 1922. Photograph.
A. A. Bakhrushin State Central Theater Museum, Moscow

escapes, and intervention by characters possessing magical powers. But in the hands of Granovsky it was transformed into a satire of the style and values it represented. The staging, with laughter at inappropriate times and bombastic music during love scenes, also aimed to mock the melodrama of the original script. The highlights of Granovsky's production were the art and music. Rabinovich assembled a Constructivist set of slanted scaffolding, ladders, and platforms protruding at various levels. It is no coincidence that Rabinovich had received some training from Exter and would later work with her on the film *Aelita* (1924). Rabinovich's training and inclinations were both firmly within the Constructivist camp. The set was influenced by Anton Lavinsky's design for the

1921 production of Vladimir Mayakovsky's *Mystery-Bouffe* at the Meyerhold Theater. Like Lavinsky's set, as well as Liubov Popova's sets for *The Magnanimous Cuckold*, the design was meant to be functional, liberating, and forward-looking, while disseminating kinetic energy throughout the auditorium. It was, in many ways, typical of the Constructivists' interest in theater as a surrogate architectural field.

Granovsky's actors danced, climbed, crawled, jumped, flipped, and somersaulted over, under, and around Rabinovich's sets. Choreographed like clockwork in accordance with biomechanical techniques, the actors moved like cogs in a machine, sporadically bursting out of their syncopated robotic mime into wild and frenzied dance. They littered the stage, filling all its open space and crevices as they crawled along the scaffolding like nimble cats or pounced out of concealed pits like leopards on the attack. Hidden behind grotesque makeup, each individual actor was but a symbol for the social class he or she represented. The collectivist movement and mass action that occupied the stage was also reminiscent of fairground entertainment. Mass spectacle was one way early avant-garde Soviet artists experimented with the creation of a proletarian art, ideally bringing the egalitarian spectacle of the fairground onto the stage. It was for this reason that early Soviet theater looked toward popular fairground entertainments as well as the circus and the carnival for inspiration. *The Sorceress*'s homage to the carnival and circus was part and parcel of contemporary currents in Soviet aesthetics to privilege entertainment genres associated with the masses. Georgy Yakulov, for instance, would famously bring the fairground into the theater with his 1920 design for *Princess Brambilla* at Tairov's Chamber Theater. Rabinovich's costume designs portrayed the characters in acrobatic positions, dancing and flipping, exuding dynamism. Joseph Akhron arranged Goldfadn's fourteen songs and wrote an additional twenty new songs, which he based on his own ethnographic studies in the former Pale of Settlement. "The Meeting of Mirele and the Sorceress," with its eerie introduction and Oriental motifs bolstering Solomon Mikhoels's wailing voice as the merchant Hotsmakh, merged well with the sets and actors' movements. The juxtaposition of Akhron's folkish melodies and Rabinovich's Futuristic sets emphasized the distinctions between old and new and followed upon Chagall's fusion of folk art with abstract Cubo-Futurism.

GOSET continued its Constructivist experimentation with its adaptation of Sholem Aleichem's *200,000*. In this "musical comedy," however, the grotesque, carnivalesque, and exotic qualities of *The Sorceress* were tempered with a less fantastical, although still far from realistic, portrayal of the quotidian lives of the rich and poor. From the opening scene of *200,000* in the workshop of the poor tailor Shimele Soroker, played by Mikhoels, the sets underlined the poverty of traditional Jewish life. When he wins the lottery, though, Shimele Soroker, now adopting the Russified name Semon Makarovich to garner more respect, leaps into the flamboyant lifestyle of the nouveau riche, only to lose his fortune again. The play's theme, emphasizing the ephemerality of material goods and wealth, was a recurring one on the Soviet Jewish stage of the 1920s. It had already been explored in *The Sorceress*

and would be revived with *Trouhadec: An Eccentric Operetta* a few years later.

As had now become common for the theater, prominent artists and musicians were recruited to design and compose for *200,000*. Aleksandr Stepanov constructed the sets, and the graphic artist Isaac Rabichev designed costumes. Stepanov designed an abstract multilayered set of wooden platforms with shapes suggesting typical shtetl houses, all crooked and slanted like the world they symbolized. In one mise-en-scène, a contorted menorah floated above center stage, mocking the false piety of the bourgeois. The costumes accentuated class differences and social types. Wearing a three-pointed hat, a symbol of Haman, the evil villain of Purim, Shimele was intended to arouse the disdain of the audience. The sharp contrast between the suddenly wealthy Shimele and his working-class background was emphasized by a split stage that poised the workers on ladders effortlessly floating above the bourgeoisie, whose obesity made them ever aware of the pull of gravity. Wealthy men and women were invariably portrayed as fat, while the women's faces dripped with makeup. Benjamin Zuskin, as the matchmaker Soloveitchik, was painted with arched eyebrows and a perpetual scowl. The costumes of the wealthy accentuated the crooked manner in which they moved across the stage. With their hands invariably stuck in their pockets the audience was reminded that the rich always have their hands on their wallets. In one mise-en-scène, Soloveitchik parachuted onto the stage, alluding to a literal interpretation of the ubiquitous *luftmentshen,* or men of air, the poverty-stricken shtetl Jews the revolution sought to reform into productive workers. In another mise-en-scène, the bloated swindler stood atop a table as the crowds swooned around him in reverence, and musicians serenaded from the scaffolding above, reminiscent of Chagall's famous images of the fiddlers on the roof. The image of the fiddler on the roof, revived in this new form, paid homage to Chagall and his time with the theater, while accentuating the impermanence and precariousness of the shtetl (fig. 4).

200,000 was an early manifestation of the Soviet attack on the shtetl that would reach fruition in the middle of the decade. To Soviet propagandists, the shtetl symbolized all they despised about the Jewish past: the petit-bourgeois economic condition of the Jewish population; the "naive" adherence to "outdated" religious beliefs and rituals; and the utopian dreams of Zion. Jewish art and literature were enlisted in the cause of destroying the shtetl and the old Jewish way

of life it represented. Thus, the theater's 1925 production of Isaac Leib Peretz's *At Night in the Old Marketplace: A Tragic Carnival* was not only an artistic tour de force, but also a powerful piece of propaganda.

In this first production of Peretz's symbolist play, Granovsky completely rewrote the text, retaining only some of the most poignant lines. At less than one thousand words, the production, billed as a "tragic carnival," was really more a conglomeration of mise-en-scènes than a fully scripted play. The story, about a wedding in a graveyard, was intended as a requiem for the old Jewish life that the theater was seeking to destroy. The theme of death and destruction permeates the text, which is ultimately about the impossibility of giving new life to that which is already deceased. As night falls in the cemetery, the dead rise from their graves to the sounds of the Kaddish, the Jewish prayer for the dead, mixed with a requiem mass. After the wedding, as dawn approaches, the wedding entertainer calls out, "Remain above the earth! Don't return to the graves!"—an appeal to abandon the metaphorical shtetls. However, fearing the rising sun and the new day, the dead return to

their graves. The attack on the shtetl was accompanied by an attack on religion. As the play ends, a voice is heard from beneath the stage, shouting "God!" to which the wedding entertainer replies, "Dead, your God . . . He is bankrupt!" (fig. 5).

The highly symbolist production was intended to evoke emotions of repulsion and eeriness in the audience. This was achieved predominantly through the musical accompaniment, composed by Aleksandr Krein, and the sets and costume design, by Robert Falk. Krein utilized dissonance to pervert traditional Jewish liturgical and klezmer music in order to set his mood. Falk, for his part, designed a series of grotesque costumes, portraying zombies with dripping flesh. Falk (1886–1958), the son of a prosperous Moscow

FIG. 5 *(above)* Robert Falk, *Shtetl (Set Design for At Night in the Old Marketplace),* 1925. Charcoal on paper, 10⅞ × 14⅞ in. (27.5 × 37.8 cm). A. A. Bakhrushin State Central Theater Museum, Moscow. Art © Estate of Robert Falk/RAO, Moscow/ VAGA, New York

FIG. 6 *(left)* Robert Falk, *Dead Bride (Costume Design for At Night in the Old Marketplace),* 1925. Pencil and tempera on cardboard, 15¾ × 9¾ in. (39.9 × 24.7 cm). A. A. Bakhrushin State Central Theater Museum, Moscow. Art © Estate of Robert Falk/RAO, Moscow/VAGA, New York.

In designing the show, Falk created a series of cutouts, serving as both costume designs and aids in blocking the production. The decrepit body of the Dead Bride shown here became emblematic of a moribund way of life.

lawyer, began his career in the Moscow School of Painting, Sculpture, and Architecture, where he was influenced by the French Post-Impressionists, particularly Henri de Toulouse-Lautrec, Paul Cézanne, and Henri Matisse. His association with these artists, though, led to accusations that he was affiliated with the political left and his expulsion from the school in 1909. After a sojourn in Italy in 1910, he affiliated himself with the Jack of Diamonds group in Moscow and met Chagall and Altman. Primarily a landscape painter, Falk found the transition to theater difficult; but he adapted well and went on to work for Habima and the Belorussian State Yiddish Theater. Falk's costumes were intended to disturb and upset conventional stereotypes. The Dead Bride, for example, reversed the nuptial connotations of purity, elegance, and joy; she was portrayed as completely desexualized, with a haggard body, lopsided breasts, and lumps

of flesh coming out of her legs—the very opposite of the type of pure beauty associated with a bride on her wedding day. The Dead Woman similarly challenged the audience's conceptions of motherhood (fig. 6). The Dead Men, for their part, retained the physical remnants of their religious beliefs, but their grotesque features resisted any associations with piety. Each was clad in traditional Jewish religious garments, wearing a prayer shawl and phylacteries, as though these were the costumes of the dead (figs. 7, 8).

Falk's elevation of the grotesque can be seen as an aesthetic reaction against the Suprematist celebration of the human figure and its attempts to perfect the body in aesthetic form. Whereas Malevich and Lissitzky presented the architecture of the human body in a streamlined form, emphasizing the harmonious relations between its parts, and the aerodynamics of slim agile bodies, Falk reversed this trajectory with

FIG. 7 Robert Falk, *Religious Men (Costume Designs for At Night in the Old Marketplace)*, 1925. Pencil, watercolor, and opaque white on cardboard, 12¼ × 6⅝ in. (31.2 × 16.8 cm). A. A. Bakhrushin State Central Theater Museum, Moscow. Art © Estate of Robert Falk/RAO, Moscow/VAGA, New York

FIG. 8 *At Night in the Old Marketplace*, 1925. Photograph, 4½ × 5½ in. (10.9 × 14 cm). Beth Hatefutsoth, Photo Archive, Tel Aviv, courtesy of Zuskin Collection.
Through prosthetic limbs and masklike expressionistic makeup, Robert Falk heightened the funereal atmosphere that pervaded the production. Second from left is Solomon Mikhoels as the first *badkhen* (wedding jester).

his crude exaggerations and asymmetrical bulky walking cadavers. His figures did not leap into the future, but rather stagnated in the past. Whereas the Suprematists emphasized functionality and human beauty, Falk highlighted the extraneous and the grotesque. This fascination with profanity and subversiveness can be seen in part as a product of the influence of Toulouse-Lautrec's barrooms and prostitutes. Like the French Post-Impressionists, Falk defamiliarized the human body through bawd imagery and crudeness.

Falk's sets merged the grotesque with Constructivism. Like GOSET's earlier Constructivist sets, the stage was multilayered, with visible stairs and platforms. But the architectural details were now reduced to background. A flurry of macabre colors graced the stage, which was set in the shadow of a huge wrinkled *hamsah,* a Kabbalistic sign in the shape of a hand, coming down from the center of the stage displaying Peretz's Hebrew initials. The stage, with its circuslike ambience full of activity, disorder, and exoticism; the contoured lines of the set; and the vivid colors, reminds one of Georgy Yakulov's sets for the Chamber Theater's 1920 production of *Princess Brambilla,* billed as a "capriccio on motifs by E. T. A. Hoffman." Like Tairov, Granovsky adapted his dramatic material into a fairground mode; his "tragic carnival," or "mystery in two parts," echoes Tairov's terminology of "mystery" and "harlequinade." *At Night in the Old Marketplace*'s homage to Jewish mysticism and superstition can also be compared with Habima's 1925 production of H. Leivick's *The Golem,* or even its earlier production of *The Dybbuk.* These plays all drew from the rich traditions of Jewish folklore and mysticism, and *The Dybbuk* and *At Night in the Old Marketplace* both imagined a porous boundary between life and death.

The year 1925 also saw the theater's first venture into film with the motion picture *Jewish Luck,* directed by Granovsky, starring Mikhoels and Zuskin and with Altman as set designer. The story follows Sholem Aleichem's hapless Menakhem Mendl as he dabbles in different ways of making a living, only to encounter at each turn the insurmountable barriers of ill fortune, or Jewish luck. The film focuses on Menakhem Mendl's attempt to make a fortune as a marriage broker. In a hilarious dream sequence, he imagines himself as a highly successful matchmaker called upon by the Jews of America to ship more brides from the Old World. Ultimately, his aspirations are foiled when he mistakenly arranges a marriage between two women—an error discovered only as the

wedding ceremony is about to begin. As in *At Night in the Old Marketplace,* the wedding ceremony, a traditional Jewish symbol of life and renewal, turns into a disaster, once again symbolizing the belief that a new beginning cannot take place within the shtetl. The new medium allowed for a more forceful attack on shtetl life. Renouncing the carnivalesque and acrobatic features that had become the hallmark of his theater, Granovsky chose instead to present a "realistic" portrait of prerevolutionary shtetl life in all its stagnancy (figs. 9, 10). The sheer starkness of the dirty town of Berdichev as depicted on the crude, grainy film was sufficiently unappetizing, especially when contrasted with the modern, revolutionary city of Odessa. Lest the audience miss the message through his straightforward narrative, Granovsky used cinematic tricks to highlight it; one scene shows the streets of Berdichev dissolving into a cemetery. The graveyard is again used as a metaphor for the shtetl.

In a rare symbiosis between artistic director and graphic designer, Altman designed the poster for the film as well. Soviet graphic designers of the 1920s, particularly those who worked in film posters, were often inspired by the cinematic techniques of montage, made famous by Sergei Eisenstein and Dziga Vertov. In particular the Stenberg brothers,

Georgy and Vladimir, who were among the most prolific and talented designers of film posters, often tried to mimic the montage of film through collage. Although photomontage was developing as a staple of Soviet avant-garde graphic artists, it was too expensive a medium to replicate in the mass-produced advertising poster. The Stenbergs often used images drawn from photography rather than actual photographic reproduction. Altman's poster for *Jewish Luck* echoed many motifs popularized by the Stenberg brothers. He combined the dynamism and sleek red and white diagonal text typical of the Soviet agitational poster with a photographic inset of a decrepit Menakhem Mendl bent over, slowly making his way out of the picture. Behind him lurks his abstracted silhouette with sleek lines in disproportionate scale. The ominous shadow seems to foretell some catastrophe to befall poor Menakhem Mendl. As if to announce the tragedy, the umbrella he clutches in the photo is reflected in the silhouette as a machine gun slung over his shoulder. This poster may have influenced the Stenberg brothers' own 1927 poster for *The Last Laugh* (*Chelovek i livreya*), which was produced with Yakov Ruklevsky and in which a shadow again contrasts with a foregrounded figure revealing two opposing dimensions of the human condition—one of success and one of failure. Both films similarly portrayed the rapid rise and fall of fortunes in the capitalist world.

Granovsky's 1927 adaptation of *Trouhadec* by the French playwright Jules Romains (1885–1972) proved that a complete break with Jewish culture—in terms of both content and provenance—could still produce fine art on GOSET's stage. The play, which mocks the self-indulgent lives of wealthy gamblers and philanderers of the Riviera, portrays the decadence of the European bourgeoisie on the model of Toulouse-Lautrec's paintings of the Moulin Rouge and Montmartre, with Altman depicting flamboyant costumes of the European urban upper class. The costume design for Sophia, for instance, resembled the dancers and prostitutes portrayed by Toulouse-Lautrec. The production mocked the vulgarity of European culture with its sexual promiscuity and inanity. Contemporary Western fads, like cancan dancing and roulette, were portrayed as mere tinsel. Here Altman borrowed motifs from Yakulov's designs for Tairov's 1922 production of Charles Lecocq's *Giroflé-Girofla*. Like Lecocq's opéra bouffe, *Trouhadec* was a musical comedy about the roller-coaster ride between debt and wealth (figs. 11, 12).

In 1928 GOSET embarked upon a highly acclaimed European tour. Granovsky, Falk, and Altman chose to remain in Europe rather than return to an increasingly stifling and repressive Soviet Union. Granovsky pursued a modest career as a film director in Germany until his 1937 death. Falk worked as Granovsky's art director before returning to the Soviet Union in 1937. Upon his return he found himself ostracized and, with the exception of a few theatrical designs, including

FIG. 9 *(opposite)* Natan Altman, *Shadkhn (Matchmaker) (Costume Design for Daniel Finkelkraut in Jewish Luck)*, 1925. Pencil on paper, 12¼ × 7½ in. (31 × 19 cm). A. A. Bakhrushin State Central Theater Museum, Moscow. Art © Estate of Natan Altman/RAO, Moscow/VAGA, New York

FIG. 10 *(right)* Natan Altman, *Zalmen (Costume Design for Moshe Goldblatt in Jewish Luck)*, 1925. Pencil on paper, 12¼ × 9 in. (31 × 23 cm). A. A. Bakhrushin State Central Theater Museum, Moscow. Art © Estate of Natan Altman/RAO, Moscow/VAGA, New York

For this harsh critique of bourgeois life in Western Europe, Altman drew upon his travels in France to create stylish and flamboyant costumes.

In this scene, Trouhadec, played by Mikhoels, stands on top of a monument to announce the foundation of the Party of Gentlemen. The baroness's daughter Jenevieve, fourth from the left, is dressed in an exaggerated, stylish costume emulating Natan Altman's design.

GOSET's *Solomon Maimon* (1940) and *Tumultuous Forest* (1946), had difficulty exhibiting in public (figs. 13, 14). Instead, he devoted himself to teaching. His art continued to have an impact, however, even after his 1957 death. When in 1962 Nikita Khrushchev visited an art display at Moscow's Manege Gallery, he famously chided the second Russian avant-garde after seeing one of Falk's nudes. Altman, for his part, remained in Paris after the 1928 tour, exhibiting with Russian émigré circles and occasionally venturing into theatrical design. Although his French work had some success, his rivalry with Chagall had come to an end, as Chagall emerged as the quintessential Jewish artist, whereas Altman languished in comparative oblivion. For GOSET, the 1928 tour along with its defections came to symbolize the end of its avant-garde phase.

Upon GOSET's return to Moscow, Mikhoels was tapped to become the theater's next director and Granovsky's successor. Mikhoels, unlike Granovsky, had grown up steeped in the Jewish religion and Yiddish culture. In contrast to Granovsky, he regarded his commitment to Jewish culture and the Jewish people as more important than his commitment to universal aesthetics. Therefore, he was willing to sacrifice the avant-garde experimentalism of the 1920s and, some would say, artistic integrity in general, for

the Jewish theater to survive in the more restricted atmosphere of the 1930s and 1940s. Indeed, what historians have termed "Stalin's Cultural Revolution" of 1928 marked the end of the avant-garde in Russia. Between 1928 and 1934, virtually all vestiges of the experimentalism of the 1920s were wiped out and replaced with an aesthetic that came to be known as Socialist Realism. It has been noted that Socialist Realism was distinct from Realism in that it portrayed the world not as it really was, but rather as some believed it ought to be. The Socialist Realist aesthetic was epitomized by grandiose portraits of workers and peasants brandishing their hammers and sickles in triumphant poses, with tables overflowing with bountiful feasts in the background. All art was henceforth required to serve the Revolution by presenting simple images of the triumphs of socialism. This aesthetic was combined with the motto "socialist in content, national in form" to refer to art produced by the Soviet Union's national minorities. All Soviet art was to use distinct national forms in order to promote a common socialist content, but national symbols and motifs were to be divorced from any parochial meaning and instead reoriented to become simply a means of expressing universal socialist ideals. In the

Jewish case, for instance, this meant that the Yiddish language was to be encouraged so long as it was not accompanied by any Jewish religious or national expression and was utilized merely as an instrument for the promotion of Soviet ideals.

Thus, in his first five years as artistic director of GOSET, Mikhoels staged a series of productions that portrayed the struggles and triumphs of the working class and the great historical victories of the Revolution: *Four Days*, by M. Daniel (pseudonym for Daniel Meyerovich), was a realist narrative of the struggle of Bolshevik partisans in Vilna (Vilnius) during the civil war; Peretz Markish's *Do Not Grieve!* was a story of the collectivization campaign in a Soviet shtetl; and David Bergelson's *Mides ha-din* was about counterrevolutionary activity in the Polish borderlands. Isaac Rabinovich, who returned to the theater to design sets for *Do Not Grieve!* and *Four Days*, toned down the Constructivist experimentalism that had been so evident in *The Sorceress*, but retained enough

FIG. 15 Isaac Rabinovich, *Set Design for Do Not Grieve!*, 1931. Pencil on paper, 10 × 12⅛ in. (25.3 × 30.8 cm). A. A. Bakhrushin State Central Theater Museum, Moscow

FIG. 16 *(left)* Aleksandr Tyshler, *King Lear (Costume Design for Solomon Mikhoels),* 1935. Watercolor on paper, 9½ × 7½ in. (24 × 19 cm). A. A. Bakhrushin State Central Theater Museum, Moscow. Art © Estate of Aleksandr Tyshler/RAO, Moscow/VAGA, New York

FIG. 17 *(below)* Aleksandr Tyshler, *King Lear (Costume Design for Solomon Mikhoels),* 1935. Watercolor on paper, 9⅞ × 6⅞ in. (24.7 × 17.6 cm). A. A. Bakhrushin State Central Theater Museum, Moscow. Art © Estate of Aleksandr Tyshler/RAO, Moscow/VAGA, New York

of the spirit of the avant-garde to invoke the ire of those critics who, following the party line, had come to disdain what they regarded as "Formalism." One critic accused the theater of presenting *Do Not Grieve!* as a "biblical scenario."[2] Rabinovich's set design of a sun rising over empty fields was too abstract and geometrical for the new era (fig. 15). These productions, all idealized portraits of recent Soviet history interpreted within highly restrictive official guidelines, offered little in the way of aesthetic innovation.

In 1935, though, GOSET achieved its greatest critical success with a production of Shakespeare's *King Lear.* For this production, the theater brought on board a new set designer, Aleksandr Tyshler, who would become one of the theater's regular collaborators. Tyshler, who had studied at Exter's studio, had been designing sets for the Belorussian and Ukrainian State Yiddish theaters before coming to Moscow in 1932. He immediately received an invitation to work with GOSET in Moscow, and spent two years working on the sets for *Lear* (figs. 16, 17). Tyshler attempted to avoid a crude reproduction of Lear's historical era, instead focusing on re-creating what he regarded

as an authentic Shakespearean reproduction. As he wrote, "In preparation for the presentation of a historical play, many artists collect encyclopedic illustrative material, mechanically transferring onto the stage individual details, costumes and even complete architectural creations. This method is not correct, as objects were misrepresented from century to century, stylized by artists and craftsmen. The approach I have chosen is to produce a spectacle on the basis of an entire presentation of Shakespeare's epoch."[3] He chose to set the play in the era in which feudalism met the Renaissance, approximately 150 years before Shakespeare's time. This was a politically opportune setting,

FIG. 18 Aleksandr Tyshler, *Costume Design for Boytre the Bandit*, 1936. Watercolor and pencil on paper, 16⅛ × 11¾ in. (41.1 × 29.8 cm). A. A. Bakhrushin State Central Theater Museum, Moscow. Art © Estate of Aleksandr Tyshler/RAO, Moscow/VAGA, New York

as it allowed for the play to be seen as a critique of feudalism and for Lear's destruction to become a metaphor for the falseness of the entire feudal order. Tyshler's main set was a two-story castle, the top half of which had gates that opened and closed in a manner reminiscent of a medieval English puppet theater. The set created an enclosed space, evoking the narrow quarters and crowded squares of the late medieval and early Renaissance eras, and forcing the actors to interact with each other on a close physical plane (see plates 97, 98). The medieval castle contrasted with the Renaissance costumes and their subdued hues. In preparation for his costume design, Tyshler constructed statues of the main characters, believing that Shakespearean protagonists with their deep character development could only be perceived in three-dimensional representations. Communist Party leader Karl Radek wrote that, with his portrayal of Lear, Mikhoels had "entered the ranks of the greatest actors of the world," and the Yiddish literary critic and Communist Party activist Moyshe Litvakov observed that GOSET could now be counted as "one of the greatest theaters in the world."[4]

Tyshler's designs the following year for the theater's production of Moyshe Kulbak's *Boytre the Bandit,* however, were regarded as problematic from an ideological point of view, still too far from the type of Socialist Realism with its boundless enthusiasm demanded of Soviet art. "Whereas for the theater the key to the play lies in its historicity, in its folkishness, lively, cheerful, and optimistic, for Tyshler it seems a pretext for a new variant of shtetl phantasmagoria," wrote one reviewer (fig. 18).[5] Indeed, Tyshler's sketches reflect some of the magical realism reminiscent of Chagallian images of the shtetl, complete with lanky fiddlers and vivid, luminous colors set against monochromatic backgrounds. By the 1930s the guardians of art in the Soviet Union had shunned this type of fantastical imagination in favor of Socialist Realism.

Tyshler continued to work with the theater throughout the decade, producing sets for *The Family Ovadis* and *Bar Kokhba* (both 1938), *The Banquet* (1939), *Wandering Stars* (1941), and *Khamza* and *Mukkana* (both 1943) (fig. 19). His most innovative sets, though, were probably those he constructed for the theater's 1945 performance of *Freylekhs,* which won GOSET the

FIG. 19 Aleksandr Tyshler, *Costume Design for Bar Kokhba*, 1938. Watercolor, black wax, and chalk on cardboard, 15½ × 11¾ in. (39 × 29.7 cm). A. A. Bakhrushin State Central Theater Museum, Moscow. Art © Estate of Aleksandr Tyshler/RAO, Moscow/VAGA, New York

Stalin Prize, the Soviet Union's most prestigious state honor. The play balanced commemoration and remembrance of the recent atrocities with an optimistic celebration of the perseverance and survival of the Jewish people. The play's loose narrative about a wedding allowed for ample innovation and creativity in the design. Tyshler set the prologue in complete darkness, evoking the recent war. Its opening scene recalled the creation myth, particularly in its Kabbalistic interpretation, as seven weak lights representing the six days of creation and the Sabbath emerge from the void. Revealing human forms representing Primal Man, the lights suddenly burst into a flurry of color. One critic described the scene:

> In the black square of the stage seven solitary lights burn. Their dim light falls on faces and hands, holding these lights. The faces are tense, their appearance is of concentration. Above shines a single star. Its bluish shining twinkle fights with the quiet melancholy of the wandering lights. The sound of a requiem fills the expanse. This Yahrzeit—a ceremonial rite for the remembrance of the dead— expresses sorrow and vows to be a grateful and eternal memorial. But suddenly a wedding jester appears—the spirit of a wedding. His ringing voice breaks the ceremonial melody— "extinguish the light, blow out the melancholy." The Requiem melody transforms itself. Joyful, ceremonial music is heard. A bright light bursts into flame. It lights up the entire stage. A demand for light. Faces are revealed with heads proudly raised. They wear bright clothing. This is the voice of the folk jester who moves, writhing like quicksilver, and who sees the wisdom of the people's faces. With great agitation he speaks of the sorrow that envelopes every blessed person with thoughts of the dead who were torn from life in the war of liberation. Let us share in a pre-eminent memorial which will be the joy of life, an affirmation of victory, and a celebration of the new life, which was fought for by the victorious people, who are immortal.[6]

The stage then fills with jesters, dressed in costumes

completely black on one side, and a patchwork of colors on the other. "Our people live!! Let's celebrate a wedding!" they declare, as they usher in a carnival of song and dance. The wedding guests then begin to arrive: an officer returning from the front, a mother who has lost her only child, and an old soldier who had been recruited into the tsarist army. A series of dances follow, beginning with the dance of the elders and ending with the dance of the future grandchildren, symbolizing the revitalization of the Jewish community through the next generation. Even the old soldier's beard was a symbol of rejuvenation. The long, scraggly beard he wears in the first scene gradually becomes shorter throughout the play, until at the end of the wedding he shaves, revealing a youthful visage. The play ends in a polar image of its beginning. Gradually a rainbow of colors merges, as in a prism, into a single shaft of white light.

The sets and costumes all celebrated the perseverance of the Jewish people, reflected in the ultimate symbol of Jewish life and new beginnings—the wedding canopy. Tyshler's wedding canopy, which covered the stage, symbolically uniting the actors under a common roof, was brightly colored with polka dots adorning the interior and colorful spirals on the outside, more reminiscent of a circus or carnival tent than a traditional white canopy. The carnivalesque represented a return to the theater's origins. Additionally, sets included a curtain decorated to resemble the walls of an Eastern European painted synagogue, complete with menorahs, zodiacal animals, and a synagogue ark, in which the Ten Commandments are replaced with the words "The voice of the bridegroom and the voice of the bride" from the Seven Blessings sung at Jewish weddings. One critic wrote of the play: "The theater performs brilliant and loud buffoonery, a sparkling carnival and parade. It performs a wise comedy of laughter through tears and tears through laughter, and in both the tears and the laughter are contained its internal vindication" (fig. 20).[7]

Rather than usher in a new period of rejuvenation, though, the play ultimately served as a requiem to the tragic end of GOSET and the further decline of Soviet Jewish life. Less than three years after the premiere of this play—intended to represent a new beginning and triumph over the threat of annihilation—Mikhoels was murdered by Stalin's agents, signifying the onset of official anti-Semitism in the Soviet Union. A year later, Mikhoels's successor and sidekick for thirty years, Benjamin Zuskin, was arrested. Whereas Mikhoels's death, disguised as a truck accident, was the occasion for public memorializing, and his body was permitted to lie in state, Zuskin was imprisoned for three and a half years before being secretly executed together with other Soviet Jewish luminaries on the night of August 12, 1952, which has since become known as the "Night of the Murdered Poets." GOSET, for its part, was officially closed in December 1949, and with it ended one of the most innovative and tragic experiments in Jewish art.

FIG. 20 Aleksandr Tyshler, *Mise-en-scène for Freylekhs*, 1945. Pencil, gouache, and watercolor on cardboard, 27½ × 22⅜ in. (69.8 × 56.7 cm). A. A. Bakhrushin State Central Theater Museum, Moscow. Art © Estate of Aleksandr Tyshler/RAO, Moscow/VAGA, New York

ART AND THEATER

Benjamin Harshav

THE MOSCOW YIDDISH THEATER

Outside, the revolutionary wave raged, and human eyes and too-human thoughts, scared and scattered, were blinking in the chaos of destruction and becoming. . . . At a time when worlds sank, cracked and changed into new worlds, a miracle occurred, perhaps still small, but very big and meaningful for us, Jews—the Yiddish theater was born.
— Solomon Mikhoels, "In Our Studio" (1919)

The Moscow Yiddish theater (1919–49) was born out of space and out of time.[1] Out of space, because it happened outside the Pale of Settlement, where five million Jews lived and spoke their own language; out of time, because it did not grow out of any organic development but emerged in a surreal moment, in the middle of World War I, and among privileged and Russian-speaking Jews who admired Russian and European cultural models. The originators, the Jewish Theater Society, founded in 1916 in Petrograd (as St. Petersburg was called at the time), were intent on building a modern, secular Jewish culture, with a theater alongside art and music, an art theater on the highest levels of the innovative theaters of Europe. The director, Aleksei Granovsky, a disciple of Max Reinhardt in Germany, projected a new conception of theater, in tacit dialogue with the most original theaters in Russia and Germany.

Some contemporaries felt that the Communist October Revolution of 1917, which provoked the revolution in all the arts, provided the impetus for this theater as well. But the idea of the Yiddish theater, as of many modernist trends, was born before the Revolution. Its logo and its first programmatic brochure, though published in 1918, were couched in national rather than Communist language. Russian intellectuals saw at the time a cognate language of Communism and the avant-garde. Even the aesthetics of mass scenes and rejection of individualism and psychologism could, on the surface, be presented as Soviet collectivism. By nationalizing the theater, the government provided it with a budget and an existence, albeit meager. But Bolshevik pressures also distorted, politicized, and crushed the modern arts.

The Moscow Yiddish theater created a mythological Jewish space and an enchanting typology of Jewish characters, a lost fictional world, based on the classics of modern Yiddish fiction. Only through a grotesque mirror or political negation of the past could the theater evoke this powerful bygone but symbolic world. If we peel off the agitprop banalities, this may be the lasting contribution of this Yiddish theater to an anti-Broadway Jewish theatrical myth. The totality of the stage experience made its performances unforgettable.

(opposite) Marc Chagall, *Costume Design for Agents,* 1920 (see pl. 40)

FIG. 1 Members of GOSET, Moscow, c. 1924. Photograph, 5½ × 8¼ in. (14 × 21 cm). The Russian State Archive of Literature and Art, Moscow

THE FAME OF THE YIDDISH AVANT-GARDE THEATER

The Moscow Yiddish theater, later known as GOSET (Gosudarstvenny Evreysky Teatr, or State Yiddish/ Jewish Theater), began as a modest actors' studio in Petrograd in 1918 and moved to the new Russian capital, Moscow, in November 1920 (fig. 1). By the mid-1920s, it was one of the most exciting companies in Russia and, indeed, Europe.

When the Yiddish theater came to Berlin's Theater des Westens in 1928, the influential theater critic Alfred Kerr began his review with these words:

> This is great art. Great art.
> External image and soul-shaking. The sound of words, the sound of blood, the sound of color, the sound of images. There are calls, voices, questions, shouts, choruses. It is enjoyment and horror . . . and in the end, human communion.
> That is, of course, pantomime with movement into eternity.
> Something wonderful.
> (Great art.)[2]

For the German Jews in the audience, who could understand only some words but still could respond to this carefully choreographed *Gesamtkunstwerk* (the Wagnerian ideal of a total, multimedia theatrical event), it was, indeed, pantomime, not dependent on words for understanding, but it was "pantomime with movement into eternity."

On a visit to Russia, the English theater critic Huntly Carter, author of several books on Russian and German theater, wrote that "the work of GOSET has no equal in Europe." The German theater critic Alfons Goldschmidt, after visiting Moscow in 1925, wrote, "The Moscow State Yiddish Theater, directed by Granovsky in ensemble with the actors, embodies at least the beginning of something entirely new, while the Western European theater, in its degeneration, looks in vain for new forms." And in 1935, after seeing the stunning performance of Solomon Mikhoels as King Lear, the distinguished Shakespearean scholar Gordon Craig wrote in the London *Times:* "Only now, after having returned from the Theater Festival in Moscow, do I understand why we have no Lear worthy of the name in Britain. The reason is quite simple: we have no actor like Mikhoels."

After all the formal inventions of the first quarter of the century, in theater as in art, it seemed that the avant-garde theater had exhausted its innovations. This new company might fulfill a need at a moment of crisis. Furthermore, for Western left-leaning intellectuals, it represented the new culture created in the wake of the October Revolution and the miraculous rebirth of the Jews, the most oppressed nation in Russia.

On November 9, 1916, with Russia still under the tsarist regime, a Jewish Theater Society was founded in Petrograd. Around World War I, a wave of national awareness and pride gave rise to new Jewish organizations, such as the Jewish Theater Society, the Society for the Promotion of Art Among Jews, the Hebrew schools network Tarbut and its Yiddish counterpart Kultur-Lige, and to a crowning achievement in publishing, the sixteen-volume Jewish Encyclopedia in Russian (*Evreyskaia entsiklopedia*).

The two revolutions of 1917 disrupted all work in the capital, but the emerging cultural powers supported the rehabilitation of the Jews as part of the new policy of elevating those oppressed by the tsarist regime. On November 29, 1918, the journal *Zhizn iskusstva* (The Life of Art) announced the establishment of a "Yiddish (or Jewish?) Workers' Theater" in Petrograd, affiliated with the department of theater and performance of the People's Commissariat of Enlightenment (Culture and Education). The Jewish Theater Society implemented that decision and published a programmatic brochure in Yiddish for the first performance. In February 1919, a theater studio was established, and Aleksei Granovsky, who had studied theater in Moscow and in Germany and been an assistant to the celebrated director Max Reinhardt, was appointed director of the Artistic Division. After five months of intensive studies, the studio was transformed into the Yiddish Chamber Theater; performances began in Petrograd on July 3, 1919.

In the eyes of the Jewish Theater Society, the task was "again to build the national, cultural life": "Isn't it strange, frightening? Jews, who have contributed the best artists, who have given the most splendid flowers to the universal altar of art, don't have their own theater to speak Yiddish with them? No! Such a theater must be. This is demanded by the honor and dignity of the Jewish people, this is demanded by our national culture."[3] Yet Granovsky's ambitions went beyond national culture: "We say: Yiddish theater is first of all a theater in general, a temple of shining art and joyous creation—a temple where the prayer is chanted in the Yiddish language. We say: *The tasks of world theater serve us as the tasks of our theater, and only language distinguishes us from others*" (emphasis mine).[4] That is, in a dialectical argument, if you want a national Jewish theater, it must be on the cutting edge of world theater and contribute to it.

It is important to keep in mind that in Russian, as in Yiddish, the same word means the language (Yiddish) and the nation (Jewish). A few times I have used "Jewish/Yiddish" to indicate the duality of the concept, but the emphasis was on the language "Yiddish." As we saw, Granovsky shared "the tasks of world theater" and insisted that "only language distinguishes us from others." And the chairman of the Jewish Theater Society, Lev Levidov, maintained that Jews needed "their own theater to speak Yiddish with them." Moreover, at the same time, another Jewish theater flourished in revolutionary Moscow, the Hebrew-language Habima (which later became the National Theater of Israel). And most important: in Soviet Russia, according to Stalin's own theory, the Jews were not considered a nation because they had no territory; Mikhoels would not have dared to defy this dogma. But Yiddish was a recognized language.

For lack of heating materials in Petrograd, the theater was closed for the 1919–20 season. But rehearsals continued, giving Granovsky the chance to educate and form an entirely new kind of well-trained and integrated repertory troupe.

In 1920, the theater moved with the Russian capital to Moscow, and was installed in a confiscated house owned by a Jewish merchant, I. L. Gurevich, who had fled the Revolution (tiles with stars of David are still embedded in the floor). The large living room on the second floor was turned into an auditorium with ninety seats, and the attached kitchen became a stage. The actors and their families lived on the first and third floors. The art critic Abram Efros, who had written a book on the art of Marc Chagall (published in Moscow in 1918), was appointed literary director of the Yiddish theater and brought Chagall to paint the backdrop.

Performances in Moscow began on January 1, 1921, surrounded by Chagall's murals (fig. 2). A year later, the theater moved to a larger auditorium with five hundred seats. In the year of purges (1937) the murals disappeared; they were stuck away until 1973 in a humid, nonfunctioning church that served as a warehouse for the Tretyakov Gallery, when they were retrieved for Chagall's signature.

In 1921, Granovsky's theater was appropriated by the state and named GOSEKT (State Yiddish Chamber Theater). Its name changed several times. In Yiddish, it was called Moskver Yidisher Melukhisher Teatr, or MIMT. In Germany in 1928, it appeared as the Moskauer Jüdische Akademische Theater (Moscow Jewish Academic Theater). In 1924, it had been renamed the State Yiddish Theater, or GOSET, and it existed under this moniker until 1949, when it was brutally liquidated.

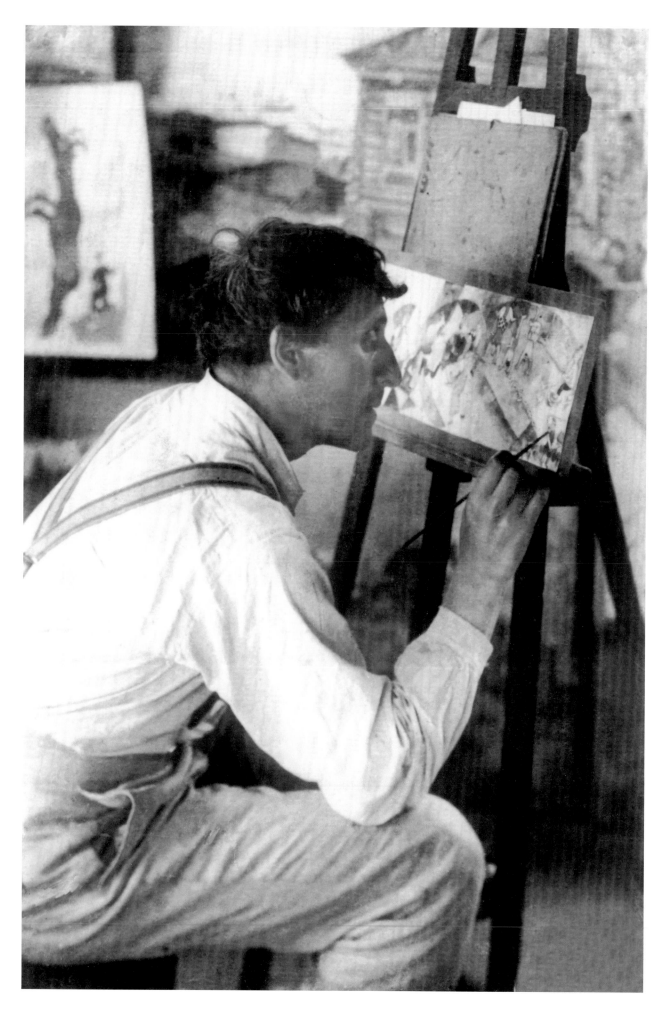

GRANOVSKY AND THEATER AS ART

The new art of the Yiddish theater was achieved in two phases, by two original artists: the director Aleksei Granovsky and the painter Marc Chagall.

Aleksei Granovsky was born Abraham Azarkh in Moscow in 1890. In 1891, some thirty thousand Moscow Jews were expelled; only five thousand remained. Granovsky's family settled in Riga (today the capital of Latvia), which had a long German tradition but had been under Russian rule for more than two centuries. Granovsky was exposed to both Russian and German culture and, through them, the culture of Western Europe. Riga, at the intersection of several empires and cultures, produced such intellectuals as the film director Sergei Eisenstein (two years older than Granovsky), whose Jewish father converted to Lutheranism and became the city architect of Riga, and the actor Solomon (Shloyme) Vovsi (or Vofsi) (Mikhoels), who, like Granovsky, was born in 1890.

Granovsky and his mentors believed in the creation of Yiddish theater as Art. The Jewish cultural renaissance of the preceding forty years had been concentrated in textual arts, literature, and ideology; now intellectuals argued that, to become a full-fledged culture, the nation needed music, plastic arts, and theater as well. Since theater was accepted as an art only in the most modern sense, they recognized no earlier Jewish theatrical tradition.

Granovsky learned from Max Reinhardt the staging of mass scenes. He erected a unified, "total work of art," using two devices: he brought all the arts—music, literature, folklore, dance—into one, total effect; and he gathered all the actors in one integrated human body that could converge in a "spot" or suddenly fall apart. In Reinhardt's conception, the director was the decisive force in the theater. Eventually, this led to a clash between the director and the artist when Granovsky told Chagall: "Who is the director here: you or I?"

Granovsky was to begin from absolute zero. As Abram Efros, the literary director of the theater, put it, "Granovsky had to build on an empty space. He was his own ancestor."

GRANOVSKY'S SYSTEM

In 1918, when Granovsky undertook his mission, he announced the search for candidates to train as actors for the new theater (fig. 3). There were only two preconditions: they must have had no previous experience with theater (the sentimental kitsch of Yiddish folk theater was anathema to him), and could be no older than twenty-seven (Granovsky himself was twenty-eight). An exception was made for Shloyme Vovsi, an intellectual who had studied law at Petrograd University and who was Granovsky's age. Vovsi had a "monkey face" so ugly that Granovsky found him beautiful. From the beginning—and under his new stage name, Mikhoels—he was Granovsky's right-hand man and his conduit to the other actors. In 1928, when Granovsky remained in the West, Mikhoels became the director as well as the leading actor of GOSET.

Granovsky trained his actors ab ovo, using the best resources of the avant-garde theater and professionals in all disciplines. He hired some of the best

FIG. 2 (opposite) Marc Chagall painting *Study for Introduction to the Jewish Theater*, 1920. Photograph, 6¼ x 9½ in. (15.9 x 24.1 cm). Private collection, Paris

FIG. 3 (right) Members of GOSEKT, Moscow, c. 1920

FIG. 4 *200,000*, 1921. Beth Hatefutsoth, Photo Archive, Tel Aviv, courtesy of Zuskin Collection

Russian teachers, who stayed in the starving capital, to instruct the actors in music, rhythm, dance, gesture, "plastic movement," and acting techniques (fig. 4). All this was done in Russian; Granovsky himself did not speak Yiddish, the language of his theater. The actors intensively studied Yiddish literature, language, folklore, and folk songs. Each was to be a master of all the theater arts, and in precise command of his body and voice. The system, similar in part to Meyerhold's "biomechanics," prepared the actors to be as agile as acrobats; the circus was an inspiration for the Yiddish theater, as it was for Meyerhold, Eisenstein, and Chagall.

Granovsky was a typical *yekke* (an East European nickname for a culturally German Jew), assimilated to high-culture German manners, and his ideal was silence, a state alien to the talkative Eastern European Jews who were his actors and audiences. As recorded by Mikhoels, he taught that "the word is the greatest weapon of stage creation. Its value lies not only in speech but in silence. . . . The normal state is silence. . . . The word is a whole event, a super-normal state of Man. . . . The intervals of silence between utterances

of phrases or words are the background from which the great, meaningful Word emerges."[5]

And in a parallel manner, Granovsky perceived movement: "The normal state [of man] is static. . . . The movement is an event, a super-normal state. . . . Every move must start from the static state, which is the gnarled background from which the meaningful move emerges. . . . A movement must be logically articulated into its basic elements, as a complex algebraic formula is broken down to its simple multipliers."[6]

Granovsky saw the theater as a temple, a religious experience, and the stage action as a choir. "Every type, everybody's movement, everybody's acting, painting, every role of individuality in the play is only a part of the architectonic whole. . . . Our artistic goal is the play as a whole. . . . And the value and significance of the smallest role is great in its relations to the whole dramatic construct. . . . One false performance of a word, or a move, not just of the central figure in a play but of the smallest and most overshadowed, can corrupt and cheapen the whole artistic image."[7] The Austrian Jewish writer Joseph Roth described Granovsky's theater in more philosophical terms: "the transformation of the accidental into the design of destiny."[8]

The theater performance was a work of art, a radical, densely orchestrated multimedia event that had nothing to do with Konstantin Stanislavsky's psychological realism. When all this was drilled perfectly, rehearsals began. Granovsky devoted between 150 and 250 rehearsals per production, chiseling every move, every word or half-word.

Modulation of movement and voice, shifts of mood and dynamics, gave life to the ensemble. It was between words and movement that the art of the ensemble was located. The text, like the actor, was treated as a means to the goal—the total performance—and the shorter the text, the better. Granovsky sought a total effect, involving every move of a multimedia polyphony. Performances were rich because they articulated each separate medium into myriad tiny steps, each foregrounded and meaningful. As Granovsky wrote in 1928: "I consider stage art an independent and sovereign domain. Therefore, all elements constituting a finished performance—the man, the script, the music, the sets, and the light—must be subordinated to a single, steadfast thought and the completed score of the production."[9]

Granovsky choreographed a polyphonic and dynamic, constantly surprising stage. He was "mathematically" precise and pedantically meticulous about every detail. The theater did not stage many productions, but almost every one was a cultural event (fig. 5). Already in the preparations for the first Moscow performance, a new force burst onto the stage, contributing a fictional world of Yiddish literature and folklore and a network of surreal devices: the art and personality of Marc Chagall.

A prominent Russian drama critic and theater professional observed:

When one sees this "Jewish acting," one cannot fail to be struck by the emotional appeal and rapidity of movement, the intensity of speech and vigor of the gestures. In its early productions, when the old repertory was being revised, poor Jews in tattered garments and comical masks or rich Jews—in frock-coats and stately, old-fashioned robes with colorful trimmings—would dart and dance about on the curious platforms and crooked staircases, in an ecstasy of delight. They were the Jews of the poorer slums. They would stand for a moment in solemn stillness, like monuments, before dashing away

FIG. 5 *The Travels of Benjamin the Third,* 1927. Photograph, 22 × 31 in. (56.2 × 78.2 cm). Beth Hatefutsoth, Photo Archive, Tel Aviv, courtesy of Zuskin Collection

FIG. 6 Marc Chagall, *Costume Design for Agents,* 1920. Pencil, ink, and gouache on paper, 10¾ × 8 in. (27.4 × 20.3 cm). Musée nationale d'arte moderne, Centre Georges Pompidou, Paris, AM 1988-254

into the hum of the marketplace, or springing from one platform to another, or rushing down a flight of stairs and away [figs. 6, 7].[10]

THE JEWISH FICTIONAL WORLD

The theater's greatness, however, did not rest solely on Granovsky's polyphonic approach, or on his mathematically calculated scores and directing. It derived rather from the fusion of these formal ideas with the surreal deformations of reality and the evocation of a Jewish fictional world, created by modern Yiddish literature and elevated to a level of art by Marc Chagall. As in Chagall's own work, another language was superimposed on the languages of avant-garde theater: a powerful, time-forged, fictional universe, with a series of generalized but unique types and situations: Menakhem Mendl, Benjamin III, and Senderl the Woman, piled-up shtetl houses with uncovered roofs, the new and precarious Jewish habitat in a train compartment (pls. 37, 38). That world was deformed, made grotesque, stood on its head—yet revitalized in a new, theatrical mythology.

This fictional world was raised to the level of a timeless myth through Granovsky's rhythm of "spots,"

which broke down the continuities of character and plot as if they were the subject matter of an Analytic Cubist painting. It was Chagall who taught him to depart from realism and continuity of space and time, and to embrace simultaneity of action on several levels—for which not Chagall, but his Constructivist followers, the artists Isaac Rabichev, Natan Altman, and Isaac Rabinovich, built multilevel stages.

Chagall and Granovsky were polar opposites: Chagall was emotional, "childish," "crazy," the very embodiment of the awakening folk type from the Jewish Pale of Settlement; Granovsky was rational, Europeanized, German-trained, and assimilated, mostly silent, precise, and disciplined. Yet Chagall, three years older, already was world-famous, accepted by the Paris avant-garde and the author of a one-man show in Berlin. They met at the very beginning of the Yiddish theater in Moscow, for a production of three minor skits by Sholem Aleichem; yet the collision of these two willful originals changed the course of the theater.

The vital link between Granovsky and Chagall was the actor Solomon Mikhoels. He was born in Dvinsk, midway between Chagall's Yiddish Vitebsk and Granovsky's Russian Riga. His father was a forest merchant and owned an estate. Before the Revolution, Dvinsk belonged to Vitebsk Province; after 1918 it was

FIG. 7 Marc Chagall, *Reb Alter (Costume Design for Solomon Mikhoels in Mazel Tov)*, 1920. Pencil and watercolor on paper, 13½ × 10 in. (34.5 × 25.5 cm). Private collection, Paris

FIG. 8 Marc Chagall, *Beyle the Cook (Costume Design for Mazel Tov)*, 1920. Ink and watercolor on paper, 11⅛ × 7⅝ in. (28.1 × 19.5 cm). Private collection, Paris

FIG. 9 Marc Chagall, *Man with Long Nose (Costume Design for It's a Lie!)*, 1920. Pencil, gouache, and red chalk on paper, 10⅜ × 7⅛ in. (26.5 × 18 cm). Private collection, Paris

incorporated into Latvia (and renamed Daugavpils). Thus it was affiliated with two different cultural worlds and assumed features of both—hence Mikhoels's closeness to the emotive, rich Yiddish folklore on the one hand, and admiration for Europe's sophisticated culture on the other. He found a common language with and admiration for both Chagall and Granovsky.

After being rejected by St. Petersburg University because he was a Jew, Mikhoels studied in Kiev. Finally, in 1915, he was admitted to the Law School of Petrograd University, from which he graduated in 1918. His attraction to acting and his commitment to Jewish culture led him to Granovsky's budding studio rather than to the practice of law. He became the lead actor in most of GOSET's plays. As an actor, Mikhoels combined his intellectual powers, a restrained, disciplined emotionalism, and the skills he had learned under Granovsky's tutelage to create one celebrated role after another. The essence of his art, however, came from Chagall: the painter was the source of the tragicomic perception of the absurdity of Jewish (and general human) existence, evoked through a demonstrative antirealism.

Under Mikhoels's guidance, the actors—all of whom came from small towns in the Pale of Settlement—recovered the gestures, movements, intonations, and sensibilities of the Jewish shtetl world from their childhood memories (fig. 10). Mikhoels and his counterpart Benjamin Zuskin collaborated to bring to light the subtle connotations and gestures of a disappearing Jewish world. This was knowledge no teacher could provide; it was the source of the emotive depth that the actors brought with them, which was then stylized and refined by Granovsky's system. Granovsky embraced the Jewish fictional world, its gestures and characters, and integrated it into his polyphonic conception, creating theater productions closer to a mythological happening than to a formalist performance.

The *Sholem Aleichem Evening*, which opened what Abram Efros called the "new birth" of the theater in Moscow, was based on character types familiar from Yiddish literature and folklore. The hero of *Agents: A Joke in One Act*[11] was Menakhem Mendl, a symbolic character based on Sholem Aleichem's book of that name, now mirrored fourfold (fig. 11). Menakhem Mendl is the prototype of a shlemiel, who seesaws between soaring fantasy and searing failure. A shtetl type, he attempts all Jewish *luft-parnoses* (professions of the air), such as matchmaking (shlemiel that he is, he brings together "a wall with a wall," a bride with a bride) and stock market speculation (with much the same success). In *Agents: A Joke in One Act*, he is placed in neither a shtetl nor Odessa, but on the road, in a train, where he tries to sell life insurance to anyone who will agree to "condemnify for death." One by one, three more agents enter the train compartment, trying to sell the same insurance to one another (fig. 12).

In 1925, Mikhoels in the role of Menakhem Mendl became the hero of the film *Jewish Luck*, which boasted Granovsky as director, Lev Pulver as composer, Isaac Babel as screenwriter, Edward Tisse (Eisenstein's cameraman) as cinematographer, and Zuskin and the GOSET cast as actors; even Chagall's (originally Sholem Aleichem's) train compartment used for the stage production was adopted and became the trademark of the film.

FIG. 10 Marc Chagall, *Costume Design for Solomon Mikhoels in It's a Lie!*, 1920. Pencil, watercolor, and ink on paper, 10⅝ × 10⅝ in. (27 × 27 cm). Private collection, Paris

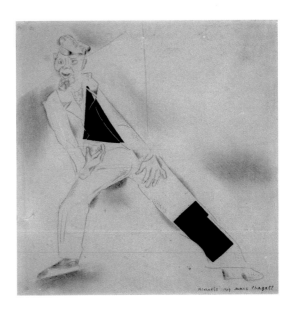

The ideological conflict of the Jewish theater was described by Mikhoels thus: "Looking for the means to reveal most sharply and conspicuously the tragic content of past Jewish life, condemned to disappear in our country, the [Moscow] theater showed a great diversity in evoking new stimuli in its development. To hone the characters, to perfect the stage devices, uncover new social kernels hidden in the atrocious, often anecdotal classical figures—this was our continuing path. *Isn't tragicomedy one of the phenomena typical of our contemporary epoch?*" (emphasis mine).[12] This tragicomic sense of humanity and Jewish destiny gave Mikhoels his singular actor's force: his grotesque or comical types carry a deep, sad overtone of tragedy, while the tragic character of King Lear is wrapped in the language and gestures of comedy. This is, of course, a Shakespearean feature, but Mikhoels drew it from his own life and times. By all accounts, Lear was his greatest role, a brilliant, tortured, unique performance.

FIG. 11 *(left)* Marc Chagall, *Menakhem Mendl (Costume Design for Agents)*, 1920. Gouache and pencil on paper, 10¾ × 8⅛ in. (27.2 × 20.5 cm). Private collection, Paris.
This costume design follows the directions of the script, which instructed that the costume be designed for "a young man . . . with a new fedora (which doesn't sit well on his head)."

FIG. 12 *(right)* Chaim Krashinski in *Agents*, 1921. Photograph, 5½ × 3¾ in. (14 × 9.5 cm). Beth Hatefutsoth, Photo Archive, Tel Aviv, courtesy of Zuskin Collection

FIG. 13 Benjamin Zuskin and Ely Ragaler in *It's a Lie!*, 1921. Photograph, 6³⁄₁₆ × 4⁷⁄₁₆ in. (15.7 × 11.3 cm). Beth Hatefutsoth, Photo Archive, Tel Aviv, courtesy of Zuskin Collection

CHAGALL'S IMPACT

A historian of the avant-garde theater in Soviet Russia wrote about this Yiddish theater:

> At the same time it is obvious from early accounts of their work that while they borrowed much from Meyerhold—his system of biomechanics, for instance—they had nothing in common with his intellectualization of theatrical form. They held his theories but expressed them with more drama and play of mood. . . . The idea of the structure is pure Meyerhold—the carrying out of the idea has the stamp of ecstasy, mystery and unfathomable sadness. A great contribution was made by such expressionists as the artists Chagall and Rabichev, and later by Nathan Altman, Rabinovich and Falk. They lit up the stage with a series of vivid pictures, always three-dimensional and mobile, which seemed to have a life of their own, which harmonized with and enhanced the grotesquerie of the stylized movements and which underlined the inherent color and richness in the Jewish character [fig. 13].[13]

An unexpected witness was the Labor Zionist leader David Ben-Gurion, who traveled from Palestine to Moscow in 1923. He went to the Yiddish theater's production of *200,000: A Musical Comedy* (based on a story by Sholem Aleichem) and recorded in his diary: "They sit on roofs, ledges and stairs, don't walk but hop, don't go up but clamber, don't come down but tumble and leap—Sholem Aleichem is unrecognizable."[14] Of course, this was a typical Chagallian vision. The artist's reading of Sholem Aleichem as a "modernist" who understood the topsy-turvy Jewish world was more on the mark.

The German critic Max Osborn saw the same performance in 1923, and on his return to Berlin he wrote an essay on Chagall. He described *200,000* in this way:

> The curtain goes up and you see a strange chaos of houses, intertwined in a Cubist manner, rising one above the other on different levels. Intersecting one another at sharp angles, they either stand below wide roofs or suddenly appear without a roof altogether, like a man taking off his hat, and display all their internal secrets. Here and there, bridges and passageways are drawn; wide streets rise and fall diagonally. Your eye perceives a fantastic interpretation of a Jewish-Russian small town, presented in the narrow confines of a stage in an unusually joyful and charming formula [fig. 14].
> Suddenly, high above the roof of one building, appears the figure of a Jew with a red beard and a green greatcoat, with a sack on his back and a staff in his hand. Instinctively I said aloud: "Chagall!" And suddenly everything

FIG. 14 Shimele Soroker's mansion in *200,000*, 1923. Photograph, 6½ × 8¾ in. (16.5 × 22.2 cm). Beth Hatefutsoth, Photo Archive, Tel Aviv, courtesy of Zuskin Collection

became clear: this is the world of Chagall. From him, everything emerged: the young artist-decorator Rabichev's creations, Granovsky's constructions, and the accompanying music of the composer Pulver. The latter, with unusual expressiveness, embodied Oriental motifs, ancient Jewish images, and Russian songs in operatic melodies, with trumpets and kettledrums.[15]

Later, in Mikhoels's dressing room, Osborn learned that, indeed, Chagall had played a decisive role in the development of the stage art of the Yiddish Chamber Theater. In this circle, he was considered the great originator and inspiration: "Like no one else in the young Russia of our days, Chagall has the stunning power of transforming the elements of an exceedingly rich and profound artistic folk culture into colorful, dreamy visions, striking our imagination."[16]

CHAGALL'S THEATER MURALS

In July 1914, Chagall had returned from Paris to Russia. After the Revolution, in August 1918, he was appointed by the Commissar of Enlightenment, A. Lunacharsky, to the post of Plenipotentiary on Matters of Art in Vitebsk and Vitebsk Province. Chagall plunged into an array of activities, including the founding of a People's Art College in Vitebsk, where he invited some of the original modern artists

as professors, including Kazimir Malevich, the founder of the abstract trend of Suprematism, and Chagall's former disciple El Lissitzky, who "converted" to the new, nonobjective art. However, the Suprematists, who were more radical than Chagall, swayed the revolutionary students and actually pushed him out of his own college. In the summer of 1920, with wife and daughter, Chagall left for Moscow. In November 1920, he accepted Granovsky's offer to paint the backdrop for three short pieces by Sholem Aleichem, staged in the new Yiddish Chamber Theater.

Chagall immersed himself feverishly in the work, and in the course of forty days in November and December 1920 he painted and furnished the stages for three short dramatic pieces by Sholem Aleichem, and he also painted the curtains, the murals that covered all the walls, the frieze under the ceiling, and even the actors' clothes and faces. Instead of a painting in a theater, he enclosed the whole theater in a painting that was dubbed "Chagall's Box." Granovsky said, "Who is the director here, you or I?"—and he never hired him again. Abram Efros, the literary director of the theater, had to keep the lights on before the play and explain what the images of the murals meant to the audience, and why the actors appeared in a frozen state on the stage and were revived on the murals.

After many efforts, the Yiddish theater was allowed to go abroad. On April 7, 1928, GOSET performed *200,000* in Berlin. More than forty reviews were published in Germany. Its reception surpassed that of any other Russian theater, and a book about it was published in German. Berlin was the center of innovative theater, and Granovsky was received there "as a new theatrical messiah, a more innovative and revolutionary director than Meyerhold, Reinhardt, and Piscator."[17]

A TOTAL PAINTING ENVIRONMENT

In a forty-day span in November–December 1920, Chagall painted an eight-meter-long canvas, *Introduction to the Yiddish Theater,* that was hung on the long, left wall. On the opposite wall, between the three windows, he placed four tall images of the Four Arts that participated in the new total theater: Music, Dance, Theater, and Literature. A long frieze under the ceiling, *The Wedding Table,* linked together the Four Arts while illustrating Sholem Aleichem's one-acter, *Mazel Tov.* And in the back, facing the audience when they left the theater, was an almost translucent and cosmopolitan square painting, *Love on the Stage,* which incorporated his Hebrew signature, SGL. Efros recalled: "He obviously considered the spectator a fly, which would soar out of its chair, sit on Mikhoels's hat and observe with the thousand tiny crystals of its fly's eye what he, Chagall, had conjured up there. . . . On the day of the premiere, just before Mikhoels's entrance on the stage, he clutched the actor's shoulder and frenziedly thrust his brush at him as at a mannequin, daubing dots on his costume and painting tiny birds and pigs no opera glass could observe on his visored cap, despite repeated, anxious summonses to the stage."[18]

The actors were thus perceived as moving Chagallian figures. This coincided with Granovsky's theory that the normal human state is silence, and actors should pop up out of the silence and fall back to it. To Chagall, the actors provided merely another degree of animation. Efros wrote of the production: "The best places were those in which Granovsky executed his system of 'spots' and the actors froze in mid-movement and gesture, from one moment to the next. The narrative line was turned into an assembly of spots. The wholeness of the spectator's impression was

complete. When the curtain rose, Chagall's wall panels and the decorations with the actors on the stage simply mirrored each other."[19]

Chagall often used geometrical shapes in his paintings, especially flat monochromatic rectangles and triangles in the Suprematist style, but he always tended to see them as real objects in a three-dimensional world, and the figures could climb under or fly above them. His own wife and child peep out from between two flat color stripes in *Introduction to the Yiddish Theater,* and the major figures of the painted theater leap above geometric space altogether. Without the geometrical shapes underneath, they would have been floating in groundless space.

THE POLYPHONIC CANVAS

As we enter the theater and look at the huge mural on the left wall, *Introduction to the Yiddish [= Jewish] Theater,* a powerful, sweeping movement carries us forward and upward; yet the movement is constantly impeded by groups of figures, bizarre activities, and ever-changing painterly events, making it a long journey indeed.

The movement upward and forward is reinforced by the band of human figures that occupies precisely half of the height of the mural and moves slowly from its lower to its upper half. This colorful band represents the story of the Yiddish theater; the paler images and vignettes in grisaille, scattered all around, represent Chagall's personal world.

The scene is divided in three rising circles (isn't life a circus?), focused around three functional groups of human figures: the theater management, the musicians, and the comedians.

Within each human grouping there is no realistic space but rather a conceptual conjunction that unites them. We cannot imagine, for example, an actual scene in which Chagall, touching Granovsky with his palette, is carried in Efros's arms; it is rather a realization of a dead metaphor, "Efros brought Chagall to Granovsky."

Space, time, and perspective are all evoked in the painting and are presented in discontinuous, disrupted bursts. The spectator's position is not taken for granted either. Chagall was furious that chairs were placed in the auditorium (of a theater!), thus fixing the place of the spectators.

AN ART OF THREE TIMES

Chagall's "supernatural" perception of both art and life—in 1912, Guillaume Apollinaire called his early art *surnaturel,* even before he coined the label *surréalisme*—his turning away from the realism, psychologism, and impressionism that still reigned in the Russian theater, his unsentimental emphasis on the vitality of traditional Jewish folk culture, infected the spirit of the theater and influenced its later achievements. Chagall's importance in the theater lay in his embracing the genre of the carnivalesque (as described by Mikhail Bakhtin), the topsy-turvy world that had reigned in medieval fairs. It was precisely through the carnival that Chagall could introduce the old, abandoned, and subverted Jewish world as a real, tangible substance of a work of art. Now the theater could fill its productions with a fictional world populated by rich archetypes, flesh-and-blood popular characters, outlandish figures. And although these characters may have been grotesque and out of touch with reality, they also were inspired by flights of fantasy and poetry, and by an ahistorical sense of absurd and comic human dignity.

One might look at the whole auditorium, "Chagall's Box," in light of Efros's understanding of Chagall and the Yiddish theater as an art sprung from nowhere, with no history or tradition, an "art of three times," encompassing its own present, past, and future. It is a celebration of Chagall's and the actors' generation as they try to enact the past, to extract its folk spirit, joy, and artistic values for the present. It is a procession onward and upward, to an unknown future, which they will reach by turning their world upside down. Yet the figures in the last group on the right of the long wall are looking not to the future but back to the present, to the performance itself.

This perception of Jewish culture entailed a foreboding of its own disaster. Secular Jewish culture, to which Chagall, Efros, and the new Yiddish theater contributed, was imported from general European culture. It was a utopian effort to create a culture of "three times." But secular Jewish culture had no true past, it had to borrow one from the religious tradition; and it had no true future of its own, it borrowed one from the Russian Revolution. Eventually, it was wiped out by that revolution itself.

INTRODUCTION TO THE YIDDISH THEATER

As we walk from left to right, in the direction of the Russian writing, a green Chagallian animal ("cow") bursts onto the scene and takes on the play with its horns. For the first-anniversary celebrations of the Revolution in Vitebsk, on November 8, 1918 (according to the new calendar), Chagall painted a green cow, indicating the new, antiacademic and antirealist revolutionary art; his students copied it and hung it all over the city (note the split in the middle of the cow, as if painted on two pieces of cardboard). Whether this story is true or not doesn't matter (fig. 15). Chagall retold it as part of his private mythology (and so did Efros). The Communist bosses did not like it: "Why is the cow green? What has that to do with Marx and Lenin?"[20] Chagall often used bright or saturated green as a challenge to realism: in his first theater work, in the Petrograd cabaret Comedians' Resting Place, he painted all the actors' faces green; his own face is green in *I and the Village* (1911), as are the faces of *The Green Jew* (1914; the revered preacher of Slutsk)

and the violinist in the Music panel on the opposite wall of the theater. In his autobiography, Chagall wrote: "I often said that I was not an artist, but some kind of a cow. I thought of placing [the cow] on my calling card." Here the painted cow represents avant-garde art and Chagall's impact on the new theater.

As Chagall tells it, the leading actor, Solomon Mikhoels, came to him to learn the nature of modern art. In Yiddish, as in some other languages, "to play the violin" and "to act on a stage" use the same verb, "to play" (*shpiln*), hence the violin is a metaphor for acting: If your fiddle is broken and you cannot *shpil* (play), you cannot *shpil* (act). The broken fiddle indicates the impasse Mikhoels saw in the old acting, and the gesture of offering it to the animal implies his willingness to learn. Mikhoels performs an acrobatic act, as taught in Granovsky's studio. The folk ornament on his pants indicates Mikhoels's link to popular culture and his fondness for Yiddish folklore, which he taught to the other actors.

In the first circle, Efros brought Chagall to the director Granovsky—here he brings him literally, a realization of the metaphor. Efros strides deter-

FIG. 15 Marc Chagall, *Study for Introduction to the Jewish Theater*, 1919–20. Pencil, ink, gouache, and watercolor on paper, mounted on board. 6¾ × 19¼ in. (17.3 × 49 cm). Musée nationale d'art moderne, Centre Georges Pompidou, Paris, AM 1988-226

minedly, left foot forward (as in Vladimir Mayakovsky's famous poem "Left March"). The Yiddish inscription on top of the first circle is written with traditional "square" Hebrew letters. It is conspicuously placed above the red arc that brings together the three dominant figures of the theater. The study for *Introduction* spells this text unambiguously: "IKSVONARG LAGASh EFROS." The first two words are inverted; when read in the opposite direction, they yield "Granovsky Shagal"—yet another expression of Chagall's ambivalence between Yiddish and Russian writing and culture. The third name is straightforward: "Efros."

On the final canvas, however, the names are distorted even further. Of "LAGASh," all that remains is "...AG...Sh," with vestiges of letters between; and

FIG. 16 Marc Chagall, *Study for Dance*, 1920. Pencil and gouache on paper, 9½ × 5 in. (24.1 × 12.7 cm). Private collection, Paris.
The Hebrew caption on the bottom reads, *Kol Chatan v'kol Kalah* (The voice of the bridegroom and voice of the bride), part of the seven marriage blessings in the Jewish wedding ceremony.

"EFROS" has only "EF . . . s," with paler outlines of the rest. Inside the words, in place of the missing letters, are tiny drawings: Chagall painting at his easel and the professorial Efros reading a book. Thus, the artist combined two systems, letters and ideograms, and two cultures, Jewish and Russian, to represent his protagonists.

The second circle shows traditional Jewish klezmers, or folk musicians, excited, with limbs strewn all around. In the third circle, three clowns wearing religious insignia stand the old Jewish world on its head. One is a religious Jew in a skullcap, turned clown. On his belt, we see a star of David ornament and an inscription in Yiddish cursive letters: *ikh bin akrob[at]* ("I am an acrobat"). Next to him is a Jew in the most solemn moment of prayer, standing on his head. Stars of David appear among the geometrical shapes on the clown's pants. Around his waist, in cursive letters, is the Yiddish inscription: *ikh bala-vezekh ikh* ("I frolic I," or: "I play pranks, am mischievous, have fun"). Between the middle clown's legs is a printed message, listing the three classical

Yiddish writers celebrated by the Yiddish Kultur-Lige and printed on their stamp: "Mend[ele-] Abramovitz Peretz Sholem Aleichem"; as well as two younger writers, friends of Chagall: "Bil [Bal-Makhshoves?] [Der] Nis[ter]."

In spite of the hilarious performance, the whole thing stands "on chicken legs" (*oyf hinershe fislekh*), that is, on a shaky foundation. Chickens are domestic animals, one of Chagall's emblems of the Jewish world. In the enclave connected to the chicken feet, we see a Jew riding on a rooster with another Chagall emblem, a fish in its mouth.

Chagall's *Introduction* is a celebration of the new Jewish art, in both painting and theater. In his manifesto "Leaves from My Notebook" (published in Yiddish in Moscow, 1922), the artist wrote: "For myself I know quite well what this little nation can achieve. Unfortunately, I am too modest and cannot say aloud what it can achieve. . . . When it wanted—it showed Christ and Christianity. When it wished—it gave Marx and Socialism. Can it be that it won't show the world some art? It will! Kill me if not."[21]

FIG. 17 Marc Chagall, *Study for Theater*, 1920. Gouache, watercolor, and pencil on squared paper, 9⅝ × 5½ in. (24.4 × 14.1 cm). Private collection, Paris. The Russian caption reads *Sketch for Badkhen mural.*

THE FOUR ARTS

In the four tall paintings representing the four arts that contributed to Granovsky's theater, Chagall painted the traditional folkloristic equivalents to the generic categories: Music, Dance, Theater, and Literature (figs. 16, 17). These traditions were linked to significant events in Jewish ritualized life and were conducted in the mundane language, Yiddish, on the margins of the Hebrew ritual texts. Indeed, in his memoirs of 1928, Chagall calls the four arts not by their general names but by the names of their traditional Jewish professions: "*klezmers* [folk musicians], women dancers, a wedding jester, a Torah scribe." Let us look at two of the arts.

Music (*Klezmers*) is a transformation of the fiddler who sits on the roof in *The Dead Man* (1908) via *The Violinist* (1912–13). In *Music*, however, he is tall (adapting to the high wall) and truly looms above the little houses and the church of the Russian provincial town. The two rows of houses create horizontal depth between them, yet, in its vertical rise, the towering figure connects the front and deep rows in a perspectival paradox. The patterns of the musician's *tallis* (prayer shawl) under his coat are translated into geometrical forms and are continued in the asymmetrically checkered pants; in Chagall's eyes, Jewish tradition provides geometrical forms, thus religious form and Cubist invention are one continuum. On the upper right, Malevich's famous black square is quoted, standing on its edge among the clouds, and the Chagall child hovers above the music like a little angel. A Chagallian animal on the lower left is enchanted by the music (see the parallel in *Literature*) and a little man on the upper left praises it between the houses. This romantic gesture of powerful, soaring music is ironized on the upper left by a little boy who defecates behind a fence, as described in Chagall's original autobiography.

Literature (*Torah Scribe*) shows a scribe, a traditional sacred profession, dedicated to the careful copying by hand of Torah scrolls written on parchment, which must be executed without a single error or blemish. He wears a prayer shawl at his holy work; yet he is writing not a sacred Hebrew text but a Yiddish folk story: "Once upon a time" ("*Amol iz [geven]*"). Yiddish literature takes over the role of religion and Hebrew. Above, behind the blue space, the same yearning animal as in *Music* moos: "SHAGAL," in Yiddish (pl. 33).

Both Chagall and the Moscow Yiddish theater started as innovative, cosmopolitan modernists and shifted to the problem of representing a culture in transformation in twentieth-century Europe.

HABIMA
AND GOSET
AN ILLUSTRATED
CHRONICLE

HABIMA

Habima (The Stage) was founded by a former Hebrew teacher, Naum Tsemakh (1887–1939), in Bialystok in 1912 and then reestablished in Moscow in 1918, after the Revolution. It was the first professional Hebrew theater in the world. As a dramatic art theater, it had as its mission to convey the ideas of Zionism and to promote the revival of the Hebrew language. Thus it performed solely in Hebrew, while stressing the continuous relationship between the heroic past of the Bible and the present.

After Habima relocated to Moscow in 1918, Konstantin Stanislavsky took the troupe under the wing of the Moscow Art Theater and became its mentor, counselor, and supporter. He appointed his protégé Evgeny Vakhtangov director of Habima. The company achieved great fame with its productions of Jewish mystical and folkloric plays that were noted for their rich visual effects and emotional intensity, including *The Dybbuk,* by S. An-sky, and *The Golem,* by H. Leivick.

Performances in Hebrew, a language unfamiliar to the majority of Russian Jews, ultimately alienated the Jewish masses. Habima's overtly religious, somewhat conservative stance underscored an uneasy relationship with governmental policy, and it was perceived as failing to adapt to the new Soviet reality. The company was harassed by the Yevsektsia, the Jewish Section of the Communist Party, which attempted to assimilate Jews into the new Soviet society and eradicate Jewish nationalist cultural expression. This pressure, together with theatrical constraints, forced the company to leave the Soviet Union for good in 1926; it eventually settled in Palestine and today is the national theater of Israel.

PLATE 1 *(left)* Natan Altman, *Poor Woman, Act 2 (Costume Design for Nechama Wiener in The Dybbuk),* 1922. Pencil and gouache on paper, 13 × 6⅞ in. (33 × 17.5 cm). Israel Goor Theater Archive and Museum, Jerusalem. Art © Estate of Natan Altman/RAO, Moscow/VAGA, New York

PLATE 2 *(right)* Natan Altman, *The Messenger (Costume Design for Aleksandr Frodkin in The Dybbuk),* 1922. Pencil and gouache on paper, 13¾ × 6⅞ in. (35 × 17.5 cm). Israel Goor Theater Archive and Museum, Jerusalem. Art © Estate of Natan Altman/RAO, Moscow/VAGA, New York

THE DYBBUK

PREMIERED **January 31, 1922**
Habima
ORIGINAL PLAY BY **S. An-sky (1914)**
TRANSLATION: **Chaim Nachman Bialik (1920)**
DIRECTION: **Evgeny Vakhtangov**
DESIGN: **Natan Altman**
MUSIC: **Joel Engel**

The Dybbuk (originally titled *Between Two Worlds*) is the tragic love story of Channan, a brilliant Talmudic scholar, and Leah, the daughter of the rich merchant Sender. The two were betrothed by their fathers before they were born, but Sender forgot this pact and promised his daughter to the son of a wealthy man. Channan tries to change this fate by employing prohibited rituals of the Kabbalah, and is struck dead. His spirit, or *dybbuk,* possesses Leah's body to prevent her from marrying another. Only through the intervention of a *tzaddik* (Hasidic sage), who threatens the *dybbuk* with excommunication, is the spirit exorcised. Nonetheless, love proves stronger than religious magic, and Leah dies so that she may join her beloved.

S. An-sky originally wrote the play in Russian for the Moscow Art Theater, but with Konstantin Stanislavsky's encouragement he translated it into Yiddish. This version was first performed by the celebrated Vilna Troupe in 1920. The poet Chaim Nachman Bialik translated the four-act play into Hebrew for Habima. Evgeny Vakhtangov interpreted the struggle of a soul between heaven and earth as a manifestation of a social and cultural revolution against the old religious order. Natan Altman designed the costumes in angular Cubo-Futurist forms, abstract geometries that relied on asymmetry to destroy the central axis of the body and intensify the traits of each character.

With this, the company's most celebrated play, Habima became one of the first theaters in Russia to embrace a newly Expressionistic acting style.

PLATE 4 Natan Altman, poster for the three-hundredth production of *The Dybbuk,* Habima, Moscow, 1926. 34 × 23 in. (86.4 × 58.4 cm). A. A. Bakhrushin State Central Theater Museum, Moscow. Art © Estate of Natan Altman/RAO, Moscow/VAGA, New York.

This is a poster for the final production of *The Dybbuk* in the Soviet Union. The text is in Russian with the name of the theater in Hebrew.

PLATE 5 Natan Altman, *The Hunchback (Costume Design for Eliyahu Weiner in The Dybbuk)*, 1922. Pencil and gouache on paper, 13¾ × 8⅝ in. (35 × 22 cm). Israel Goor Theater Archive and Museum, Jerusalem. Art © Estate of Natan Altman/RAO, Moscow/VAGA, New York.

Of his costume designs for *The Dybbuk* Natan Altman wrote, "The people . . . were tragically broken and twisted, like trees growing on a dry and bare soil. Colors of tragedy were inherent in them. Their movements and gestures were exaggerated and strained. I aimed at the utmost expression of the form. The forms, mainly, were meant to affect spectators since the Hebrew words were incomprehensible to most of them."

PLATE 6 Natan Altman, *Henoch, Friend of Channan (Costume Design for Benjamin Tsemach in The Dybbuk)*, 1922. Pencil on paper, 11¾ × 8½ in. (30 × 21.5 cm). Israel Goor Theater Archive and Museum, Jerusalem. Art © Estate of Natan Altman/RAO, Moscow/VAGA, New York

PLATE 9 *(above)* The Court of the *Tzaddik* in *The Dybbuk,* 1922. Photograph, 5⅞ × 8⅝ in. (15 × 22 cm). A. A. Bakhrushin State Central Theater Museum, Moscow.

In this scene, Sender has brought his daughter Leah to the court of a *tzaddik,* or miracle-working rabbi, to free her from the spirit of Channan. The *tzaddik,* wearing a fur-trimmed hat and seated on a high throne, orders the dybbuk to leave Leah's body, but the spirit, speaking through Leah, refuses. The Hebrew inscription above the *tzaddik*'s throne reads, *Hasha'ar L'Hashem* (The Gate of the Lord), a verse from Psalm 118 that is often placed above the ark in a synagogue.

PLATE 10 *(left)* Natan Altman, *Leah (Costume Design for Hanna Rovina in The Dybbuk),* 1922. Silk and cotton, height 63 in. (160 cm). Habima National Theater of Israel, Hanna Rovina Collection, Tel Aviv. Art © Estate of Natan Altman/RAO, Moscow/VAGA, New York.

Hanna Rovina performed the role of Leah wearing a white dress, which distinguished her from the other, black-clad actors. *The Dybbuk* established Rovina as the greatest actress in the Hebrew-language theater, and her original costume and dressing room from Moscow are currently enshrined in the Habima Theater in Tel Aviv.

THE GOLEM

PREMIERED **March 15, 1925**
Habima
ORIGINAL PLAY BY **H. Leivick (1924)**
TRANSLATION: **M. Caspi**
DIRECTION: **Boris Ilich Vershilov**
DESIGN: **Ignaty Nivinsky**
MUSIC: **Moshe Milner**

The Golem was based on the legend of Rabbi Judah Loew, also known as the Maharal (an acronym for Moreinu Ha-rav Loew, or "our teacher the Rabbi Loew") of Prague (c. 1512–1609). He was a student of the Kabbalah who learned the ineffable Name of God and used it to create a mystical creature out of clay. He endowed this *golem* with monstrous strength to protect the Jews against their oppressors and enemies, but eventually the Golem turned on his own people and had to be destroyed. Leivick's play is an expression of the traditional Jewish quest for the Messiah: the Maharal, impatient with God's promise of Redemption, takes matters into his own hands. His attempts fail, and Redemption remains beyond human reach.

Habima's production presented the Golem as a symbol of the Revolution—a monster created with the best of intentions. This allusion escaped the Soviet censors, but not Habima's sympathetic Jewish audience.

Ignaty Nivinsky's set design described a foreboding, ruined synagogue. Drawing on Jewish and Russian folklore, as well as on contemporary science fiction, his colorful costume designs envisioned beggars, phantasmagorical hybrid creatures, and figures that echoed the ancient amulets and the spirit of the Kabbalah.

PLATE 12 Ignaty Nivinsky, *The Fifth Tower (Set Design for The Golem),* 1924. Pencil, gouache, ink, and bronze paint on paper, mounted on cardboard, 18 × 24⅞ in. (45.7 × 63.2 cm). A. A. Bakhrushin State Central Theater Museum, Moscow. The plaque on the right says *Mizrach* ("East," which is the direction of Jerusalem and where Jews face when they pray).

PLATE 13 The Fifth Tower (Scene from *The Golem*), 1925.
Photograph, 7⅛ × 9½ in. (18 × 24 cm). A. A. Bakhrushin State
Central Theater Museum, Moscow.

This scene depicts the Fifth Tower, a ruined fortress where
the Jews of Prague took refuge from a pogrom. The two men
on the far right are the Messiah and the Prophet Elijah,
disguised as beggars. They have come to save the Jews from
the pogrom and ask permission to spend the night in the
tower. Only the madman, Tanchum, recognizes the Messiah
and rebukes him for wanting to sleep when the Jewish people
are threatened. The Maharal (center, with staff) arrives and
also recognizes the Messiah and Elijah. Alarmed that they
might interfere with his plans to save the Jews himself, the
Maharal orders them to leave the tower. The inscription on
the wall reads *Mizrach*, indicating that the tower was once a
place of Jewish worship.

PLATE 14 Ignaty Nivinsky, *Tallit with Tefillin (Costume Design for The Golem)*, 1925. Pencil, gouache, and tempera on cardboard, 13⅜ × 9¾ in. (33.8 × 24.7 cm). A. A. Bakhrushin State Central Theater Museum, Moscow

PLATE 15 Ignaty Nivinsky, *The Rabbanit, Wife of the Maharal (Costume Design for The Golem)*, 1925. Pencil, gouache, tempera, and ink on cardboard, 13½ × 9½ in. (34.2 × 24.1 cm). A. A. Bakhrushin State Central Theater Museum, Moscow

PLATE 18 Ignaty Nivinsky, *Frog (Tsefardeya) (Costume Design for The Golem)*, 1925. Pencil and watercolor on paper, 9⅛ × 5⅞ in. (23 × 15 cm). The Russian State Archive of Literature and Art, Moscow.

This is another rendition of the figure of the Golem, here portrayed as a mechanized, robotlike creature. One tradition of depicting the Golem was to emphasize its strength and mechanization in movement and behavior. The idea of an "artificial man" along with the new technology was popular in Nivinsky's time.

PLATE 19 Ignaty Nivinsky, *Fire (Esh) (Costume Design for The Golem)*, 1925. Pencil and watercolor on paper, 9⅛ × 5⅞ in. (23 × 15 cm). The Russian State Archive of Literature and Art, Moscow.

The Hebrew letters on the body do not have a meaning and are intended to invoke the magical aspect that is at the center of this play. As is the case with other drawings Nivinsky created for *The Golem,* this work incorporates elements of contemporary science fiction, along with his own imagination. These costume designs, as well as those for the other nonhuman figures, were designed by Nivinsky as evocations of magic, but were probably not used as actual costumes.

PLATE 20 *(below top)* Ignaty Nivinsky, *Golem (Costume Design for The Golem),* 1925. Pencil and tempera on cardboard, 18⅝ × 13½ in. (47.2 × 34.2 cm). A. A. Bakhrushin State Central Theater Museum, Moscow.

The Hebrew word at right, *Tit,* means clay, the substance from which the Golem is made.

PLATE 21 *(below bottom)* Ignaty Nivinsky, *Fish (Dag) (Costume Design for The Golem),* 1925. Pencil, gouache, and watercolor on cardboard, 18½ × 13 in. (46.8 × 32.9 cm). A. A. Bakhrushin State Central Theater Museum, Moscow

PLATE 22 Ignaty Nivinsky, *Bird (Tzippor) (Costume Design for The Golem),* 1925. Pencil and watercolor on paper, 9⅛ × 5⅞ in. (23 × 15 cm). The Russian State Archive of Literature and Art, Moscow.

In depicting the Golem, Nivinsky tried to go beyond a traditional anthropomorphic approach and reinvented the creature as a hybrid of various animals, human, and mechanical elements. However, the director of the play rejected the fantastic and phantasmagorical designs, and in all likelihood they were not translated into actual costumes.

PLATE 23 *(top left)* Ignaty Nivinsky, *Amulet (Costume Design for The Golem),* 1925. Pencil, gouache, and silver paint on cardboard, 9½ × 6¾ in. (24.2 × 17 cm). A. A. Bakhrushin State Central Theater Museum, Moscow.

These amulets, with Hebrew letters suggesting kabalistic names, were common in popular Jewish culture and were reproduced in the *Jewish Encyclopedia,* the major Russian reference book on Jewish tradition and history in the early 1900s. Ignaty Nivinsky was likely familiar with the *Jewish Encyclopedia* and saw an amulet reproduced in the book. The reproduction of the amulet had three bird figures with the names of the three angels—Senoi, Sansenoi, and Sammangelof—who were sent by God to punish Lilith after she fled from Adam in the Garden of Eden.

PLATE 24 *(top right)* Ignaty Nivinsky, *Amulet (Costume Design for The Golem),* 1925. Pencil, gouache, and ink on cardboard, 9⅝ × 6¾ in. (24.4 × 17 cm). A. A. Bakhrushin State Central Theater Museum, Moscow

PLATE 25 *(right)* Ignaty Nivinsky, *Amulet (Costume Design for The Golem),* 1925. Pencil and gouache on cardboard, 9½ × 6⅝ in. (24 × 16.7 cm). A. A. Bakhrushin State Central Theater Museum, Moscow

PLATE 26 Ignaty Nivinsky, *Amulet (Costume Design for The Golem),* 1925. Pencil and gouache on cardboard, 9½ × 6¾ in. (24.1 × 17 cm). A. A. Bakhrushin State Central Theater Museum, Moscow

PLATE 27 Ignaty Nivinsky, *Amulet (Costume Design for The Golem),* 1925. Pencil, gouache, watercolor, and bronze paint on cardboard, 9½ × 6¾ in. (24.1 × 17.2 cm). A. A. Bakhrushin State Central Theater Museum, Moscow

STATE YIDDISH THEATER

(GOSUDARSTVENNY EVREYSKY TEATR, GOSET)

The Yiddish Chamber Theater was founded in 1918 in Petrograd and presented its first public performance there on July 3, 1919. In 1920 the troupe relocated to Moscow, and in 1921 the theater received the patronage of the government. Thus it was renamed the State Yiddish Chamber Theater (GOSEKT). Marc Chagall was invited by the director, Aleksei Granovsky, to design the sets and costumes for the inaugural production in Moscow, *An Evening of Sholem Aleichem*, on January 1, 1921. The artist covered the auditorium with his murals, establishing a creative direction for the company through his stage sets, costumes, and makeup. Even the extreme stylization of the actors' gestures, for which the company became known, distinguished GOSET as one of the most innovative theaters in Moscow.

From the beginning, the Yiddish theater was supported by the Yevsektsia, the Jewish Section of the Communist Party, which considered it a propaganda tool that would address the Jewish masses in their own language. It was the theater for the proletariat, which could convey the corruption of capitalism and the death of the old shtetl lifestyle. Under the direction of Granovsky, and later the troupe's leading actor, Solomon Mikhoels, the company offered daring productions of traditional and contemporary Yiddish dramas, transformed to accord with the ideas of the Revolution. Ostensibly, the plays were supportive of the Soviet state, but a closer reading suggests that they actually contained veiled critiques of Stalin's regime. In its early years the theater cultivated an avant-garde approach, which combined strikingly reductive Constructivist-inspired set designs with an exaggerated, almost Expressionistic acting style.

In 1924, the theater received its final name, State Yiddish Theater, better known by its Russian acronym, GOSET. It performed for another twenty-five years, attracting a large audience, and its productions evolved in response to events in the Soviet Union. In 1928, as a result of GOSET's tremendous success in Moscow, the Soviet authorities decided to send the company on a tour of Western Europe. When the troupe was summoned back to Moscow, Granovsky decided to remain behind because of mounting restrictions imposed by the Soviet regime, and Mikhoels became the director while continuing as principal actor. In 1948, he was murdered on Joseph Stalin's orders, in what was officially designated an accident. The next year, after another leading actor, Benjamin Zuskin, had served briefly as director, GOSET was shut down by authorities.

THEATER MURALS BY MARC CHAGALL

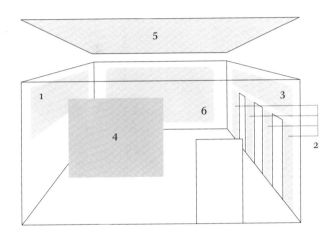

PLATE 28 Layout for Chagall's murals for the State Yiddish Chamber Theater, Moscow. 1. *Introduction to the Jewish Theater.* 2. Between the windows: *Music, Dance, Theater, Literature.* 3. Frieze: *The Wedding Feast.* 4. Exit wall: *Love on the Stage.* 5. Ceiling. 6. Stage.

Marc Chagall's murals for the original GOSEKT on Greater Chernishevksy Street served as an "Introduction to the Jewish Theater," and were composed of individual panels devoted to allegorical depictions of music, dance, theater, and literature. The artist recalled the folkloric imagery of his childhood in a Jewish village, but also made visual allusions to contemporary trends in Russian avant-garde art. His work, which contains many Yiddish puns and literary references, represents an attempt to combine all aspects of the theater into an integrated whole.

Chagall created an entire environment for his work, taking over the auditorium of the theater, and in several frenzied weeks painted murals to cover the walls, ceiling, and even the curtain on the stage. It was his intention for the action on the stage to embrace the audience, blurring the division between art and reality. The auditorium became known as "Chagall's Box." All the murals were executed in tempera and gouache on canvas, which could be taken down and thus preserved.

Chagall incorporated portraits of real people as well as imaginary characters. In one section of the painting, the Jewish theater critic Abram Efros carries the painter. Alongside this pair, GOSEKT director Aleksei Granovsky breaks into a dance. Above the heads of Efros and Chagall, and to Granovsky's left, Chagall painted their surnames in an arch of Hebrew letters.

Geometric squares, triangles, and segments of circles dance across the painting like shafts of light. The geometric surfaces, broken views, and distortions of Cubism are, however, modified in Chagall's work. The colored areas in the murals are reminiscent of Suprematist motifs, though Chagall uses them to heighten the rhythm and dynamism. Ultimately the formal composition is inseparable from the elaborate figurative content of the painting.

In the aftermath of the political turmoil of 1937, Chagall's murals vanished from public view. Until 1973, when Chagall returned to the Soviet Union to sign the murals, they were stored by the Tretyakov Gallery in an offsite warehouse. Beginning in 1990, the murals were seen publicly in the West and elsewhere.

PLATE 29 Marc Chagall, *Introduction to the Jewish Theater,* 1920. Tempera, gouache, and opaque white on canvas, 111⅞ × 309⅞ in. (284 × 787 cm). State Tretyakov Gallery, Moscow. Chagall incorporated many Yiddish puns and literary references, along with portraits of real people as well as imaginary characters. Entering the theater from the left is a portrait of the Jewish theater critic Abram Efros, who is carrying Chagall. Alongside this pair, GOSEKT director Aleksei Granovsky pirouettes. Above the heads of Efros and Chagall and to Granovsky's left are their surnames written in an arch of Hebrew letters. Chagall is greeted by a dwarflike character and an improvised orchestra. The conductor, in frock coat and cap, directs a lively tune, to the beat of which the principal actor, Solomon Mikhoels, is dancing. Lev Pulver, the theater's resident composer, plays the flute. This group, along with a goat, is placed on a disk, which turns about a central axis formed by the violinist, whose head, complete with jester's hat, has separated from his body. Mikhoels appears three times in the painting—as a dancer in the center, at the far left with a violin (doing a split), and once in normal dress, with a tie and a hat, behind the circus artists standing on their heads. The lower right-hand corner echoes the motif of the boy relieving himself in *Study for Introduction to the Jewish Theater* (1917).

PLATE 30 Marc Chagall, *Music,* 1920. Tempera, gouache, and opaque white on canvas, 83⅞ × 41 in. (213 × 104 cm). State Tretyakov Gallery, Moscow.

The *klezmer* (violinist) stands above the *shtetl* housetops and church. He wears a prayer shawl underneath his coat, suggesting a connection between religion and music. The panel includes multiple references to previous Chagall works, and the piece itself is based on several of the artist's earlier works, such as *The Violinist,* 1912–13. In addition, Chagall refers to artistic rival Kazimir Malevich's famous *Black Square* (1915), balancing it on one corner of the house on the upper right.

PLATE 31 Marc Chagall, *Dance,* 1920. Tempera, gouache, and opaque white on canvas, 84¼ × 42½ in. (214 × 108.5 cm). State Tretyakov Gallery, Moscow.

Symbolizing the joy of a wedding, this image features a female dancer who is surrounded by elements of celebration, including various instruments of a Jewish klezmer band and an acrobatic man standing on his head in carnival mode. Painted both inside and around the yellow ring upon which she dances is the phrase *Kol Chatan v'kol Kalah* (the voice of the groom, the voice of the bride), a verse from the Hebrew wedding song. In the upper left a boy gathers up and carries away the *chuppah* (wedding canopy).

PLATE 32 Marc Chagall, *Theater*, 1920. Tempera, gouache, and opaque white on canvas, 83¾ × 42¼ in. (212.6 × 107.2 cm). State Tretyakov Gallery, Moscow.

The central figure in this panel is that of the *badkhen* (wedding jester), who serves both to entertain his audiences with poems and bawdy humor as well as to emphasize the bittersweetness of weddings. His joyous expression juxtaposed with the weeping bride and groom is a testament to the dual function of the *badkhen*. Behind him, the bride's parents flank the purple *chuppah* (wedding canopy), under which a rabbi waits.

PLATE 33 Marc Chagall, *Literature,* 1920. Tempera, gouache, and opaque white on canvas, 85 × 32 in. (216 × 81.3 cm). State Tretyakov Gallery, Moscow.

Chagall depicts the figure of a Torah scribe in the process of copying sacred texts. The text he is transcribing, however, is not bibilical but rather the beginning of a Yiddish folk story that reads, "Once upon a time," underscoring the significance of Yiddish literature and folklore. Behind the blue space upon which the scribe is seated, a cow moos "SHAGAL" in Yiddish. In the far background, a boy carries a chair with a sign on which the letters "Th" for "Theater" are written.

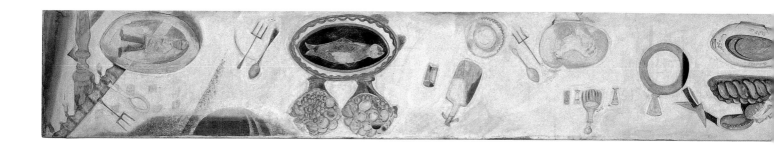

PLATE 34 Marc Chagall, *Wedding Feast,* 1920. Tempera, gouache, and opaque white on canvas, 25¼ × 314½ in. (64 × 799 cm). State Tretyakov Gallery, Moscow.

The long frieze, stretching the entire length of the wall above the four allegorical figures, depicts the wedding table with all the ritual dishes. It served to heighten the festive, ceremonial atmosphere that surrounded the celebration of the wedding.

PLATE 35 *(opposite)* Marc Chagall, *Love on the Stage,* 1920. Tempera, gouache, and opaque white on canvas, 111½ × 97⅝ in. (283 × 248 cm). State Tretyakov Gallery, Moscow.

Located on the end wall opposite the stage, *Love on the Stage* is based on the classic ballet pas de deux. The disembodied silhouettes of the ballerina and her partner have been liberated from their traditional ballet poses. They dance amid an array of circles, squares, lines, and triangles. The down-to-earth scene at the lower portion of the canvas contrasts with the ecstasy of love above.

AN EVENING OF SHOLEM ALEICHEM

PREMIERED **January 1, 1921**
State Yiddish Chamber Theater (GOSEKT)
BASED ON **the Menakhem Mendl stories of Sholem Aleichem**
DIRECTION: **Aleksei Granovsky**
DESIGN: **Marc Chagall**

The Yiddish theater's first production in Moscow combined three short plays derived from the Menakhem Mendl stories of the Russian Yiddish-language author Sholem Aleichem (1859–1916). *An Evening of Sholem Aleichem* consisted of *Agents: A Joke in One Act, Mazel Tov,* and *The Spoiled Celebration.* The last was replaced by *It's a Lie! Dialogue in Galicia* in September 1921. *An Evening* was later extended to include *Der get* (The Divorce), another one-act play, and the four plays collectively ran as *The Masks of Sholem Aleichem* from 1924.

Sholem Aleichem's themes, which were closely aligned with those of the Revolution, equated capitalism and religion. According to the actor Solomon Mikhoels, they demonstrated the "bankruptcy of the old world when many still believed that everything was in good working order." Mikhoels portrayed Sholem Aleichem's famous recurring character Menakhem Mendl, a *luftmentsh,* or "man of air," whose failure to find a place in society despite repeated (and often ludicrous) attempts at financial success reveals the inherent corruption of capitalism. The first production of *An Evening of Sholem Aleichem* took place on Moscow's Greater Chernishevsky Street in a small theater that held only ninety spectators. It featured costume and set designs by Marc Chagall, whose murals for the auditorium fused the action on the stage with the art on the surrounding walls.

AGENTS

A JOKE IN ONE ACT

PREMIERED **January 1, 1921 (part of *An Evening of Sholem Aleichem*)**
State Yiddish Chamber Theater (GOSEKT)
BASED ON **the Menakhem Mendl stories of Sholem Aleichem**
DIRECTION: **Aleksei Granovsky**
DESIGN: **Marc Chagall**

In this one-act comedy, which takes place in a third-class train car, Menakhem Mendl—Sholem Aleichem's most celebrated character—endeavors to sell life insurance. As with his other ventures, this one ends in failure.

Menakhem Mendl makes his first sales pitch when a gentleman takes the seat next to him. As the conversation between the two unfolds, the audience apprehends that both are insurance agents. When a third gentleman, another insurance agent, enters the car, the scenario repeats itself. Finally, a fourth man enters the car, with his wife and five ill-mannered children. The three agents try to convince him of the necessity of life insurance. When he attempts the same with them, each realizes that they are all insurance agents, and that none of them can make a sale.

Although the play provides only a glimpse into the life of Menakhem Mendl, the audience was expected to recognize the *luftmentsh* ("man of air") that this character embodies: an impractical dreamer with no single career or income, drifting from one failed get-rich-quick scheme to another. The *luftmentsh* would be an emblem for the Jew of the old shtetl.

Marc Chagall's set included a white arch that sprang from the floor, suggesting railroad tracks, which carried a toy locomotive up an incline. The Yiddish inscription indicated that this was a "Smoking Car."

PLATE 37 *(opposite)* Third-Class Train Car in *Agents,* 1921. Photograph, 6 × 8½ in. (15.5 × 21.5 cm). Austrian Theater Museum, Vienna, PSA 299.497

PLATE 38 Marc Chagall, *Third-Class Train Car (Set Design for Agents),* 1920. Pencil, gouache, and ink on paper, 10⅛ × 13½ in. (25.6 × 34.2 cm). Musée nationale d'art moderne, Centre Georges Pompidou, Paris, AM 1988-253

PLATE 39 Marc Chagall, *Woman with Child (Costume Design for Agents),* 1920. Pencil and gouache on paper, 10⅞ × 8 in. (27.7 × 20.3 cm). Private collection, Paris

PLATE 40 Marc Chagall, *Costume Design for Agents*, 1920.
Gouache, watercolor, and pencil on paper, 10¾ × 8⅛ in.
(27.2 × 20.5 cm). Private collection, Paris

MAZEL TOV

PREMIERED **January 1, 1921 (part of *An Evening of Sholem Aleichem*)**
State Yiddish Chamber Theater (GOSEKT)
BASED ON **the Menakhem Mendl stories of Sholem Aleichem**
DIRECTION: **Aleksei Granovsky**
DESIGN: **Marc Chagall**

Set in the kitchen of a wealthy home, *Mazel Tov* features a conversation between the bookseller Reb Alter and the cook Beyle. Reb Alter, a kindhearted dreamer, complains that his customers are more interested in socialist literature than in old books, which hurts his business. Beyle, a widow in her mid-thirties, is irritated by the world's injustice. After becoming slightly drunk, Reb Alter tells her about Zionist and socialist principles, about which he has only slight knowledge. A mutual sympathy grows between the two, and the play concludes with their decision to get married. Simultaneously, the servant Fradl and the neighbor valet Chaim decide to do the same.

In his stage set, Marc Chagall rendered a Jewish kitchen dreamlike with an upside-down goat—a recurring motif of his—and a decorative scheme of Hebrew letters on the fire screen. When read sideways, the letters spelled "Alei," the beginning of the name Aleichem—short for Sholem Aleichem.

PLATE 41 *(left)* Marc Chagall (left) with Solomon Mikhoels (right) as Reb Alter in *Mazel Tov,* 1921. Photograph. Courtesy of Jacob Baal-Teshuva, New York

PLATE 42 *(opposite)* Marc Chagall, *Young Man (Costume Design for Mazel Tov),* 1920. Gouache and pencil on paper, 10⅛ × 4⅞ in. (25.6 × 12.3 cm). Private collection, Paris

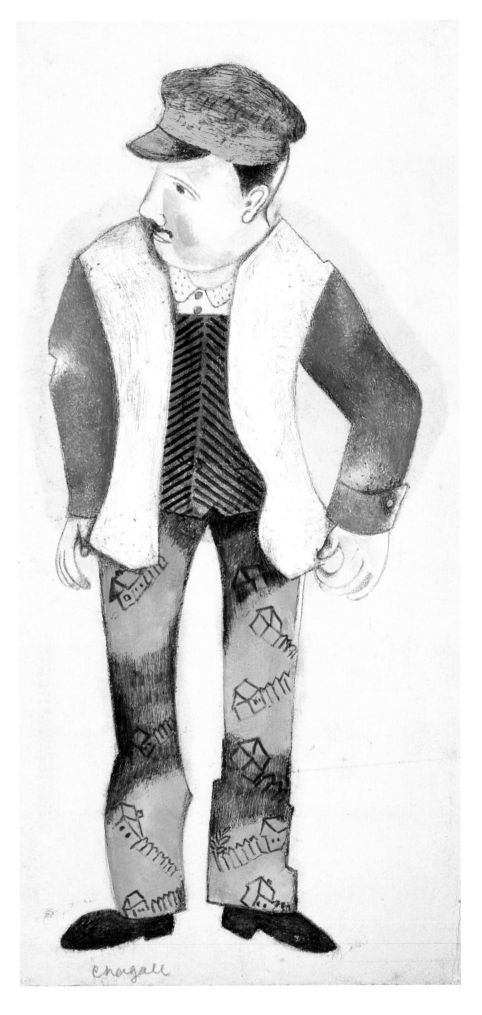

PLATE 43 Solomon Mikhoels as Reb Alter and Mikhail Shteiman as Chaim in *Mazel Tov,* 1921. Photograph, 4½ × 6⅛ in. (11.5 × 15.7 cm). Beth Hatefutsoth, Photo Archive, Tel Aviv, courtesy of Zuskin Collection.

In this photograph Chaim, the neighbor's valet, walks into Beyle's kitchen, where Reb Alter is sitting, to announce his engagement to Fradl the servant.

IT'S A LIE! DIALOGUE IN GALICIA

PREMIERED September 1921 (part of *An Evening of Sholem Aleichem*)
State Yiddish Chamber Theater (GOSEKT)
BASED ON the Menakhem Mendl stories of Sholem Aleichem
DIRECTION: Aleksei Granovsky
DESIGN: Marc Chagall
SET DESIGN: Natan Altman

It's a Lie! Dialogue in Galicia is a dialogue between two Jewish men riding in a railroad car. When one discovers that the other is from the town of Kolomea, he attempts to obtain as much information as possible about the town's wealthiest resident. The man from Kolomea reveals the information, but in order not to appear a gossipmonger, he prefaces everything with the words "They say" and ends with "But it's a lie."

The play took as its theme the destructive force of gossip and mocked false piety. Under Aleksei Granovsky's direction, the two actors used extravagant gestures in the manner of marionettes. *It's a Lie!* marked the beginning of Benjamin Zuskin's career as a Yiddish actor.

Although Marc Chagall left the theater after the first production of *An Evening of Sholem Aleichem,* when *It's a Lie!* was not yet a part of its repertoire, he designed the set and costumes for the play. His costume designs were used in the September production, but his set designs were regarded as too abstract. Designs by Natan Altman, his first for GOSEKT, replaced Chagall's. Altman's set designs unfortunately have not survived.

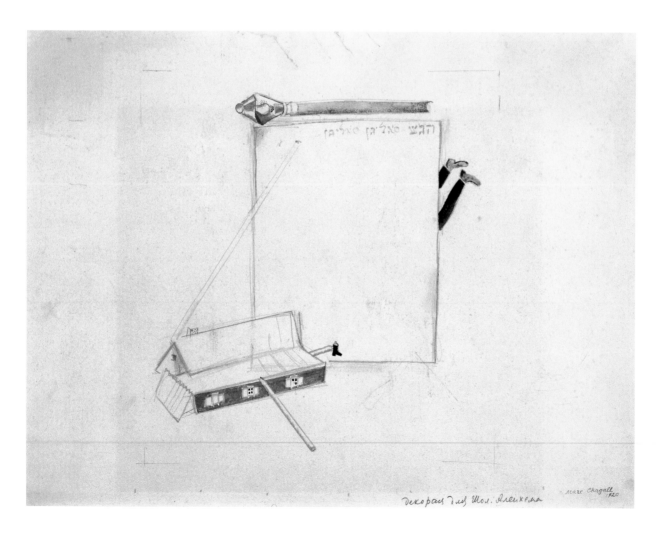

PLATE 45 *(opposite)* Marc Chagall, *Set Design for It's a Lie! Dialogue in Galicia,* 1921. Pencil and gouache on paper, 8⅞ × 11¾ in. (22.5 × 30 cm). Private collection, Paris.
The Yiddish inscription on the flat reads HGSh S'ALIGN S'ALIGN: the first word should be read from left to right (and not the Yiddish right to left) and is a distortion of the inverted word *Shagal* (Chagall). The other two mean "it's a lie." According to Benjamin Harshav, Chagall's design was regarded as too abstract and was replaced with a set by Natan Altman.

PLATE 46 *(above)* Marc Chagall, *Costume Design for It's a Lie!,* 1920. Pencil, gouache, and ink on paper, 10⅝ × 7⅝ in. (27 × 19.3 cm). Private collection, Paris.
This fanciful costume design for *It's a Lie!* includes the title of the play embroidered in both Yiddish (S'Align) and Hebrew (Sheker) on the pants leg.

GOD OF VENGEANCE

PREMIERED 1921
State Yiddish Chamber Theater (GOSEKT)
ORIGINAL PLAY BY Sholem Asch (1907)
DIRECTION: Aleksei Granovsky
DESIGN: Isaac Rabinovich
MUSIC: S. Rozovsky

God of Vengeance is the story of Yankel Tshaptshovitsh, a Jewish brothel owner who tries to shield his daughter from his immoral occupation. His hopes for her redemption are crushed when she falls in love with a prostitute from his brothel. One of the first European plays to deal explicitly with a lesbian theme, *God of Vengeance* had already gained notoriety in German-, Russian-, and English-language productions before GOSEKT's performance.

Aleksei Granovsky chose to emphasize the play's didactic and political message—that is, the inherent connection between sinful behavior and capitalism—over its risqué subject matter.

God of Vengeance marked a new artistic direction for the theater, after Marc Chagall's departure. Isaac Rabinovich designed colorful sets and costumes for the production, his first work for GOSEKT. His stage designs accentuated the dichotomy between the bourgeois propriety of the apartment and the squalor of the brothel beneath it (the setting for the second act), thereby capturing the split between Tshaptshovitsh's two worlds.

PLATE 47 Poster for *200,000, The Sorceress, God of Vengeance,* and *Three Jewish Raisins,* GOSEKT, Moscow, 1924. 28 × 21 in. (71 × 53.5 cm). The Russian State Archive of Literature and Art, Moscow

PLATE 48 *(top)* Isaac Rabinovich, *The Apartment of Yankel Tshaptshovitsh, the Brothel Owner (Set Design for God of Vengeance),* 1921. Pencil and oil on paper, 13 × 17¾ in. (33 × 45.2 cm). A. A. Bakhrushin State Central Theater Museum, Moscow

PLATE 49 *(bottom)* Isaac Rabinovich, *Costume Designs for God of Vengeance,* 1921. Pencil and oil on paper, mounted on cardboard, 13⅛ × 38¾ in. (33.3 × 98.5 cm). A. A. Bakhrushin State Central Theater Museum, Moscow

URIEL ACOSTA

PREMIERED **July 3, 1919**
REVIVED **April 9, 1922**
State Yiddish Chamber Theater (GOSEKT)
ORIGINAL PLAY: **Karl Gutzkow (1846)**
ADAPTATION FOR THE 1922 PRODUCTION: **Moshe Litvakov
      and Mark Rivesman**
DIRECTION: **Aleksei Granovsky**
DESIGN: **Natan Altman**
MUSIC: **S. Rosovsky**

Karl Gutzkow's classic German drama is based on the
life of Uriel Acosta, a seventeenth-century Portuguese
converso, or involuntary convert to Christianity, who fled
to Amsterdam in search of religious freedom. Once he
was there, however, the strict orthodoxy of the Jewish
community drove him to suicide. Because of its implied
criticism of religion and superstition, the play appealed
to Soviet authorities.

　　The sets by Natan Altman—consisting of black walls
and an empty stage, with only a few geometric forms to
suggest furniture and aid the actors in their movements—
reflected the peak of Constructivist design. The abstract
set contrasted with the actors' realistic performance.

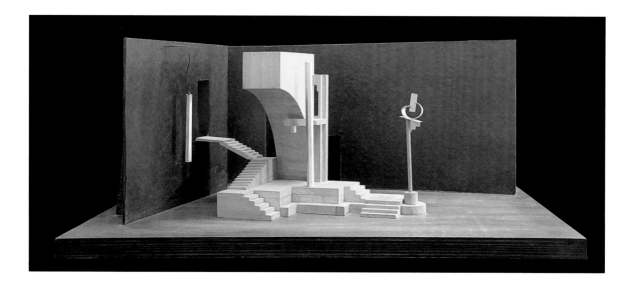

PLATE 50 *Set Model for Uriel Acosta,* based on original design
by Natan Altman, 1922, (reconstructed later). Wood and
metal, 12½ × 29 × 20¼ in. (31.8 × 73.7 × 54.4 cm). Israel Goor
Theater Archive and Museum, Jerusalem

PLATE 51 Poster for *The Sorceress* and *Uriel Acosta* (on the bottom), GOSEKT, Moscow, 1923. 28 × 40 in. (71.1 × 101.6 cm). The Russian State Archive of Literature and Art, Moscow

PLATE 52 Natan Altman, *Library in the House of De Silva
(Set Design for Uriel Acosta)*, 1922. Ink, tempera, lacquer,
and collage on cardboard, 13⅝ × 18⅞ in. (34.6 × 48 cm). A. A.
Bakhrushin State Central Theater Museum, Moscow. Art ©
Estate of Natan Altman/RAO, Moscow/VAGA, New York.
Altman designed the all-black set of *Uriel Acosta* as different
levels of platforms and stairs, devoid of any furniture.
Constructions, or geometrical forms, replaced painted deco-
rations, epitomizing the avant-garde's rejection of illusionist
sets as antiquated and bourgeois.

THE SORCERESS AN ECCENTRIC JEWISH PLAY

PREMIERED **December 2, 1922**
State Yiddish Chamber Theater (GOSEKT)
ORIGINAL PLAY BY **Avrom Goldfadn (1882)**
ADAPTATION: **Yekhezkel Dobrushin and Moshe Litvakov**
DIRECTION: **Aleksei Granovsky**
DESIGN: **Isaac Rabinovich**
MUSIC: **Joseph Akhron**

The Sorceress: An Eccentric Jewish Play contains all of the hair-raising adventures, improbable coincidences, and magical interventions typical of nineteenth-century Yiddish melodrama. The play opens at the home of a wealthy Jew, Reb Avremtse, where his daughter Mirele is celebrating her birthday. The festivities come to an abrupt halt when a tsarist officer enters to arrest Avremtse. Mirele is left in the care of her evil stepmother, Vasia, who, aided by a sorceress, kidnaps Mirele and sells her into slavery in Istanbul. Though the play has a happy ending—Mirele's beloved rescues her, and her father is released from custody—Yekhezkel Dobrushin and Moshe Litvakov transformed Avrom Goldfadn's melodrama into a harsh critique of capitalism and of the early Yiddish theatrical tradition, through acrobatics, inappropriate laughter, and bombastic music. The production was nonetheless criticized as reactionary by Soviet authorities for returning to the themes of traditional Yiddish theater.

Isaac Rabinovich's Constructivist set comprised scaffolding, ladders, and platforms built atop and beside one another to allow for exuberant movements by the actors. The stage resembled a construction site, a symbol of progress familiar to the proletarian audience. Joseph Akhron wrote twenty songs, inspired by his ethnographic studies in the former Pale of Settlement. The juxtaposition of his traditional melodies with Rabinovich's modern set emphasized the discrepancy between old and new.

PLATE 54 *(opposite top)* Poster for *The Sorceress*, GOSEKT, Moscow, 1922. 28 × 34 in. (71.1 × 86.4 cm). The Russian State Archive of Literature and Art, Moscow.
This poster was made for the fiftieth performance of *The Sorceress.*

PLATE 55 *(opposite bottom) Set Model for The Sorceress,* based on original design by Isaac Rabinovich, 1922 (reconstructed later). Wood, metal, and cloth, 17 × 24 × 11 in. (42.3 × 62 × 29 cm). Israel Goor Theater Archive and Museum, Jerusalem.
Set designs for *The Sorceress* incorporate screens, furniture, ladders, platforms, and construction materials in various configurations. Each act established its own distinct setting, from a family home to a crowded Istanbul marketplace.

ГОСУДАРСТВЕННЫЙ ЕВРЕЙСКИЙ КАМЕРНЫЙ ТЕАТР

Малая Бронная 2 (у Никитских ворот) Тел. 1-69-10.

СУББОТА 21 АПРЕЛЯ

в **50** раз в **50** раз

КОЛДУНЬЯ

ЦЕНЫ ПОВЫШЕННЫЕ.

Начало в 8 часов.

Билеты в кассе (11-9) и в театр. кассах.

PLATE 56 The Marketplace in *The Sorceress*, 1922. Photograph, 8½ × 28½ in. (21.5 × 72.5 cm). A. A. Bakhrushin State Central Theater Museum, Moscow

PLATE 57 Isaac Rabinovich, *Costume Designs for The Sorceress,* 1922. Pencil, crayon, ink, and oil on paper, mounted on cardboard, 15¾ × 37⅝ in. (40 × 95.5 cm). A. A. Bakhrushin State Central Theater Museum, Moscow

PLATE 59 Benjamin Zuskin in the title role of *The Sorceress*, 1922. Photograph, 10 × 6½ in. (25.4 × 16.5 cm). Courtesy of Ala Zuskin-Perelman, Or-Yehuda, Israel.

Caked in grotesque makeup and wearing a prosthetic nose, Benjamin Zuskin played the Sorceress, his first leading role in a GOSEKT production. The title character was written to be played by a male actor.

200,000 A MUSICAL COMEDY

PREMIERED June 28, 1923
State Yiddish Chamber Theater (GOSEKT)
BASED ON The Big Win by Sholem Aleichem (1915)
ADAPTATION: Yekhezkel Dobrushin
DIRECTION: Aleksei Granovsky
SET DESIGN: Aleksandr Stepanov
COSTUME DESIGN: Isaac Rabichev
MUSIC: Lev Pulver

200,000: A Musical Comedy tells the story of Shimele Soroker, a poor tailor who wins 200,000 rubles in the lottery. After becoming rich overnight, Shimele tries to ingratiate himself with the local bourgeoisie by throwing a lavish ball and investing in a movie theater. But he mistakenly writes an extra zero on the check for the theater, thus paying out more money than he actually has and losing his newfound wealth. In Sholem Aleichem's original version, Shimele gives much of his fortune to charity, but Granovsky sought to portray characters as social types, and in GOSEKT's production Shimele represents the immorality and decadence of the nouveau riche.

The social status of the various characters was underscored by a split stage: workers floated on ladders above the obese bourgeoisie. A highlight of the production was the entrance of Soloveitchik the matchmaker, played by Benjamin Zuskin, who descended onto the stage with a parachute to arrange the marriage between Shimele's daughter and a wealthy man. This was a visualization of the Yiddish term *luftmentsh*, or "man of air," a schemer without substance. The GOSEKT production transformed Sholem Aleichem's lighthearted and comical treatment of class conflict into a scathing and farcical critique of capitalism.

PLATE 60 Poster for *200,000*, GOSET, Moscow, 1935. 18 × 24¾ in. (45.7 × 62.9 cm). A. A. Bakhrushin State Central Theater Museum, Moscow.
The Russian text reads: "GOSET for the Metro Workers." The subway system was one of the most remarkable symbols of propaganda and was portrayed in newspaper articles, paintings, and poetry. Concerts and plays, including productions by GOSET, were produced for subway construction crews.

PLATE 6I *(top)* Isaac Rabichev, *Tailor Shop Workers and Rich Men (Costume Designs for 200,000),* 1923. Pencil, crayon, ink, and watercolor on paper, 13¾ × 30 in. (76 × 34.8 cm). A. A. Bakhrushin State Central Theater Museum, Moscow. In this drawing, Solomon, the son of Mr. Fein, a rich man, comes to Soroker's tailor shop in order to try on a new suit. Creditors are seen here on the right, grouped around an unseen Soroker. Soloveitchik the Matchmaker stands right of center with his umbrella, dressed in black. This sketch shows the contrast between the clothes of the wealthy and the proletarian characters.

PLATE 62 *(bottom)* Benjamin Zuskin as Soloveitchik the Matchmaker with four wealthy women (left to right: Eva Itskhoki, Evgeniia Epstein, Rakhl Imenitova, Esther Karchmer), in *200,000,* 1923. Photograph, 3½ × 5¼ in. (8.9 × 13.3 cm). Beth Hatefutsoth, Photo Archive, Tel Aviv, courtesy of Zuskin Collection

PLATE 63 Benjamin Zuskin as Soloveitchik the Matchmaker, in *200,000*, 1923. Photograph, 5¾ × 3⅝ in. (14.6 × 9.2 cm). Beth Hatefutsoth, Photo Archive, Tel Aviv, courtesy of Zuskin Collection

JEWISH LUCK (FILM)

RELEASED 1925
State Yiddish Theater (GOSET)
SCREENPLAY BASED ON **the Menakhem Mendl stories by Sholem Aleichem**
SCREENWRITER: **Isaac Babel**
DIRECTION: **Aleksei Granovsky and Grigory Gricher-Cherikover**
CINEMATOGRAPHY: **Eduard Tissé**
DESIGN: **Natan Altman**
MUSIC: **Lev Pulver**

GOSET's first venture into film returned to Sholem Aleichem's hapless *luftmentsh* Menakhem Mendl to cast a curious glance at the dying traditions of shtetl life. Humorous in tone, *Jewish Luck* depicts the Belorussian village of Berdichev through the lens of the preposterous exploits of Mendl and his assistant, whose love for the daughter of a rich man sets up the principal tension between old and new value systems. A large Jewish community in the former Russian empire, Berdichev, with its humble buildings that represent the continuity of generations, here becomes a half-dead place. The director, Aleksei Granovsky, employed the camera to forge the same parallel between shtetl and graveyard made in the play *At Night in the Old Marketplace: A Tragic Carnival* (also of 1925).

Jewish Luck is at times a prosaic document, at times a comedic masterpiece, and was notorious for its scenes of Jewish brides as cargo—a pointed criticism of match-making practices, which Granovsky felt were archaic. The balance between realism and comedy informs the film throughout, and the line between the two is often obscured. Trying his hand at matchmaking, Mendl accidentally arranges the marriage of two brides—a sharp condemnation veiled as comedy. Only by coincidence are the film's actual lovers united and the farcical dignity of shtetl life preserved. The events in the play serve both to explicate and to call into question the role of the shtetl in the modern world.

PLATE 64 Natan Altman, *Poster for Jewish Luck,* 1925. Printed on paper, 40 × 28 in. (100 × 71.5 cm). Collection of Merrill C. Berman, Rye, New York. Art © Estate of Natan Altman/RAO, Moscow/VAGA, New York

PLATE 65 *Jewish Luck*, 1925. Solomon Mikhoels is third from left. Film still courtesy Sovkino/Photofest, New York

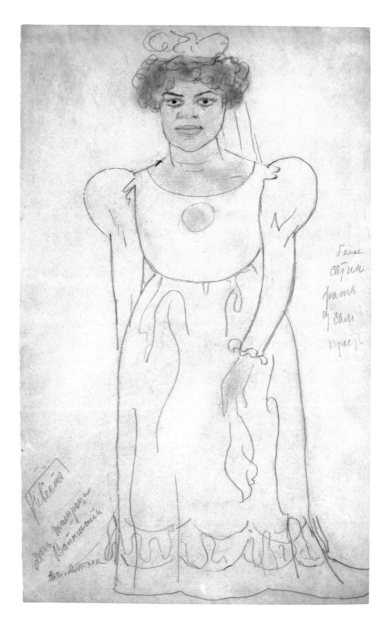

PLATE 69 Natan Altman, *Mrs. Kimbak (Costume Design for Jewish Luck)*, 1925. Pencil on paper, 13¾ × 8¾ in. (35 × 22.3 cm). © St. Petersburg State Museum of Theater and Music. Art © Estate of Natan Altman/RAO, Moscow/VAGA, New York.

The words to the side of the drawing are instructions: "The dress is either cream or gray with large flowers."

AT NIGHT IN THE OLD MARKETPLACE

A TRAGIC CARNIVAL

PREMIERED **February 1925**
State Yiddish Theater (GOSET)
ORIGINAL PLAY BY **I. L. Peretz (1907)**
ADAPTATION AND DIRECTION: **Aleksei Granovsky**
DESIGN: **Robert Falk**
MUSIC: **Aleksandr Krein**

Written by I. L. Peretz as a mystical play about the dawn of modernity, *At Night in the Old Marketplace: A Tragic Carnival* was transformed into a tragedy in Aleksei Granovsky's adaptation. A plotless array of disparate images, it opens on an old shtetl market as night falls. In the course of the play, the market turns into a graveyard, and the living figures of children, drunkards, and prostitutes are replaced by their ghostly equivalents. The wedding of a dead bride and groom brings the play to its eerie climax, as the morning star appears and the dead must flee back to their graves. Throughout the play, a pair of *badkhonim,* or wedding jesters—played by Solomon Mikhoels and Benjamin Zuskin—provide mocking, blasphemous commentary, and conclude the play shouting, "Dead your God. . . . He is bankrupt!"

Establishing parallels between the living and the dead, shtetls and graveyards, GOSET's production of *At Night in the Old Marketplace* intentionally sounded the death knell for the traditional Russian Jewish way of life. The wedding of the dead in the cemetery reinforced the belief that a new beginning cannot arise from a moribund world.

Since the text for the play was only a thousand words long, its success depended on the stage decoration, the costumes, and the music. Aleksandr Krein's musical score incorporated klezmer tunes and religious elements with modern motifs. Robert Falk's grotesque costumes of dead skeletal figures and living zombies with dripping flesh, inspired by what he had seen in visits to Moscow's Institute of Forensic Medicine, were among GOSET's most memorable designs. Falk recalled his preparation for the play, saying that he "made sketches of drowned men and the decomposed bodies of those murdered . . . for, in fact, reality is the most fantastic thing."

PLATE 70 Robert Falk, *Poster for At Night in the Old Marketplace,* GOSET, Moscow, 1925. 42 × 28 in. (106.7 × 71.1 cm). The Russian State Archive of Literature and Art, Moscow. Art © Estate of Robert Falk/RAO, Moscow/VAGA, New York

PLATE 71 *At Night in the Old Marketplace,* 1925. Photograph, 6⅝ × 8¹³⁄₁₆ in. (16.8 × 22.4 cm). Courtesy of Vladislav Ivanov, Moscow.
A large, bony hand hanging over the stage displayed the Hebrew initials of the play's author, I. L. Peretz.

PLATE 72 Robert Falk, *Prostitute (Costume Design for At Night in the Old Marketplace)*, 1925. Pencil, watercolor, ink, and opaque white on paper, 15½ × 10⅜ in. (39.3 × 26.2 cm). A. A. Bakhrushin State Central Theater Museum, Moscow. Art © Estate of Robert Falk/RAO, Moscow/VAGA, New York

PLATE 74 (above) Robert Falk, *Dead Woman (Costume Design for At Night in the Old Marketplace)*, 1925. Pencil, tempera, and ink on cardboard, 12¼ × 3⅜ in. (31.5 × 8.7 cm). A. A. Bakhrushin State Central Theater Museum, Moscow. Art © Estate of Robert Falk/RAO, Moscow/VAGA, New York

PLATE 75 (right) Robert Falk, *Dead Religious Man with Tallit and Tefillin (Costume Design for At Night in the Old Marketplace)*, 1925. Tempera on cardboard, 13⅛ × 4¾ in. (33.6 × 12 cm). A. A. Bakhrushin State Central Theater Museum, Moscow. Art © Estate of Robert Falk/RAO, Moscow/VAGA, New York

PLATE 76 Robert Falk, *Benjamin Zuskin and Solomon Mikhoels as Badkhonim in At Night in the Old Marketplace*, 1925. Tempera on cardboard, 25½ × 20¾ in. (64.6 × 52.5 cm). A. A. Bakhrushin State Central Theater Museum, Moscow. Art © Estate of Robert Falk/RAO, Moscow/VAGA, New York

PLATE 77 Robert Falk, *Religious Man with Tefillin (Costume Design for At Night in the Old Marketplace)*, 1925. Pencil, ink, watercolor, and gouache on paper, 13⅝ × 6¾ in. (34.5 × 17 cm). A. A. Bakhrushin State Central Theater Museum, Moscow. Art © Estate of Robert Falk/RAO, Moscow/VAGA, New York

THE TENTH COMMANDMENT

A PAMPHLET OPERETTA

PREMIERED 1926
State Yiddish Theater (GOSET)
ORIGINAL PLAY BY **Avrom Goldfadn** (1887)
ADAPTATION: **Yekhezkel Dobrushin**
DIRECTION: **Aleksei Granovsky**
DESIGN: **Natan Altman**
MUSIC: **Lev Pulver**

Avrom Goldfadn's operetta relates the story of two angels, one evil and one good, who wager on the efficacy of the Tenth Commandment: "Thou shalt not covet thy neighbor's wife." The evil angel, played by Solomon Mikhoels, arguing that the commandment is obsolete, bets that even a righteous person will break it. When he sees the manner in which the German bourgeoisie swap wives, the good angel surrenders. Thus *The Tenth Commandment: A Pamphlet Operetta* exposes the corruption and decadence of Western Europe, while mocking traditional Jewish definitions of good and evil.

With settings in heaven and contemporary Palestine and Germany, GOSET injected the original material with a heavy dose of Soviet propaganda, criticizing traditional piety, bourgeois values, and Zionism. Nevertheless, the play maintained the operetta form and the humor of Goldfadn's original. Lyrics written especially for the GOSET production were praised by Soviet critics for their accessibility to a mass audience and their commitment to the Revolution.

PLATE 78 Poster for opening night of *The Tenth Commandment*, GOSET, Moscow, 1926. 40 × 30 in. (101.6 × 76.2 cm). The Russian State Archive of Literature and Art, Moscow

PLATE 79 Natan Altman, *Young Hasid (Costume Design for The Tenth Commandment)*, 1926. Pencil and gouache on paper, 13¾ × 8¼ in. (35 × 21 cm). A. A. Bakhrushin State Central Theater Museum, Moscow. Art © Estate of Natan Altman/RAO, Moscow/VAGA, New York

PLATE 80 Eda Berkovskaia as a young Hasid in *The Tenth Commandment*, 1926. Photograph, 6½ × 3½ in. (16.5 × 8.9 cm). Beth Hatefutsoth, Photo Archive, Tel Aviv, courtesy of Zuskin Collection

PLATE 81 Natan Altman, *The Evil Angel Akhitoifel (Costume Design for Solomon Mikhoels in The Tenth Commandment),* 1926. Pencil on paper, 13¾ × 8¾ in. (35.2 × 22.3 cm). A. A. Bakhrushin State Central Theater Museum, Moscow. Art © Estate of Natan Altman/RAO, Moscow/VAGA, New York.

Natan Altman's designs for *The Tenth Commandment* satirized European fashions and politics: the Evil Angel played by Mikhoels wore the dapper suit of a capitalist businessman.

PLATE 82 Natan Altman, *The Good Angel Friedl (Costume Design for Benjamin Zuskin in The Tenth Commandment),* 1926. Pencil on paper, 14 × 8½ in. (35.5 × 21.5 cm). © St. Petersburg State Museum of Theater and Music. Art © Estate of Natan Altman/RAO, Moscow/VAGA, New York.

In contrast to the Evil Angel's dapper suit, Natan Altman dressed the Good Angel in the outfit of a Hasidic Jew, using the Good Angel's gullibility to poke fun at the naïveté of traditional religious belief.

THE TRAVELS OF BENJAMIN THE THIRD

EPOS IN THREE ACTS

PREMIERED **April 20, 1927**
State Yiddish Theater (GOSET)
BASED ON **an unfinished short story**
    by Mendele Mocher Seforim (1835–1917)
ADAPTATION: **Yekhezkel Dobrushin**
DIRECTION: **Aleksei Granovsky**
DESIGN: **Robert Falk**
MUSIC: **Lev Pulver**

GOSET returned to the foundations of Yiddish literature with its production of *The Travels of Benjamin the Third: Epos in Three Acts,* which was based on Miguel de Cervantes's *Don Quixote.* Benjamin and his friend Senderl, both naive shtetl-dwellers from Tuneiadovka (Droneville), embark on an adventure to find the "Land of Israel." After an arduous journey, they arrive in what is in fact the neighboring town of Glupskie (Dimwit Town), which Senderl, a submissive househusband, mistakes for Istanbul. Benjamin and Senderl believe they have walked all the way around the world and back. Benjamin succumbs to a fantastical dream filled with strange creatures and imagines himself a great king, Benjamin III, married to the daughter of Alexander the Great. In reality, the two men recognize that this is their shtetl and that Russia is their rightful home.

By emphasizing the foolishness of Benjamin and Senderl, the GOSET production offered a barely hidden critique of Zionism, of Jewish emigration from Soviet Russia, and of shtetl life. Ironically, when Golda Meir attended a revival of the play in 1948, during the first Israeli diplomatic mission to the USSR, Soviet authorities accused GOSET of espousing the very Zionist sympathies that the play had originally intended to disparage. The composer Lev Pulver incorporated the Zionist anthem and future national anthem of Israel, "Ha-tikvah," into the play's traditional Ukrainian melodic motif, thus asserting the Soviet Union as the true homeland.

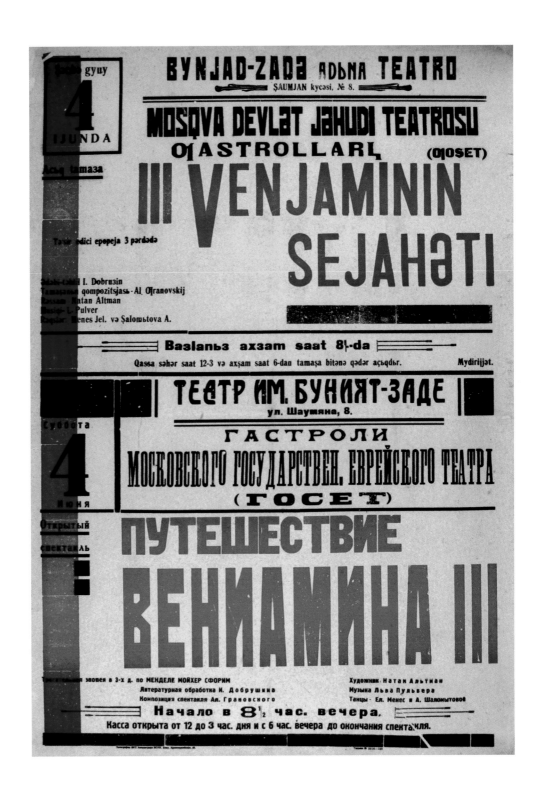

PLATE 83 Poster for *The Travels of Benjamin the Third*, GOSET, Baku, 1927. 41 × 29 in. (104.1 × 73.7 cm). A. A. Bakhrushin State Central Theater Museum, Moscow.
The text is in Azerbaijani and Russian.

PLATE 86 Robert Falk, *Senderl the Housewife (Costume Design for Benjamin Zuskin in The Travels of Benjamin the Third)*, 1927. Pencil and gouache on paper, 13⅞ × 8⅜ in. (35.2 × 21.4 cm). A. A. Bakhrushin State Central Theater Museum, Moscow. Art © Estate of Robert Falk/RAO, Moscow/VAGA, New York. The character of Senderl, played by Benjamin Zuskin, is so dominated by his wife that the villagers call him *Senderl Baba*, Senderl the Housewife. Robert Falk's costume design for Zuskin played upon this nickname by dressing Senderl in a woman's coat and scarf, as well as padded pants that gave him rounded, matronly hips.

PLATE 87 *(opposite left)* Robert Falk, *Alexander the Great (Costume Design for Joseph Shidlo in The Travels of Benjamin the Third)*, 1927. Pencil, gouache, watercolor, and tempera on paper, 14⅛ × 8⅞ in. (35.8 × 22.7 cm). A. A. Bakhrushin State Central Theater Museum, Moscow. Art © Estate of Robert Falk/RAO, Moscow/VAGA, New York. Benjamin's dream sequence features a parade of fantastically dressed characters, including the figure of Alexander the Great, who anoints Benjamin king of the redheaded Jews, and weds him to his daughter, Rahav the Whore.

PLATE 88 Robert Falk, *Rahav the Whore (Costume Design for The Travels of Benjamin the Third)*, 1927. Pencil, watercolor, gouache, ink, and bronze paint on paper, 14⅜ × 8⅛ in. (36.6 × 20.6 cm). A. A. Bakhrushin State Central Theater Museum, Moscow. Art © Estate of Robert Falk/RAO, Moscow/VAGA, New York

TROUHADEC

AN ECCENTRIC OPERETTA

PREMIERED **January 1927**
State Yiddish Theater (GOSET)
ORIGINAL PLAY BY **Jules Romains (1923)**
ADAPTATION AND DIRECTION: **Aleksei Granovsky**
DESIGN: **Natan Altman**
MUSIC: **Lev Pulver**
CHOREOGRAPHY: **Helena Menes**

Trouhadec: An Eccentric Operetta, originally written in French, was the first GOSET production without any explicit Jewish content, and marked the first performance of a work by Jules Romains onstage. Set in the luxurious world of a Monte Carlo casino, the play tells the story of Yves Le Trouhadec, a French professor who turns to gambling to win the love of the Parisian actress Mademoiselle Rolande. After a winning streak at the casinos, Trouhadec stages an elaborate banquet to impress his beloved, but he experiences a run of bad luck during the preparations; he loses everything and is nearly driven to suicide. Then a friend, who is a baron, offers him the job of police commissioner for the principality of Monaco, and Trouhadec moves up the social ladder. Now a part of the elite, he determines to marry a baroness—only to have to abandon his plans when a pregnant Rolande appears, demanding that he take responsibility for his unborn child.

Trouhadec presented a weighty communist critique of capitalism. Evoking the decadent glamour of a Western city, Natan Altman's set designs included mock streetlights and French-language signs. The advertisement for *modes,* or fashions, emphasized what the Soviets saw as the Western obsession with consumption. While the flamboyance of Altman's costumes, based on what he had seen on his travels in France, reflected the excesses of bourgeoisie life, the play itself revealed the author's rejection of the value placed on individual wealth in a capitalist society.

PLATE 89 Natan Altman, *Poster for Trouhadec,* GOSET, Moscow, 1927. 42 × 28⅜ in. (106.7 × 71.9 cm). The Russian State Archive of Literature and Art, Moscow. Art © Estate of Natan Altman/RAO, Moscow/VAGA, New York

PLATE 90 Natan Altman, *Mademoiselle Rolande (Costume Design for Sara Rotbaum in Trouhadec)*, 1927. Pencil and crayon on paper, 14⅛ × 8⅝ in. (35.7 × 22 cm). A. A. Bakhrushin State Central Theater Museum, Moscow. Art © Estate of Natan Altman/RAO, Moscow/VAGA, New York.
The words on the right side of the drawing are instructions: "black oilcloth." On the left is Natan Altman's signature.

PLATE 91 Natan Altman, *Sophie the Maid (Costume Design for Trouhadec)*, 1927. Pencil, colored pencil, and brown chalk on paper, 14⅛ × 8⅝ in. (36 × 22 cm). A. A. Bakhrushin State Central Theater Museum, Moscow. Art © Estate of Natan Altman/RAO, Moscow/VAGA, New York

PLATE 92 Natan Altman, *Sophie (Costume Design for Trou-hadec)*, 1927. Pencil, colored pencil, and brown chalk on paper, 14⅛ × 8⅝ in. (36 × 22 cm). A. A. Bakhrushin State Central Theater Museum, Moscow. Art © Estate of Natan Altman/ RAO, Moscow/VAGA, New York.

It has been suggested that there are two sides to the character of Sophie: she may be Trouhadec's maid by day and a prosti-tute by night.

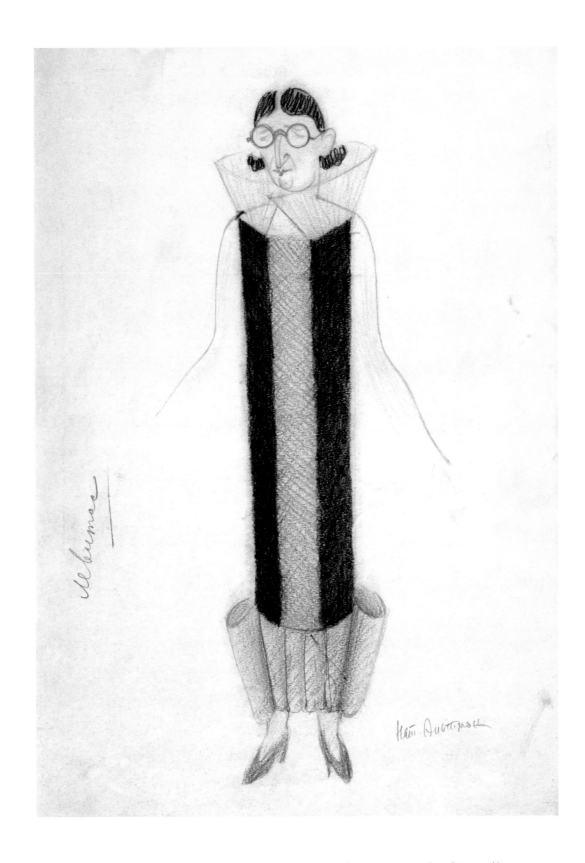

PLATE 93 Natan Altman, *Jenevieve Gentil Duran (Costume Design for Eugenia Levitas in Trouhadec)*, 1927. Pencil, crayon, and opaque white on paper, 14⅛ × 9⅞ in. (36 × 25 cm). A. A. Bakhrushin State Central Theater Museum, Moscow. Art © Estate of Natan Altman/RAO, Moscow/VAGA, New York

GOSET ON TOUR

Given GOSET's tremendous success in Moscow, the Soviet authorities decided to send the company on a tour of Western Europe in order to demonstrate the accomplishments of the new Soviet state. From April 1928 to January 1929, GOSET toured throughout Western Europe, performing *200,000*, *Trouhadec*, *The Sorceress*, and *The Travels of Benjamin the Third*. Visiting Warsaw, Berlin, Paris, and Vienna, the troupe enjoyed many favorable reviews from Western audiences; the actors' meetings with Zionist activists abroad, however, were criticized in the Soviet press. GOSET's director, Aleksei Granovsky, had long chafed under the constant interference of Soviet authorities in his work, and on his reception in Berlin "as a new theatrical messiah," he chose to remain there rather than return to the USSR when the troupe was summoned home because of government suspicions.

PLATE 94 Poster for *The Travels of Benjamin the Third, The Sorceress, 200,000, and Trouhadec,* GOSET on tour, Paris, 1928; 37½ × 25¼ in. (95.3 × 64.1 cm). A. A. Bakhrushin State Central Theater Museum, Moscow

KING LEAR

PREMIERED **February 10, 1935**
State Yiddish Theater (GOSET)
ORIGINAL PLAY BY **William Shakespeare (1606)**
TRANSLATION: **Shmuel Halkin**
DIRECTION: **Sergei Radlov and Les Kurbas**
DESIGN: **Aleksandr Tyshler**
MUSIC: **Lev Pulver**

GOSET's 1935 version of *King Lear* reflected the widespread popularity of Shakespeare's plays in Soviet Russia at the time. After Joseph Stalin's 1932 decree that all artistic endeavors conform to the goals of the Revolution, the classic status of Shakespeare's works, translated from Russian to Yiddish by Shmuel Halkin, made them safe vehicles for disguised political commentary. Solomon Mikhoels was able to translate his role as an egocentric and despotic King Lear into a critical portrait of Stalin, who was persecuting many of his original supporters in much the same way as Lear rejects his one loyal daughter.

King Lear marked the pinnacle of Mikhoels's collaboration with Benjamin Zuskin, who played the Fool. Mikhoels felt that he and Zuskin were not playing two separate roles, but, in fact, two sides of a single role. The interaction between their two characters reflected the stark dichotomies that marked Stalin's Soviet Union. The emphasis on individual psychological paradoxes was far removed from the stylization of social types that Granovsky had extracted from the writings of Sholem Aleichem and Avrom Goldfadn.

Aleksandr Tyshler's two-story set depicted a medieval village with a castle and sculpted figures. The play, which confirmed GOSET as one of the world's leading theaters, would be performed two hundred times in less than four years. Of Mikhoels's performance, the Shakespearean actor and director Gordon Craig commented, "I understand why we have no Lear worthy of the name in Britain. The reason is quite simple: we have no actor like Mikhoels."

PLATE 96 Poster for *King Lear*, GOSET, Moscow Theater Festival, 1935. 36¼ × 24¼ in. (92.1 × 61.6 cm). A. A. Bakhrushin State Central Theater Museum, Moscow

PLATE 97 *(opposite)* Aleksandr Tyshler, *Mise-en-scène from King Lear*, 1935. Watercolor on paper, 25¼ × 18¾ in. (64 × 47.5 cm). A. A. Bakhrushin State Central Theater Museum, Moscow. Art © Estate of Aleksandr Tyshler/RAO, Moscow/VAGA, New York. Tyshler's preliminary drawing depicts Lear's departure from the Earl of Gloucester's castle, where his daughter Regan is staying. Both Regan and her sister Goneril have refused to shelter Lear as long as he maintains his royal retinue, and he has chosen to depart for the wilderness rather than give up his kingly privileges. Lear's villainous daughters stand to the left in elaborate costumes, while the Fool, in the costume of a court jester, pokes his head out from behind Lear's back.

PLATE 98 Aleksandr Tyshler, *Set Model for King Lear*, 1935 (reconstructed in 1991). Gouache on cardboard and wood, 9½ × 13⅜ × 9½ in. (24 × 34 × 24 cm). A. A. Bakhrushin State Central Theater Museum, Moscow. Art © Estate of Aleksandr Tyshler/RAO, Moscow/VAGA, New York.

Aleksandr Tyshler's two-story stage incorporated elements from medieval architecture, with carved sculptural figures and a thatched roof. The two movable wings opening on the second story resemble the structures of an altarpiece and enhance the flexibility of the set. The sculptural figures are similar to the carved columns of cathedrals.

PLATE 99 Benjamin Zuskin as the Fool in *King Lear*, 1935. Photograph, 22⅛ × 29⁷⁄₁₆ in. (56.2 × 74.7 cm). Beth Hatefutsoth, Photo Archive, Tel Aviv, courtesy of Zuskin Collection

PLATE 100 *(top left)* Aleksandr Tyshler, *King Lear (Costume Design for Solomon Mikhoels)*, 1935. Watercolor on paper, 9⅝ × 6⅞ in. (24.6 × 17.6 cm). A. A. Bakhrushin State Central Theater Museum, Moscow. Art © Estate of Aleksandr Tyshler/ RAO, Moscow/VAGA, New York

PLATE 101 *(top right)* Aleksandr Tyshler, *Drawing of Solomon Mikhoels as King Lear*, 1935. Watercolor on paper, 9¾ × 6⅞ in. (24.8 × 17.6 cm). A. A. Bakhrushin State Central Theater Museum, Moscow. Art © Estate of Aleksandr Tyshler/RAO, Moscow/VAGA, New York

PLATE 102 *(right)* Solomon Mikhoels's costume and wig for *King Lear*, 1935. Israel Goor Theater Archive and Museum, Jerusalem

PLATE 103 *(opposite)* Solomon Mikhoels as King Lear, 1935. Photograph, 8⅞ × 5⅞ in. (22.8 × 14.9 cm). A. A. Bakhrushin State Central Theater Museum, Moscow

GOSET THE FINAL CHAPTER

After the 1941 German invasion of the Soviet Union, the need for international assistance was dire. Crucial to the Soviet government's push to promote international support and national solidarity was the formation, in 1942, of the Jewish Anti-Fascist Committee, a group dedicated to enlisting the aid of Jews worldwide for the Soviet war effort. As secretary-general of the Committee, Solomon Mikhoels became the de facto leader of the Soviet Jewish community, organizing several Moscow rallies with important Jewish figures.

In 1943, in an effort to muster political and financial support for the Soviet cause, a delegation from the Jewish Anti-Fascist Committee embarked on a world tour. With the Yiddish poet Itzik Fefer, who was sent by the Soviet authorities to monitor Mikhoels's activities, the actor traveled for nearly eight months in the Middle East, England, and North America, making stops in major cities across the United States, Mexico, and Canada. In New York, a rally at the Polo Grounds attracted forty-seven thousand people, as well as the alarm of the U.S. government, which looked unfavorably on reports of the crowd's overwhelming approval of Soviet leadership. In meeting with such luminaries as Albert Einstein, Charlie Chaplin, and Upton Sinclair, Mikhoels put a human face on the Soviet Union and, perhaps more significant, on Soviet Jewry.

Mikhoels is shown holding a radio rally on August 24, 1941. Front row, left to right: author Samuel Marshak, poet Peretz Markish, novelist David Bergelson, architect Boris Iofan, author Ilya Ehrenburg. Back row, left to right: cellist Yacov Flier, violinist David Oistrakh, critic Isaac Nusinov, actor Solomon Mikhoels, pianist Yacov Zak, actor Benjamin Zuskin, artist Aleksandr Tyshler, journalist Shakhno Epstein.

PLATE 105 Pages from Solomon Mikhoels's diary of his trip to the United States as head of the Jewish Anti-Fascist Committee, 1943. Handwritten manuscript, 18 pages. Two sizes: 9½ × 6 in., and 7 × 4 in. (24.2 × 15.2 cm and 17.8 × 9.5 cm). The Russian State Archive of Literature and Art, Moscow

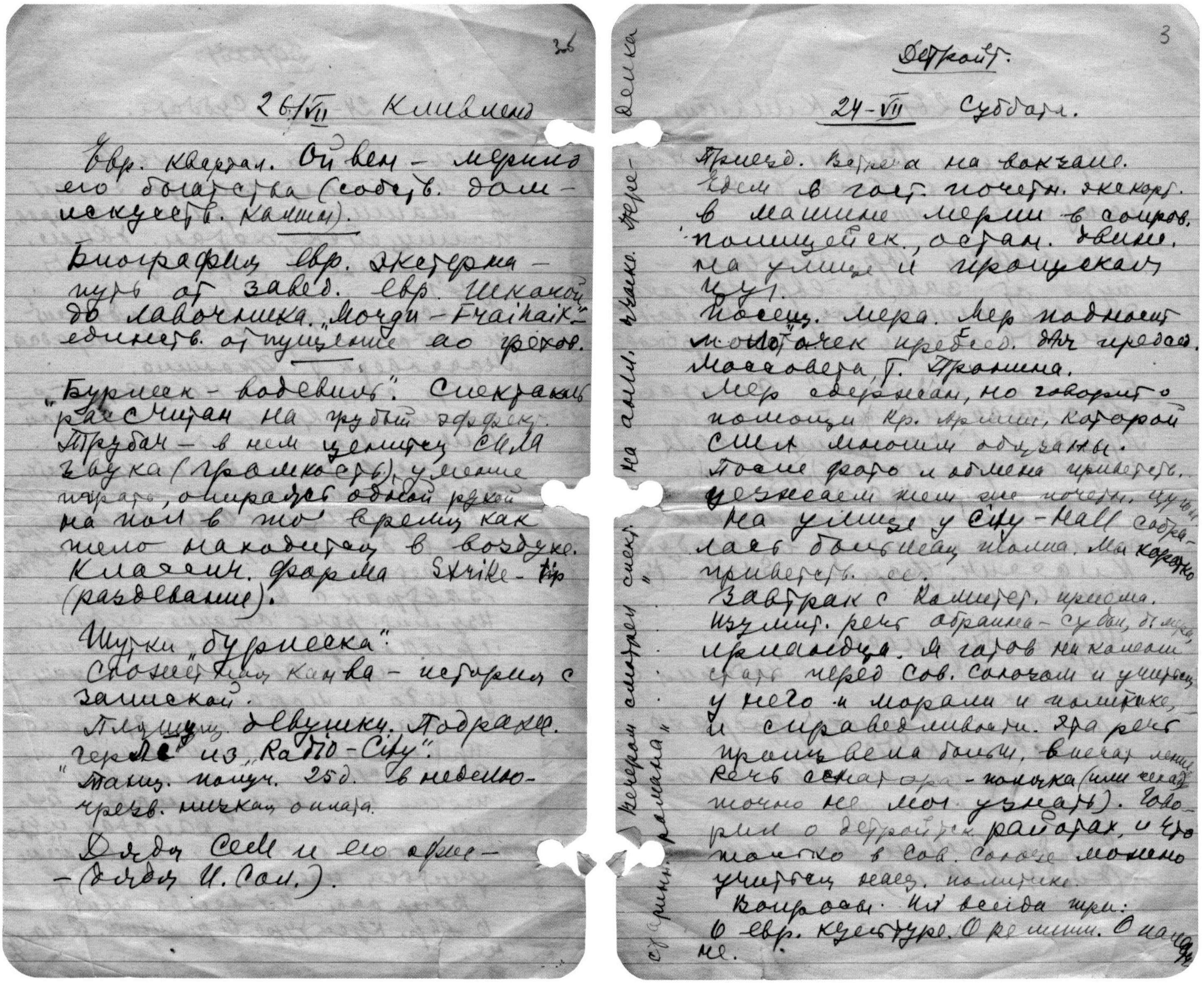

3б

26/VII Кливленд

Евр. квартал. [illegible] – мерило его богатства (собств. дом – искусств. камин).

Биография евр. экстерна – путь от завед. евр. школой до лавочника. „[illegible]" – [illegible] от [illegible] грехов.

„Бурлеск – водевиль". Спектакль рассчитан на грубый эффект. Трубач – в нем ценится сила звука (громкость), умение играть, опираясь одной рукой на пол в то время как тело находится в воздухе. Клоун. Форма Strike-tip (раздевание).

Шутки „бурлеска":
[illegible] канва – история с запиской.
[illegible] девушки. Подраж. героине из „Radio-City".
Танц. получ. 25д. в неделю. [illegible] оплата.

Дядя Сем и его армия – (дядя И. Сол.).

3

Детройт.

24-VII Суббота.

Приезд. Встреча на вокзале. Едем в гост. почетн. эскорт. в машине мэрии в сопров. полицейск., остан. движ. на улице и пропускают нас.
Посещ. мэра. [illegible]
[illegible]
Мэр сдержан, но говорит о помощи Кр. Армии, которой [illegible]
[illegible]
На улице у City-Hall [illegible]
Завтрак с [illegible]
[illegible]
Вопросы [illegible]: о евр. культуре. О религии. О [illegible]

PLATE 106 Itzik Fefer, Albert Einstein, and Solomon Mikhoels, Princeton, New Jersey, June 1943. Photograph, 10 × 8 in. (25.4 × 20.3 cm). Archives of the YIVO Institute for Jewish Research, New York.

The Soviet authorities sent the Yiddish poet and Secret Police informant Itzik Fefer to accompany Solomon Mikhoels on his tour of the United States to monitor his activities. Although Mikhoels was criticized by many American Jews as a Soviet puppet during his travels, his wartime efforts were intended to foster international Jewish solidarity and later exposed him to charges of Zionism from the Soviet authorities.

SOLOMON MIKHOELS'S DEATH

In December 1947, shortly after the United Nations voted to establish a Jewish state in Palestine, Solomon Mikhoels made a speech in which he expressed support for the vote, disclosing for the first time his Jewish national sympathies. Believing it necessary to silence such a powerful exponent of the Jewish solidarity movement then growing in popularity among Soviet Jews, Joseph Stalin ordered the actor's assassination. In January 1948, Mikhoels was dispatched to Minsk on the pretext of judging a play for the Stalin Prize. On January 12, the actor and his traveling companion, the critic Vladimir Golubov-Potapov, were driven from their hotel room to the dacha of Lavrenty Tsanava, head of Belorussian security services, where they were murdered. Their bodies were dumped on a snowy road outside Minsk, disguised to appear as the victims of a traffic accident. Tsanava later received the Order of Lenin "for exemplary execution of a special assignment from the government."

A tremendous outpouring of grief met the news of Mikhoels's death. Over the course of two days, more than ten thousand people viewed the body while it lay in state at the GOSET theater. It is said that during the funeral, despite the bitter cold, a fiddler climbed onto a nearby fence to play in tribute to the actor.

Most Soviet Jews remained unaware of the real nature of Mikhoels's death, believing the official explanation. The directorship of GOSET passed to Benjamin Zuskin, but the theater's days were numbered. Within a year, he was arrested along with other eminent Jewish cultural figures; by the close of 1949, the liquidation of the theater had been ordered. Zuskin and twelve others were executed on the night of August 12, 1952. What became known as the Night of the Murdered Poets signaled the brutal end of an extraordinarily creative era.

PLATE 107 *(opposite left)* Solomon Mikhoels (first row, center) the day before his assassination, Minsk, January, 1948. Photograph, 3¼ × 4¼ in. (8.3 × 10.8 cm). Archives of the YIVO Institute for Jewish Research, New York.
This is the last known photograph of Solomon Mikhoels, taken during his ill-fated journey to Minsk to judge a play for the Stalin Prize Committee. Standing on the far right is his traveling companion Vladimir Golubov-Potapov, who was murdered along with Mikhoels.

PLATE 108 *(opposite right)* Solomon Mikhoels lying in state, Moscow, 1948. Photograph, 4 × 6 in. (10.2 × 15.2 cm). Israel Goor Theater Archive and Museum, Jerusalem

PLATE 109 Sarah Lebedeva, *Head of Solomon Mikhoels*, 1939. Bronze, 13¾ × 10 × 9⅞ in. (35 × 25.5 × 25 cm). The State Tretyakov Gallery, Moscow. Art © Estate of Sarah Lebedeva/RAO, Moscow/VAGA, New York.
The Russian sculptor Sarah Lebedeva (1892–1967) was known for her monumental portraits of prominent Soviet figures. This portrayal of Mikhoels reveals her characteristic psychological sensitivity to her sitters.

Natan Altman

JOSEPH AKHRON
(Lozdzieje, Poland, 1886–1943, Hollywood, California)
Composer

The Blind, The Sorceress: An Eccentric Jewish Play

Joseph Akhron is known for compositions drawn from traditional Jewish harmonies and influenced by the Hebrew language. He first gained notice as a young violinist, and entered the St. Petersburg Conservatory in 1899. After graduating in 1904 with a gold medal, he performed extensively throughout Russia. In 1908, alongside such musicians as Moshe Milner and Aleksandr Krein, he helped found the Society for Jewish Folk Music.

He composed original scores for the GOSEKT productions *The Blind* in 1919 and *The Sorceress* in 1922. Juxtaposed with Isaac Rabinovich's Futuristic sets, Akhron's folksy melodies for the latter play emphasized the distinction between old and new. After a three-year world tour, Akhron settled in New York in 1925. He moved to Hollywood in 1935, where he lived until his death.

FURTHER READING
Moddel, *Joseph Achron*.
Veidlinger, *The Moscow State Yiddish Theater*, 34, 46–47.

SHOLEM ALEICHEM
(SHOLEM YAKOV RABINOVITZ)
(Pereyaslav, 1859–1916, New York)
Author

Agents: A Joke in One Act, The Enchanted Tailor, Der get (The Divorce), *It's a Lie! Dialogue in Galicia, Luftmentshen, Mazel Tov, The Spoiled Celebration, Tevye the Dairyman, 200,000: A Musical Comedy*

One of the first authors to establish Yiddish as a literary language, Sholem Aleichem advocated it as a national Jewish language. Born to a well-to-do Jewish family (who later lost their savings), he adopted the pseudonym Sholem Aleichem, derived from the common greeting meaning "Peace be with you." He attended a traditional *heder* until he was fourteen years old; his father's interest in the Haskala (Jewish Enlightenment) led the young Rabinovitz to transfer his childhood passion from acting to writing. He became the author of many novels and plays, and his most famous stories, featuring Tevye the Dairyman, were later adapted for the musical *Fiddler on the Roof*.

Upon immigrating to New York in 1914, Sholem Aleichem tried to make a living as a writer for the Yiddish theater and press. He died in 1916 while working on a novel. His funeral, one of the largest in the history of New York at the time, drew an estimated hundred thousand mourners.

FURTHER READING
Baker, "Yiddish in Form and Socialist in Content."
Belenky, *Shalom-Aleikhem—pisatel i chelovek*.
Encyclopaedia Judaica (1978), vol. 14, 1272–1286.
Finkel, *Sholem Aleykhem*.
Frieden, *Classic Yiddish Fiction*.
Levy, *The Habima, Israel's National Theater, 1917–1977*, 119–121.
Mikhoels, "Sholem Aleichem."
Samuel, *The World of Sholem Aleichem*.
Sandrow, *Vagabond Stars*, 35, 179–183, 229.
Veidlinger, *The Moscow State Yiddish Theater*, 177–178, 206–209.
Waife-Goldberg, *My Father, Sholom Aleichem*.
Weitzner, *Sholem Aleichem in the Theater*.
Di yidishe drame fun 20stn yorhundert.

NATAN ISAEVICH ALTMAN
(Vinnitsa, 1889–1970, Leningrad)
Artist

Arn Fridman, The Dybbuk, Jewish Luck, The Tenth Commandment: A Pamphlet Operetta, Trouhadec: An Eccentric Operetta, Uriel Acosta

Natan Altman was a leading avant-garde artist with intimate ties to the Soviet Jewish theater movement. He studied at the Odessa Art School, but, discontented with its dominant realist approach, he returned in 1907 to Vinnitsa, where he began to incorporate Jewish themes into his paintings. He moved to Paris in 1910; there he studied at the Free Russian Academy, worked in the studio of Vladimir Baranoff-Rossiné, and forged connections with Marc Chagall, Aleksandr Archipenko, David Shterenberg, and other artists. Altman familiarized himself with contemporary Western Impressionism and Cubism, yet associated with the Makhmadim artists, who were working collectively to create a modern Jewish art.

Around 1916, Altman helped found the Jewish Society for the Encouragement of the Arts in Petrograd. After the Bolshevik Revolution, which he eagerly supported, his work incorporated innovative Futurist elements. His most striking public design was an ambitious decorative scheme for Uritsky

Square in Petrograd to mark the first anniversary of the 1917 revolution. He became a member of IZO Narkompros (Department of Fine Arts of the People's Commissariat for Education), the visual arts section of the Soviet agency charged with "enlightening" the people. In 1919, as a leader of the Communist Futurists (Komfut) in Petrograd, he worked on Vladimir Lenin's Plan for Monumental Propaganda.

In 1921, Altman moved to Moscow and was named chief of IZO Narkompros. Until 1928, he created stage designs for Habima and GOSET in Moscow, mingling decorations derived from Jewish folk and religious art with geometric planes suspended from the theater flies.

Altman accompanied GOSET on its 1928 European tour but did not return to the Soviet Union until 1931, when he once again designed sets for Moscow theaters. He was named an Honored Arts Worker in 1968.

FURTHER READING

Arbatov, *Natan Altman.*
Efros, *Portret Natana Altmana; Profili,* 247–288.
Etkind, *Natan Altman.*
Goodman, *Russian Jewish Artists,* 30–31, 42–44, 46–51, 55–64, 72–73.
Lozowick, "The Art of Nathan Altman."
Veidlinger, *The Moscow State Yiddish Theater,* 44–45, 65, 77, 103, 108, 204.

S. AN-SKY (SOLOMON ZAINWIL RAPAPORT)
(Vitebsk, 1863–1920, Warsaw)
Author
The Dybbuk

Best known by the nom de plume S. An-sky, Solomon Zainwil Rapaport immersed himself in the literature of the Jewish Enlightenment, or Haskala, and embraced socialism. Born to a landowner's agent and an innkeeper, he was drawn to the life of the Russian peasants and as a young man lived and worked among them. He began his career writing for Russian-language publications but was influenced by the work of I. L. Peretz to write in Yiddish, composing folk legends, Hasidic tales, and short stories about social issues.

An-sky's 1914 play *Between Two Worlds,* later renamed *The Dybbuk,* was based on ethnographic expeditions he organized from 1911 to 1914 through the Ukrainian provinces of Volhynia and Podolia, where he encountered the practice

of *dybbuk* exorcism among the Hasidim. An-sky translated the play from Yiddish into Russian for the Vilna Troupe, which became the first to perform it, in 1920, two months after his death. The poet Chaim Nachman Bialik translated it into Hebrew, combining and revising An-sky's significantly different Yiddish and Russian versions. Habima first performed Bialik's version, to great acclaim, in Moscow in 1922.

FURTHER READING

An-sky, *The Jewish Artistic Heritage.*
Encyclopaedia Judaica (1978), vol. 3, 34–35.
Goodman, *Russian Jewish Artists,* 45–49.
Mlotek, *S. Ansky.*
Safran and Zipperstein, *The Worlds of S. An-sky.*

SHOLEM ASCH
(Kutno, Poland, 1880–1957, London)
Author
God of Vengeance, In Winter, The Older Sister, Prologue, Sin

The prolific Yiddish author Sholem Asch rebelled against his Orthodox upbringing by devoting himself to literature. Though his early education was entirely religious, Asch's exploration of literature, both sacred and secular, deeply worried his devout parents and ultimately precipitated his move away from home. He began his career writing in Hebrew, but the prominent author I. L. Peretz urged him to write in Yiddish. Known from his early works as a "poet of the shtetl," Asch increasingly sought to break free from Jewish conventions, often engendering controversy. Despite his rift with the Yiddish community, his writing evinced a deep attachment to the Jewish past, while expanding the horizons of Yiddish literature beyond the confines of the shtetl and bridging the Yiddish world and mainstream Western culture. Asch spent the final years of his life in Israel before his death in London.

FURTHER READING

Asch, *Tales of My People.*
Encyclopaedia Judaica (1978), vol. 3, 684–687.
"Sholem Asch Reconsidered."
Stahl, *Sholem Asch Reconsidered.*
Zuskin-Perelman, *Puteshestvie Veniamina,* 77, 103, 390, 395, 439.

Marc Chagall

ISAAC IMMANUILOVICH BABEL
(Odessa, 1894–1940, Moscow)
Screenwriter
Jewish Luck

Although he published only a few collections of short stories, Isaac Babel is considered one of the greatest Russian writers of the twentieth century. He was raised in the cosmopolitan, Yiddish-speaking milieu of Odessa, yet his works often speak to the difficulties Jews faced while adapting to the violent, tumultuous world of revolutionary Russia. Babel wrote the screenplay for Aleksei Granovsky's film *Jewish Luck,* an adaptation from Sholem Aleichem. The work denounced the moneymaking schemes of the shtetl, as well as such traditional practices as matchmaking.

Despite his support for the Revolution, Babel fell from favor after the death of his protector, Maxim Gorky. Arrested in May 1939 for allegedly conspiring with foreign agents against the Soviet Union, Babel was forced to sign a confession, which implicated the actor Solomon Mikhoels and the film director Sergei Eisenstein. Babel was executed in January 1940.

FURTHER READING
Carden, *The Art of Isaac Babel.*
Charyn, *Savage Shorthand.*
Encyclopaedia Judaica (1978), vol. 4, 18–22.
Falen, *Isaac Babel.*
Zuskin-Perelman, *Massaot Biniamin Zuskin*, 163, 241, 459;
      Puteshestvie Veniamina, 168, 246.

MARC CHAGALL
(MOISEI ZAKHAROVICH SHAGAL)
(Vitebsk, 1887–1985, St.-Paul-de-Vence, France)
Artist
Murals for GOSEKT; *An Evening of Sholem Aleichem*

One of the most important artists of the twentieth century, Marc Chagall was born to a Hasidic family. Displaying artistic talent at an early age, the young Chagall became an artist's apprentice in Vitebsk and attended Yehuda Pen's art school. In 1908, he left his beloved hometown for St. Petersburg, where he was recommended to work and study with Leon Bakst, the director of the Svanseva art school.

In 1911, supported by a stipend from the art patron Maxim Vinaver, Chagall traveled to France; he used this formative period to develop his artistic style, and he established close relationships with leading artists. Chagall derided the efforts of the Makhmadim, who published an art magazine to promote a modern Jewish style, even as he began producing a body of work dealing with shtetl life and other Jewish themes.

In 1920, Chagall received an invitation from Aleksei Granovsky and the noted art critic Abram Efros to design the interior of the newly established State Yiddish Chamber Theater (GOSEKT). His first works in Moscow were a series of murals on canvas to be placed on the ceiling and walls. With these paintings, which were infused with Yiddish puns and literary references—and later, with costume and set designs—Chagall sought to combine all aspects of the theater into an integrated whole.

He participated in the *Exhibition of the Three* with Natan Altman and David Shterenberg in 1922; during that year, Anatoly Lunacharsky obtained a passport for Chagall to travel to Lithuania and, from there, permanently, to the West. Chagall first lived in Berlin, then settled in France in 1924. He returned to the Soviet Union only once, in 1973, to sign and date his murals, which had been preserved by fellow artists and were later stored by the State Tretyakov Gallery in Moscow; they were not seen again until 1990. Chagall died at age ninety-seven in the south of France.

FURTHER READING
Amishai-Maisels, "Chagall's Jewish In-Jokes."
Baal-Teshuva, *Marc Chagall.*
Chagall, *My Life.*
Compton, *Chagall: Love and the Stage; Marc Chagall.*
Frost, "Marc Chagall and the Jewish State Chamber Theatre."
Goodman, *Marc Chagall.*
Harshav, *Marc Chagall and His Times; Marc Chagall and the Lost Jewish World.*
Kamensky, *Chagall.*
Marc Chagall and the Jewish Theater.
Meyer, *Marc Chagall.*
Vitali, *Marc Chagall.*

Robert Falk

YEKHEZKEL DOBRUSHIN
(Ukraine, 1883–1953, Siberia)
Author, adapter for the stage
Carnival of the Jewish Masks, Marvelous History, On the Sixty-second, The Sorceress: An Eccentric Jewish Play, The Specialist, Three Jewish Raisins, The Travels of Benjamin the Third: Epos in Three Acts, 200,000: A Musical Comedy

A prominent Yiddish author, literary critic, and playwright, Yekhezkel Dobrushin collaborated frequently with GOSET. The son of a Ukrainian lumber merchant, he received his education at the Sorbonne in Paris, then returned to Russia in 1909. In 1918 he cofounded the Kiev Kultur-Lige, a secular organization that sought to establish Yiddish as the official language for the transmission of Jewish education and culture. Dobrushin wrote Yiddish poetry and short stories, and he was named secretary of the Yiddish Writers' Union in 1920. His interest in national identity led him to write about Jewish folk art, seeking to define its unique characteristics.

A member of the Jewish Anti-Fascist Committee during World War II, Dobrushin was arrested in February 1949 and deported to a Siberian labor camp, where he died four years later.

FURTHER READING
Encyclopaedia Judaica (1978), vol. 6, 144.
Kampf, *Jewish Experience in the Art of the Twentieth Century*, 29–30.
Veidlinger, *The Moscow State Yiddish Theater*, 42, 46, 48, 78, 84, 118, 179, 263, 269.

JOEL (YULY DMITREVICH) ENGEL
(Berdyansk, 1868–1927, Tel Aviv)
Composer
The Dybbuk

The Russian composer, critic, lexicographer, and folklorist Joel Engel initially pursued law but then turned to music, studying theory and composition at the Moscow Conservatory. After working as a music critic for *Russkie vedomosti*, he started performing and publishing the songs of Eastern European Jews; he gave public lectures and wrote newspaper articles to promote the subject. He helped found the Society for Jewish Folk Music, and joined S. An-sky on an ethnographic expedition to Jewish villages in southern Russia. Engel later

composed music for the celebrated 1922 Habima production of An-sky's *The Dybbuk*. That same year, he left the Soviet Union; he later settled in Tel Aviv.

FURTHER READING
Kunin, *Glazami sovremennika.*
Rabinovich, *Of Jewish Music, Ancient and Modern.*
Ravina, *Yo'el Engel veha-muzikah ha-yehudit.*
Soroker, *Rossiiskie muzykanty-yevrei*, 38–39.
Veidlinger, *The Moscow State Yiddish Theater*, 25–26.
Weinberg, "Joel Engel."
Weisser, *The Modern Renaissance of Jewish Music, Events, and Figures.*

ROBERT RAFAILOVICH FALK
(Moscow, 1886–1958, Moscow)
Artist
At Night in the Old Marketplace: A Tragic Carnival, Solomon Maimon, The Travels of Benjamin the Third: Epos in Three Acts, Tumultuous Forest

One of Russia's preeminent avant-garde painters, Robert Falk was known for his somber landscapes and Cubo-Futurist portraits, the stability of his compositions, and his harmonious, restrained use of color. Born to a prosperous Moscow family, he entered the Moscow School of Painting, Sculpture, and Architecture in 1905; he studied with Abram Arkhipov, Viktor Vasnetsov, and Leonid Pasternak. His early paintings were influenced by Paul Cézanne and by the Post-Impressionist style of his Moscow teachers. After returning from a trip to Italy in 1910, he joined artists with a similar outlook to found the Bubovny Valet (Jack of Diamonds) group, through which he met Marc Chagall and Natan Altman. In the late 1910s, Falk adopted a sharper, Cubist style, with flashes of Fauvist color.

After the revolution, Falk entered the world of theater, creating stage and costume designs for several of GOSET's productions. His designs for *At Night in the Old Marketplace: A Tragic Carnival* were among the most memorable in the company's history—for the costumes, he drew inspiration from visits to the Institute of Forensic Medicine in Moscow—though they did not elude the disapproval of the critic Abram Efros, who attacked Falk's use of space.

As the head of the Painting Department at the VKhUTEIN institute, Falk was awarded a trip to Paris in 1928 to study

Aleksei Granovsky

Western art; he remained there until 1937. After his return to Moscow, he designed sets for GOSET in 1940–41, as well as for Jewish theaters in Belorussia, until they were closed in 1948.

Apart from his role in the Jewish theater, Falk was active in Soviet artistic life. He participated frequently in exhibitions in Moscow and abroad. During World War II, he was evacuated to Samarkand in Central Asia, where he was inspired by local art forms. In the 1950s, his work significantly influenced the rising generation of nonconformist Soviet artists.

FURTHER READING
Azarkh-Granovskaia, *Vospominania.*
Basner, *Robert Falk.*
Besançon, "R. R. Falk (1886–1958)."
Efros, "Khudozhniki teatra Granovskogo."
Falk, *Besedy ob iskusstve, pisma, vospominania o khudozhnike.*
Goodman, *Russian Jewish Artists,* 164–165.
Rudnitsky, *Russian and Soviet Theatre,* 160.
Sarabyanov, *Robert Falk.*

AVROM GOLDFADN
(Staro Konstantinov, 1840–1908, New York)
Author

Bar Kokhba, Shulamis, The Sorceress: An Eccentric Jewish Play, Two Kuni-Lemls

The poet and playwright Avrom Goldfadn is credited with founding the first professional Yiddish theater troupe, in Jassy, Romania, in 1876. He later directed the company's productions throughout the Russian empire and Western Europe, and in New York. Goldfadn's plays, for which he also wrote original music, were generally farces or melodramas, in which he sought to convey the reality of shtetl life with the latest stage effects, inserting traditional imagery into modern contexts. The performances were immensely popular in Russia and drew crowds of Jewish intellectuals, but they gradually lost favor with both the tsarist government and conservative members of the Jewish community. In 1922, GOSEKT adapted Goldfadn's 1882 play *The Sorceress: An Eccentric Jewish Play,* undermining its original melodramatic nature.

Goldfadn first moved to New York in 1887 and later returned in 1903. Called the "Yiddish Shakespeare" and "a poet and a prophet" by the *New York Times,* he had a profound impact on Jewish literature and culture.

FURTHER READING
Berkowitz, "Avrom Goldfaden and the Modern Yiddish Theater";
    "The Tallis or the Cross."
"Burial of a Yiddish Poet."
Encyclopaedia Judaica (1978), vol. 7, 715–717.
"Noted Jewish Bard Dead."
Sandrow, *Vagabond Stars,* 39–69.
"75,000 at Poet's Funeral."
Shatsky, *Hunderd yor Goldfadn.*

ALEKSEI MIKHAILOVICH GRANOVSKY
(Moscow, 1890–1937, Paris)
Director

Agents: A Joke in One Act, God of Vengeance, It's a Lie! Dialogue in Galicia, Jewish Luck, Mazel Tov, At Night in the Old Market-place: A Tragic Carnival, The Sorceress: An Eccentric Jewish Play, The Spoiled Celebration, The Tenth Commandment: A Pamphlet Operetta, Three Jewish Raisins, The Travels of Benjamin the Third: Epos in Three Acts, Trouhadec: An Eccentric Operetta, 200,000: A Musical Comedy, Uriel Acosta

Aleksei Granovsky was the founding director of GOSET and the key figure in its establishment as a major Russian theater. Born Avraham Azarkh, he was the son of Moshe Azarkh, one of the wealthiest Jews in Russia and among the few allowed to live in Moscow. The family moved to Riga in Granovsky's infancy, assimilating into the dominant German population. In 1910, Granovsky went to St. Petersburg to study theater; there he was influenced by Vsevolod Meyerhold's experimental studio. Three years later, he went to Berlin to study under Max Reinhardt, one of the pioneers of Expressionist theater. In 1918, Granovsky was named director of the Jewish Theatrical Society's new Yiddish Chamber Theater in Petrograd. He envisioned this as a studio school that would mold a troupe of amateurs to meet his exacting standards. With an offer of state support, the troupe moved to Moscow in 1920; it became the State Yiddish Chamber Theater, or GOSEKT (which became GOSET in 1924).

Granovsky had little exposure to Yiddish culture before his direction of GOSEKT. He did not even speak Yiddish; his German had to suffice until he learned enough from the actors. His productions were dominated by Expressionist and Symbolist aesthetics, in which characters represented exaggerated stereotypes rather than realistic individuals. Appealing to the burgeoning postrevolutionary Jewish population of Moscow, GOSET became the center of Jewish cultural activity in the capital.

During the company's European tour in 1928, Granovsky neutralized the political message of his productions and ran a deficit, both of which angered Soviet authorities. Having failed to receive permission to extend the tour to America, GOSET was recalled to the Soviet Union. Granovsky remained in Berlin. Though Stalinist authorities purged him from GOSET's official history, his artistic career continued. He worked with the Jewish theater Habima in the 1930s and later became a filmmaker. In 1933, Granovsky fled Nazi Germany and resettled in Paris, where he died four years later.

FURTHER READING

Adler, "Alexis Granovsky and the Jewish State Theatre of Moscow."

Altshuler, *Ha-teatron ha-yeuidi bebrit Ha-mietsot*, 15–20, 216–221, 228–231, 259–269.

Azarkh-Granovskaia, *Vospominania*.

Rudnitsky, *Russian and Soviet Theatre*, 106–108.

Sandrow, *Vagabond Stars*, 226–239.

Veidlinger, *The Moscow State Yiddish Theater*, 4, 22, 55, 60, 67–73.

Vovsi-Mikhoels, *Moi otets Solomon Mikhoels*, 39.

Zuskin-Perelman, *Massaot Biniamin Zuskin*, 53–60, 65–68, 70–73, 79–82, 109–112, 165–167; *Puteshestvie Veniamina*, 51–53, 55–60, 65–67, 71–73, 80–83, 109–115, 436–438.

KARL GUTZKOW
(Berlin, 1811–1878, Kesselstadt bei Hanau, Germany)
Author
Uriel Acosta

The German writer Karl Gutzkow began his career as a student of theology and philosophy under Georg Hegel and Friedrich Schleiermacher, and soon became a principal figure in the Young Germany literary movement. A fervent nationalist, he entangled himself in literary feuds with such liberals as the German Jewish poet Heinrich Heine. In 1836, Gutzkow was convicted of blasphemy and sentenced to a month in prison. In the early 1840s he turned his attention to theater. He achieved his greatest dramatic triumph with the 1846 premiere of *Uriel Acosta,* based on the life of a seventeenth-century Jewish philosopher who rebelled against the strict orthodoxy of his community. Gutzkow continued to write prolifically until his death in a fire in 1878.

FURTHER READING

Dobert, *Karl Gutzkow und seine Zeit*.

Jones, "Authorial Intent and Public Response to *Uriel Acosta* and *Freiheit in Krähwinkel*."

Morse, "Karl Gutzkow and the Modern Novel."

Steinecke, "Gutzkow, die Juden und das Judentum."

ALEKSANDR ABRAMOVICH KREIN
(Nizhny Novgorod, 1883–1951, Staraya Ruza)
Composer
In Winter, King Lear, At Night in the Old Marketplace: A Tragic Carnival

Born into a well-known family of professional musicians, Aleksandr Krein studied cello and composition at the Moscow Conservatory, where he later became a professor. He enjoyed great success in the 1920s as a composer of stage music, and was active in the Society for Jewish Folk Music, for which he was a staunch advocate. Admired for their rich orchestration, lyrical impressionism, and Jewish folk motifs, Krein's musical compositions accompanied the GOSET productions of *King Lear* and *At Night in the Old Marketplace: A Tragic Carnival*. His partnership with GOSET lasted for more than two decades.

FURTHER READING

Encyclopaedia Judaica (1978), vol. 10, 1252–1253.

Veidlinger, *The Moscow State Yiddish Theater*, 33–34, 209–210.

Weisser, *The Modern Renaissance of Jewish Music, Events, and Figures*.

SARAH DMITRIEVNA LEBEDEVA
(St. Petersburg, 1892–1967, Moscow)
Sculptor

Born Sarah Dmitrievna Darmolatova, Lebedeva trained in the studios of several noted Russian artists. Her exposure to ancient and Renaissance sculpture in the museums of Paris, Berlin, and Vienna strengthened her proclivity toward the Western classical tradition. During the first two decades of the twentieth century, Lebedeva worked as a theater decorator and a teacher, and made portrait busts of the French revolutionaries Georges Danton and Maximilien Robespierre. During those years she worked primarily in two media, sheet iron and porcelain. Her preferred genre was portrait sculpture of well-known figures, in which she combined traditional figuration with impressionistic modeling; her work displays great sensitivity toward the psychology of her sitters. From 1925 she lived in Moscow, rendering remarkable portraits of eminent personalities in Soviet politics and culture, including a 1939 bust of Solomon Mikhoels. She was married to the noted Russian artist V. V. Lebedev.

FURTHER READING
Alpatov, *Trois sculpteurs soviétiques.*
Lebedeva, *Album.*
Ternovets, *Sarra Lebedeva.*
Yablonskaya, *Women Artists of Russia's New Age 1900–1935.*

H. LEIVICK (LEYVICH HALPERN)
(Igumen, 1886–1962, New York)
Author
The Golem

The poet and playwright H. Leivick, born Leyvich Halpern, received a traditional religious education. He was, however, expelled from his yeshiva at age fifteen for reading Abraham Mapu's romantic Haskala novel *Love of Zion.* Two years later he became active in the left-wing Jewish Bund. After several arrests, he was sentenced to forced labor and exile for life in Siberia, but in 1913 he was able to escape to the United States. Leivick's 1921 masterpiece *The Golem* was written in Yiddish in New York. Translated into Hebrew by M. Caspi, it was first produced and performed by Habima in 1925. In subsequent decades, after resettling in Israel, the company continued to restage the play. Between 1917 and 1920, Leivick wrote four apocalyptic, visionary poems reflecting the waves of pogroms in Eastern Europe. Late in life he edited several important anthologies of Yiddish writing.

FURTHER READING
Biletzky, *H. Leivik.*
Niger, *H. Leyvik.*
Sandrow, *Vagabond Stars,* 189–192.
Shtudyes in Leyvik.
Waldman, *H. Leivik, poète yiddish.*

MOSHE LITVAKOV
(Cherkassy, 1875–1937, Minsk)
Author
Translated *Uriel Acosta*; adapted *The Sorceress: An Eccentric Jewish Play*

After receiving a traditional Jewish education and becoming active in the labor Zionist movement, Moshe Litvakov chose a secular education at the Sorbonne in Paris over religious training. Upon his return to Russia in 1905, he cofounded the Society for Friends of the State Yiddish Theater and became head of the Jewish Writers' Section and editor-in-chief of the Yiddish communist daily *Der emes* (The Truth). Despite his earlier Zionist sympathies, he was a vehement opponent of Zionism and the Hebrew language. From his platform as a member of the State Yiddish Theater's governing board, he actively promoted Yiddish theatrical arts as the only appropriate medium for the expression of revolutionary ideas.

Litvakov translated Karl Gutzkow's *Uriel Acosta* into Yiddish and adapted Avrom Goldfadn's *The Sorceress: An Eccentric Jewish Play* for the stage. Both productions were performed by GOSEKT. Criticized by the authorities for reactionary and nationalistic sentiments, Litvakov was arrested in 1937 during one of Joseph Stalin's purges; he was shot in prison.

FURTHER READING
Encyclopaedia Judaica (1978), vol. 11, 404–405.
Veidlinger, *The Moscow State Yiddish Theater,* 21–22, 56–57, 129–130, 185–188.
Zuskin-Perelman, *Massaot Biniamin Zuskin,* 56, 66, 101–103, 105, 118, 184, 452; *Puteshestvie Veniamina,* 56, 66, 104, 106, 108, 121, 169.

MENDELE MOCHER SEFORIM
(SHOLEM YAKOV ABRAMOVICH)
(Kapuli, 1835–1917, Odessa)
Author
The Travels of Benjamin the Third: Epos in Three Acts

Often described as the founder of modern Jewish literature, Sholem Yakov Abramovich adopted the Hebrew pseudonym Mendele Mocher Seforim (Little Mendel the Book Peddler) to hide from his Hebraist colleagues the fact that he had begun writing in Yiddish. Mendele's childhood was marked by uprootedness after the death of his father. He attended several *yeshivot,* then traveled on his own throughout Russia

Solomon Mikhoels

and the Ukraine. These early experiences provided inspiration for his later writings. Drawing on Yiddish folk culture in addition to biblical writings and modern European literature, Mendele reinvigorated Hebrew and Yiddish prose, creating highly popular works. Enamored as he was with the ideology of the Haskala (Jewish Enlightenment) and Zionism, his writings urged Russian Jews to free themselves from the physical and intellectual restraints of the ghetto. Typical of his works is the story "The Travels of Benjamin the Third," which Yekhezkel Dobrushin adapted into a play for GOSET in 1927. Based on *Don Quixote*, the story features a sharply critical attitude toward Russian shtetl life that exemplifies Mendele's efforts to modernize Jewish life through literature.

FURTHER READING

Encyclopaedia Judaica (1978), vol. 11, 1317–1323.

Klinger, *Mendele Mocher Sforim.*

Liptzin, *A History of Yiddish Literature*, 40–45.

Steinberg, *Mendele Mocher Seforim.*

Zuskin-Perelman, *Massaot Biniamin Zuskin*, 88, 94, 95, 127, 241, 303, 392, 440, 450, 476; *Puteshestvie Veniamina*, 87, 89, 93, 98, 130, 309, 398, 456.

SOLOMON MIKHAILOVICH MIKHOELS (SHLOMO VOVSI)
(Dvinsk, 1890–1948, Minsk)
Actor, director

Actor: *The Deaf, An Evening of Sholem Aleichem, Family Ovadis, King Lear, At Night in the Old Marketplace: A Tragic Carnival, Solomon Maimon, The Specialist, Tevye the Dairyman, The Travels of Benjamin the Third: Epos in Three Acts, 200,000: A Musical Comedy*
Director: *Bar Kokhba, Boytre the Bandit, Do Not Grieve!, Freylekhs, Solomon Maimon, Tumultuous Forest*

Solomon Mikhoels was the principal actor in GOSET from its inception until nearly its end. In addition, he served as its director from 1928 to 1948. Born Shlomo Vovsi to a traditional Hasidic family, he studied law in Petrograd. He left his studies at age twenty-nine to join Aleksei Granovsky's studio, indulging a lifelong passion for the theater. With his extraordinarily expressive style, he quickly became the troupe's leading actor, rising to fame in GOSEKT's 1921 production of *An Evening of Sholem Aleichem*. Among his remarkable roles

were Benjamin in *The Travels of Benjamin the Third: Epos in Three Acts* by Mendele Mocher Seforim, Tevye in Sholem Aleichem's *Tevye the Dairyman*, and the title role in *King Lear*, a 1935 GOSET production.

In 1929, after GOSET returned to the Soviet Union from its European tour without Granovsky, Mikhoels assumed the directorship. While he never rejected Judaism, he did drift away from the traditional religious lifestyle in which he was raised, just as he resisted being caught up in the socialist and populist circles that enticed so many Jewish intellectuals. He was therefore well suited to directing an accessible form of theater when, in 1932, Socialist Realism was mandated as the national artistic form.

Because of his visibility as actor and director, Mikhoels was appointed head of the Jewish Anti-Fascist Committee in 1942. He traveled to the United States, Canada, Mexico, and England on its behalf, mobilizing support for the Soviet Union in the war against Nazi Germany.

Mikhoels's public actions for the restoration of Jewish life in the Soviet Union after the war, as well as his growing Zionist sympathies, left him open to charges of Jewish nationalism and cosmopolitanism. On January 13, 1948, while on a business assignment in Minsk, he was brutally murdered, on Joseph Stalin's orders, in what was officially termed a car accident. At his funeral in Moscow, thousands paid their respects. His murder signaled the beginning of the end for Yiddish culture in the Soviet Union. GOSET would close in 1949.

FURTHER READING

Altshuler, *Ha-teatron ha-yeuidi bebrit Ha-mietsot*, 47–49, 56–59, 213–237, 251–253, 255–322.

Azarkh-Granovskaia, *Vospominania*, 7, 8, 50–60, 97–145, 155.

Dobrushin, *Mikhoels der aktior.*

Folkovitsch, *Mikhoels, 1890–1948.*

Geizer, *Mikhoels; Mikhoels: zhizn i smert.*

Goldenberg, *Zhizn i sudba Solomona Mikhoelsa.*

Kostyrchenko, *Out of the Red Shadow*, 33–55, 63–69, 81–90, 109–114, 121–123, 132–138, 142–144, 225–228, 282–284, 297–299.

Liubomirsky, *Af di lebnsvegn*, 132–184.

Rubinstein and Naumov, *Stalin's Secret Pogrom.*

Rudnitsky, *Russian and Soviet Theatre*, 106–107, 160.

Veidlinger, *The Moscow State Yiddish Theater.*

Vovsi-Mikhoels, *Moi otets Solomon Mikhoels.*

Zuskin-Perelman, *Massaot Biniamin Zuskin; Puteshestvie Veniamina.*

Ignaty Nivinsky

MOSHE MILNER (MIKHAIL ARNOLDOVICH)
(Rokitno, 1886–1953, Leningrad)
Composer
The Flood, The Golem, Jacob's Dream

Moshe Milner first gained notice when, in 1914, his songs were published by the Society for Jewish Folk Music, an organization he had helped found. His career was informed by a childhood spent as a member of choirs directed by well-respected cantors and as a student at the Kiev and St. Petersburg conservatories. Milner's works pioneered the use of traditional melodic material in the dramatic style of Modest Mussorgsky (1839–1881). Milner's 1923 opera *Die himlen brenen*, based on S. An-sky's *The Dybbuk*, did not fare well. The first Russian Yiddish opera, it was denounced as reactionary after two performances, and all future showings were forbidden. He went on to compose the music for Habima's 1925 production of *The Golem*, which enjoyed tremendous critical success. Heavily influenced by Jewish folk songs and liturgical texts, Milner's music lent itself well to H. Leivick's ominous drama.

FURTHER READING
Encyclopaedia Judaica (1978), vol. 11, 1586.
Kopytova, "Moissej Milner und seine Oper 'Die himlen brenen.'"

IGNATY IGNATIEVICH NIVINSKY
(Moscow, 1881–1933, Moscow)
Artist
The Golem

Ignaty Nivinsky was a Russian graphic artist, muralist, and teacher, best known for his etchings based on travels in Italy, the Caucasus, and the Crimea. Among his murals was a series based on ancient Egypt, painted at the Museum of Fine Arts in Moscow in 1912. His involvement with the Russian avant-garde theater began in 1921, when he collaborated with Evgeny Vakhtangov on *Erik XIV* and *Princess Turandot* at the Moscow Art Theater. Nivinsky created set and costume designs for Habima's 1925 production of *The Golem*. Despite his non-Jewish origins, his designs for the play revealed a profound knowledge of Jewish tradition and culture.

FURTHER READING
Dokuchaeva, *Ignaty Ignatievich Nivinsky.*
Rudnitsky, *Russian and Soviet Theatre,* 53–54.

ISAAC LEIB PERETZ
(Zamosc, Poland, 1852–1915, Warsaw)
Author
The Fire, At Night in the Old Marketplace: A Tragic Carnival

I. L. Peretz was a celebrated Yiddish author and playwright, and a founding member of the Yiddish Theatrical Society in Warsaw. He was raised in a traditional family by deeply religious parents, and his private education emphasized languages, Hebrew, German, and Russian in particular. Peretz began his career writing in Polish and Hebrew, but adopted Yiddish after the widespread pogroms in the 1880s, which awoke his interest in Jewish nationalism. He also reviewed Yiddish plays in the press and called for the "democratization" of theater, with greater access for the masses. In 1925, Aleksei Granovsky transformed Peretz's mystical 1907 play *At Night in the Old Marketplace: A Tragic Carnival* into a tragedy, leaving little of the original intent. Instead, Granovsky's version of the play dovetailed with the new agenda of the Jewish Section of the Communist Party.

FURTHER READING
Altshuler, *Ha-teatron ha-yeuidi bebrit Ha-mietsot,* 239–258.
Encyclopaedia Judaica (1978), vol. 13, 279–283.
Frieden, *Classic Yiddish Fiction.*
Wisse, *I. L. Peretz and the Making of the Modern Jewish Culture.*
Yudel, *I. L. Peretz, 1852–1915.*

LEV PULVER
(Yekaterinoslav, 1883–1970, Moscow)
Composer
Bar Kokhba, The Deaf, King Lear, Luftmentshen, Tevye the Dairyman, The Travels of Benjamin the Third: Epos in Three Acts, Trouhadec: An Eccentric Operetta

GOSET's primary composer, Lev Pulver was born to a renowned family of klezmer players in Yekaterinoslav, a shtetl on Russia's western frontier. After graduating from the St. Petersburg Conservatory in 1908, he played in the orchestra of the Bolshoi Theater as a violin soloist for fourteen years. He later served as the concertmaster and conductor of symphony orchestras in Kiev, Kharkov, and Minsk, and as a musical advisor to GOSET. Drawing heavily on Eastern European Jewish folk music, his catchy musical scores became a signature of the company's productions. They were also performed at the

Isaac Rabinovich

World's Fair in New York in 1939, when Pulver was named an Honored Artist of the Republic. He was one of the few GOSET artists to escape Joseph Stalin's later purges.

FURTHER READING

Braun, "Jews in Soviet Music."

Veidlinger, *The Moscow State Yiddish Theater*, 49, 84, 139, 171, 211.

Zuskin-Perelman, *Massaot Biniamin Zuskin*, 84, 89, 110, 189, 212, 244, 247, 249, 260, 266, 281, 348, 431; *Puteshestvie Veniamina*, 85, 91, 113, 195, 218, 249, 251, 253, 254, 269, 288, 354, 448.

ISAAC BENICH RABICHEV
(Kiev, 1896–1957, Moscow)
Artist

Carnival of the Jewish Masks, Three Jewish Raisins, 200,000: A Musical Comedy

Isaac Rabichev is known for his set designs and graphic art. He studied at the Brodsky Art School in Kiev, before continuing his training in Moscow. He worked for the newspaper *Pravda* as a graphic artist and designed propaganda posters, the most famous of which bore such slogans as "Proletarians of All Countries, Unite!" and "The Enemy Will Find No Place to Hide from the People."

In 1923, collaborating with Aleksandr Stepanov, Rabichev designed the sets for a number of Aleksei Granovsky's GOSEKT productions, including *Carnival of the Jewish Masks*, by Yekhezkel Dobrushin, Nahum Oislender, and Aaron Kushnirov; *Three Jewish Raisins*, an adaptation by Dobrushin and Oislender; and *200,000: A Musical Comedy*, by Sholem Aleichem. His work was featured in Russian exhibitions in the late 1920s and early 1930s.

FURTHER READING

Apter-Gabriel, *Tradition and Revolution*, 39, 136, 242.

Picon-Vallin, *Le théâtre juif soviétique pendant les années vingt*.

Veidlinger, *The Moscow State Yiddish Theater*, 49.

ISAAC MOISEYEVICH RABINOVICH
(Kiev, 1894–1961, Moscow)
Artist

The Deaf, Do Not Grieve!, God of Vengeance, Holiday in Kasrilevka, Prince Reubeni, The Sorceress: An Eccentric Jewish Play, Tevye the Dairyman, The Trial Is Going On

After Marc Chagall's departure from GOSEKT in 1922, the company hired an unknown young artist, Isaac Rabinovich, as his replacement. Educated at the Kiev Art School, Rabinovich studied under the acclaimed art historian Adrian Prakhov. He created his first stage design in 1911 for a production of Hans Christian Andersen's fairy tales performed at Kiev's Bergone Theater. He continued his stage design work at the Solovtsovsky Theater and took part in the outdoor decoration of Kiev and Kharkov for the May Day celebrations of 1919 and 1920.

In 1921, Rabinovich moved to Moscow, where he joined GOSEKT. His first contribution to the theater was the set design for Granovsky's production of Sholem Asch's *God of Vengeance*. The following year he devised the set for Avrom Goldfadn's *The Sorceress: An Eccentric Jewish Play* in a Futuristic-Constructivist style that reflected his commitment to revolutionary principles. He designed the sets for GOSET's 1926 production of Sholem Aleichem's *Holiday in Kasrilevka* and its 1928 productions of *The Deaf* and *The Trial Is Going On*, as well as the Yiddish productions of *Earth and Four Days* (1930–31), *Tevye the Dairyman* (1939), and *Prince Reubeni* (1946).

Beyond the Yiddish theater, Rabinovich played a key role in the development of Russian stage and film design. He was responsible for the production design for a number of Moscow's major theaters until the late 1950s.

FURTHER READING

Apter-Gabriel, *Tradition and Revolution*, 127–128, 136–137, 139, 150, 242.

Goodman, *Russian Jewish Artists*, 30, 32, 45, 48, 76.

Rudnitsky, *Russian and Soviet Theatre*, 48, 106–107.

Veidlinger, *The Moscow State Yiddish Theater*, 43, 46–47, 74, 116, 178, 188, 218.

Hanna Rovina

Naum Tsemakh

JULES ROMAINS
(LOUIS-HENRI-JEAN FARIGOULE)
(St.-Julien-Chapteuil, 1885–1972, Paris)
Author

Trouhadec: An Eccentric Operetta

A novelist, poet, and playwright, Jules Romains was prominent in French literary and theatrical circles. Born in southeastern France, he studied science and philosophy at the École Normale Supérieure in Paris. Before embarking on a full-time writing career, he taught philosophy, which inspired him to found the literary movement Unanimism that advocated a belief in universal brotherhood and a collective consciousness. Romains's philosophical beliefs were reflected in his literary works throughout his career.

Written in 1923, the play *Trouhadec: An Eccentric Operetta* critiqued the capitalist emphasis on individualism and wealth. Aleksei Granovksy adapted it for the GOSET stage in 1927. It was the theater's first successful production with a secular theme. Romains's most popular work to date remains *Knock, ou le triomphe de la médecine* (1923; *Dr. Knock*, 1925).

FURTHER READING
"Jules Romains."

HANNA ROVINA
(Berezino, 1889–1980, Tel Aviv)
Actress

The Dybbuk, The Eternal Jew, Mirele Efros

Attracted to the theater by her love of the Hebrew language, this internationally celebrated actress was recognized as the first lady of the Hebrew theater. Hanna Rovina was educated at a yeshiva for girls, and school plays introduced her to the world of theater. She trained as a kindergarten teacher in Warsaw and operated an institute for refugee children during World War I. In 1917, together with Naum Tsemakh and Menachem Gnesin, she was a founding member of the Habima theater company in Moscow.

In Habima's groundbreaking 1922 production of S. An-sky's *The Dybbuk*, Rovina played the spirit-possessed Leah. She reprised the role in Leningrad in 1925, in Riga in 1926, and on Habima's tours of Western Europe and the United States thereafter. Arriving with the company in Palestine in 1928, she was quickly acclaimed the country's leading actress.

FURTHER READING
Finkel, *Hanah Rovina.*
Gai, *Ha-malkah nas'ah be-otobus.*
Levy, *The Habima,* 6–8, 12–13, 15–16, 164–166.

ALEKSANDR FEDOROVICH STEPANOV
(1894–1965, Moscow)
Artist

Carnival of the Jewish Masks, The Specialist, Three Jewish Raisins, 200,000: A Musical Comedy

Aleksandr Stepanov received his early education at Stroganov-skoe Art Industrial School in Moscow, and continued his education at VKhUTEMAS (Higher Artistic and Technical Studios). In 1922 he joined GOSEKT as part of the stage management team. The following year he and Isaac Rabichev collaborated on the landmark stage productions *Carnival of the Jewish Masks* and *200,000: A Musical Comedy;* for the latter, Stepanov conceived the sets, while Rabichev was costume designer. In 1924 the pair created the designs for another GOSEKT production, *Three Jewish Raisins.* Stepanov was primary designer for GOSET's *The Specialist* in 1932. He remained with GOSET until its closing in 1949, working for much of that time as technical director.

NAUM TSEMAKH
(Volkovysk, 1887–1939, New York)
Founding director, Habima

A gifted fund-raiser, motivator, organizer, and actor, Naum Tsemakh was considered the father of the Hebrew theater. Born to a lower-middle-class family, he received a religious education until age sixteen, when his father died. To earn money for his family, Tsemakh taught Hebrew. His passion, however, was the stage. After several theatrical ventures, in 1917 he founded and recruited acting talent for a new Hebrew-language company, Habima. Despite the lack of a Hebrew-speaking audience in Russia, he expended great effort in the organization and development of the theater.

Tsemakh was the logistical leader and spokesman for Habima until 1931, when, after a six-year world tour, long-running tensions caused the troupe to split in two. His minority group settled in the United States, while the other members eventually relocated permanently to Palestine, where they established a new company. Finding little success, Habima in

Aleksandr Tyshler

Evgeny Vakhtangov

the United States disintegrated, and Tsemakh's career stalled. He served briefly as the manager of the Jewish Theater Unit of the WPA's Federal Theatre Project in 1937. He tried but failed to reconcile with Habima in Palestine, before his death in 1939.

FURTHER READING
Encyclopaedia Judaica (1978), vol. 16, 981–982.
Kohansky, *The Hebrew Theatre.*

ALEKSANDR GRIGOREVICH TYSHLER
(Melitpol, 1898–1980, Moscow)
Artist
Bar Kokhba, Boytre the Bandit, An Eye for an Eye, Freylekhs, King Lear

Maintaining a distinct and individualistic style throughout his career, Aleksandr Tyshler created a singular type of fantasy painting with personal allegorical significance often drawn from Jewish life and folklore. After completing his art studies at the Kiev Art School in 1917, he frequented the studio of the theater designer Aleksandra Exter. From 1927 until the mid-1930s, he designed sets for GOSET in Minsk, the Kharkov Jewish Theater, and the Gypsy Theater. In 1935, Solomon Mikhoels invited Tyshler to design the sets and costumes for the GOSET production of *King Lear* in Moscow, and the artist collaborated with GOSET until 1949.

In addition to his theatrical work, Tyshler illustrated books by well-known authors, including Sholem Aleichem, and painted portraits of Mikhoels and other celebrities. Tyshler's work was often criticized for its fantastical elements and for his formalist style. In 1945 he designed the sets and costumes for GOSET's famed production of Z. M. Shneer's *Freylekhs.* Tyshler was awarded the Stalin Prize in 1946.

FURTHER READING
A. G. Tyshler: Teatr, zhivopis, grafika.
A. Tyshler: Zhivopis, grafika, skulptura.
Aleksandr Tyshler 1898–1980.
Goodman, *Russian Jewish Artists,* 78–79, 89–90, 234–235.
Syrkina, *Aleksandr G. Tyshler.*

EVGENY BAGRATIONOVICH VAKHTANGOV
(Vladikavkaz, 1883–1922, Moscow)
Director
The Dybbuk

A renowned director affiliated with the Moscow Art Theater in the 1910s, Evgeny Vakhtangov was memorialized with the Vakhtangov Theater, established four years after his death. Born to Armenian parents in Vladikavkaz, he entered the Moscow Art Theater, founded by Konstantin Stanislavsky, as an actor and director in 1911, and became a devotee of Stanislavsky's innovative technique. Vakhtangov's productions typically used music, dance, abstract costumes, masks, and avant-garde sets.

In 1918, when Habima produced its first productions in Moscow, Vakhtangov was appointed its director. He immediately grounded the company in his acting principles, encouraging the actors to consider themselves onstage as priests performing the rites of the temple. Vakhtangov thus fostered in Habima a theatrical cult, one for which there could be no distinction between the actors' lives on and off stage. In this revolutionary period of Russian and Jewish history, the actors of Habima were distinguished by their conception of theater as a vehicle for spiritual expression, an ideology considered somewhat reactionary in the heady progressivism of the day.

Though devoted to Stanislavsky's method, Vakhtangov sought to develop his own distinct style. He amplified the sets, costumes, and acting in his productions, while striving for truthful depictions of human nature. His efforts allowed Habima to engage in an Expressionist style of acting that attained a realism through theatrical means, as opposed to the more literal realism championed by Stanislavsky. Vakhtangov's 1922 production of S. An-sky's *The Dybbuk,* Habima's most successful and identifiable play, brought renown to him and to the company. He died that year at age thirty-nine, and the company struggled to find a replacement with similar enthusiasm for the theater.

FURTHER READING
Apter-Gabriel, *Tradition and Revolution,* 132–135.
Ivanov, "Poetika metamorfoz."
Ivanov and Krivitsky, *Vakhtangov i vakhtangovtsy.*
Kampf, *Jewish Experience in the Art of the Twentieth Century,* 38.

Benjamin Zuskin

Levy, *The Habima.*
Rudnitsky, *Russian and Soviet Theatre,* 21, 52–55, 76–83.
Sandrow, *Vagabond Stars,* 218, 225, 280.
Simonov, *Stanislavsky's Protégé.*
Vakhtangov, Evgeny, 1883–1922.
Worrall, *Modernism to Realism on the Soviet Stage.*

BENJAMIN ZUSKIN
(Ponevezh, Lithuania, 1899–1952, Moscow)
Actor

Arn Fridman, The Deaf, Do Not Grieve!, The Enchanted Tailor, An Evening of Sholem Aleichem, An Eye for an Eye, Freylekhs, King Lear, The Millionaire, the Dentist, and the Pauper, At Night in the Old Marketplace: A Tragic Carnival, Solomon Maimon, The Sorceress: An Eccentric Jewish Play, The Specialist, The Travels of Benjamin the Third: Epos in Three Acts, Tumultuous Forest, 200,000: A Musical Comedy, Wandering Stars

A principal actor for the State Yiddish Theater, Benjamin Zuskin was once called a "treasure of expressiveness" by Marc Chagall. Zuskin left his hometown in Lithuania after the 1915 expulsion of Jews from the Baltic States, and eventually settled in Moscow, where he attended the Moscow Mining Institute. He abandoned his studies to join Aleksei Granovsky's Yiddish theater studio, developing his acting style and experiencing success quickly. His first performance was in September 1921 in *It's a Lie! Dialogue in Galicia,* a segment of *An Evening of Sholem Aleichem.* In 1922, with his first leading role—in *The Sorceress: An Eccentric Jewish Play*—he positioned himself as Solomon Mikhoels's onstage cohort for years to come.

Zuskin's acting style embodied the grotesque irony advocated by Granovsky. At the same time, he added original psychological dimensions to the roles he played, conveyed through nuanced improvisation and a striking sense of rhythm. In particular, he captured the simultaneously tragic and comic contradictions of Jewish village life. Throughout his career, he provided a crucial counterpart to Solomon Mikhoels's dramatic pathos, specializing in roles that were both earthy and melancholic, such as Senderl in Mendele Mocher Seforim's *The Travels of Benjamin the Third: Epos in Three Acts* and the Fool in *King Lear.*

Zuskin also worked as a film actor and theatrical director, and taught at the acting studio attached to GOSET. In 1939 he was awarded the title of Honored Artist of the Republic by the Soviet regime. After the assassination of Mikhoels in 1948, Zuskin served briefly as director of GOSET before falling ill. He was arrested while in the hospital in 1949, charged with promoting "Jewish nationalism," and imprisoned. Together with twelve other Jews, some of them major cultural figures, Zuskin was executed in Lubyanka Prison on August 12, 1952, now known as the Night of the Murdered Poets.

FURTHER READING
Altshuler, *Ha-teatron ha-yeuidi bebrit Ha-mietsot,* 14–17, 48–52.
Azarkh-Granovskaia, *Vospominania,* 126–137, 140–144.
Liubomirsky, *Af di lebnsvegn,* 185–245.
Rudnitsky, *Russian and Soviet Theatre,* 106–107, 160–161.
Veidlinger, *The Moscow State Yiddish Theater,* 36–37, 217–218, 241–242, 268–272.
Zuskin-Perelman, *Massaot Biniamin Zuskin; Puteshestvie Veniamina.*

TIMELINE

Bold type = Historical Events

Roman type = Jewish Cultural Events in the Soviet Union

1917

February Revolution: Tsar Nicholas II is forced to abdicate, and thus the Romanov dynasty ends. A provisional parliamentary government takes over, under Aleksandr Kerensky.

Emancipation of the Russian Jews. The Pale of Settlement is officially abolished.

October Revolution: The Bolsheviks, led by Vladimir Lenin, overthrow the provisional government and declare a Soviet republic.

The Jewish Society for the Encouragement of the Arts sponsors an exhibition of painting and sculpture by Jewish artists at the Lemercier Gallery in Moscow. El Lissitzky designs the catalogue.

First Habima production in Moscow, with four one-act plays performed in Hebrew.

1918

The Treaty of Brest-Litovsk marks the end of World War I in Russia.

The Russian capital moves from Petrograd (St. Petersburg) to Moscow.

The Bolsheviks establish a Jewish Section of the Communist Party, the Yevsektsia, to enlist Jewish support for the new Soviet government.

The civil war begins. Bolshevik "Red" forces battle nationalist, monarchist, and other groups united under the banner of the "White" armies, led by former imperial generals. Jews and other minorities suffer at the hands of the Whites and Ukrainian nationalist forces; more than fifty thousand Jews die. Red troops prevent further pogroms and garner widespread Jewish support.

Habima, founded in Bialystok in 1912, is established in Moscow by Naum Tsemakh and gives its first performance *(The Eternal Jew)* under the artistic leadership of director Evgeny Vakhtangov.

Anatoly Lunacharsky, the people's commissar of enlightenment, names Marc Chagall the commissar of art in Vitebsk.

The Kultur-Lige, a Yiddish cultural organization, is founded in Kiev and other cities to revive Yiddish art and culture.

The Yiddish Chamber Theater is founded by Aleksei Granovsky in Petrograd.

Natan Altman, in his role as art commissar of Petrograd, designs decorations in the city's Palace Square for the first anniversary of the Revolution.

The audience at Habima's first public performance, October 8, 1918

(left) Benjamin Zuskin (second from right) as Shlomke in *God of Vengeance*, 1921. Photograph, 3½ × 5½ in. (18.9 × 14 cm). Beth Hatefutsoth, Photo Archive, Tel Aviv, courtesy of Zuskin Collection

(right) Brochure for the exhibition of Marc Chagall's murals in the Moscow State Yiddish Chamber Theater, June 1921. Private collection, Paris. In an effort to make his murals known to a wider audience, Chagall instigated an exhibition of his work, held at the GOSEKT theater in 1921. The following year the Moscow League of Culture organized a second exhibition at the theater, featuring designs by Natan Altman and David Shterenberg in addition to Chagall. Both exhibitions received extensive coverage in the press, helping to solidify Chagall's reputation in the Moscow art world.

(opposite right) Poster for the Yiddish Chamber (Kamerny) Theater, 1919; 32 × 24 in. (81.3 × 6.1 cm). The Russian State Archive of Literature and Art, Moscow. At upper right is the theater's logo, used on its early programs, depicting stage curtains pulled back to reveal a menorah, with the letters EKT in Russian and AKT in Yiddish (the acronym of Yiddish Chamber Theater). The logo was designed by the Russian artist and stage designer Mstislav Dobuzhinskii (1875–1957), a central figure in the World of Art movement, and Chagall's drawing teacher.

The art critics Abram Efros and Yakov Tugendhold publish the first monograph on Marc Chagall. I. Rybak and B. Aronson publish "The Paths of Jewish Painting" in the Kiev Yiddish journal *Oifgang*.

1919

Habima becomes a Soviet state theater.

The Yiddish Chamber Theater opens in Petrograd with Maurice Maeterlinck's *The Blind* and Sholem Asch's *The Sin* and *Amman and Tamar*.

The Kultur-Lige publishes *Chad Gadya*, illustrated by El Lissitzky.

1920

The Yiddish Chamber Theater moves from Petrograd to Moscow and is renamed State Yiddish Chamber Theater (GOSEKT).

Marc Chagall moves to Moscow and joins GOSEKT.

1921

The civil war ends with a Bolshevik victory. The government initiates a New Economic Policy to aid in recovery from the war. Restrictions against private enterprise are temporarily relaxed.

A new GOSEKT opens to the public with *An Evening of Sholem Aleichem*, directed by Granovsky and with costume and set design by Chagall.

God of Vengeance and *Before Sunrise*, GOSEKT.

1922

Formation of the Union of Soviet Socialist Republics (USSR).

Exhibition of the Three, featuring works by Marc Chagall, Natan Altman, and David Shterenberg, is organized by the Kultur-Lige in Moscow.

The Sorceress: An Eccentric Jewish Play and *Uriel Acosta*, GOSEKT.

The Dybbuk, Habima.

Marc Chagall leaves Moscow for Paris.

The Sorceress, 1922. Photograph,
4½ × 7¼ in. (11.4 × 18.4 cm)

Poster for *200,000* and *Three Jewish Raisins*, GOSEKT, Moscow, c. 1922–24; 40 × 30 in. (101.6 × 76.2 cm). The Russian State Archive of Literature and Art, Moscow

1923

To strengthen socialism among Soviet national minorities, the government promotes a policy that is "socialist in content, nationalist in form." Among Jews, a socialist Yiddish-language culture begins to flourish. Nonsocialist aspects of Jewish culture, such as religion and Zionism, are suppressed.

Masks, GOSEKT.

200,000: A Musical Comedy, GOSEKT.

The Yevsektsia promotes the state funding of Yiddish culture as part of the effort to strengthen socialism.

Isaac Babel publishes *Red Cavalry*, a fictionalized account of his experiences in the Red Army.

1924

Vladimir Lenin dies.

Petrograd is renamed Leningrad.

GOSEKT becomes the State Yiddish Theater (GOSET).

Three Jewish Raisins, GOSET.

1925

Premiere of the film *Jewish Luck*, based on stories by Sholem Aleichem

At Night in the Old Marketplace: A Tragic Carnival, GOSET.

The Golem, Jacob's Dream, and *The Flood*, Habima.

1926

The Ukrainian Academy of Sciences in Kiev establishes a department of Jewish culture.

After touring Europe, Habima leaves the Soviet Union permanently, and eventually relocates to Palestine. It will become the national theater of Israel.

The Tenth Commandment: A Pamphlet Operetta and *137 Children's Houses*, GOSET.

1927

All publications in Hebrew in the Soviet Union cease.

Leon Trotsky, the first commissar of foreign affairs and the first leader of the Red Army, is expelled from the Communist Party's Central Committee, and later from the party itself.

The Travels of Benjamin III: Epos in Three Acts and *Trouhadec*, GOSET.

(left) The Inquisitor Tadeush in *The Golem,* Habima, Moscow, 1925. Photograph, 7³⁄₁₆ × 5¹⁄₁₆ in. (18.3 × 12.9 cm). Courtesy of Vladislav Ivanov, Moscow

(right) Natan Altman, *Evreiskoe Shchast'e (Jewish Luck),* 1926. Book cover with lithographed lettering and illustration on front, and lithographed illustration on back, 11⅞ × 8¹⁵⁄₁₆ in. (30.2 × 22.7 cm). The Museum of Modern Art, New York, Gift of The Judith Rothschild Foundation

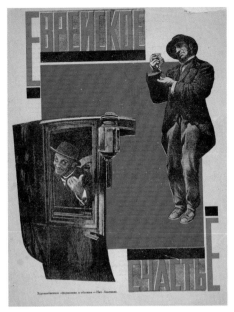

1928

Joseph Stalin assumes power.

The Soviet "Cultural Revolution" clamps down on avant-garde art.

End of the New Economic Policy, and declaration of the first Five-Year Plan, a blueprint for the radical transformation of the rural Soviet Union into an industrialized socialist society.

Birobidzhan, the Jewish Autonomous Region in the Soviet Far East, is created as an alternative to Zionism; it represents the culmination of an agricultural resettlement program for urban Jews.

Luftmentshen, GOSET.

GOSET tours Europe. At tour's end, Aleksei Granovsky, Robert Falk, and Natan Altman remain in Germany; Solomon Mikhoels becomes director of the company.

1929

Most Yiddish schools and cultural institutions across the Soviet Union are closed.

1930

The Yevsektsia is dissolved.

The Deaf, written by David Bergelson, GOSET.

Soviet artists and writers are forced to become members of a union in their field. The establishment of new artistic associations is banned.

1931

Natan Altman returns to the Soviet Union.

Four Days, written by M. Daniel (Daniel Meyerovich), and *Do Not Grieve!,* written by Peretz Markish, GOSET.

1932

The government resolution "On the Reconstruction of Literary and Artistic Organizations" is passed, promoting the ideology of Socialist Realism and severely limiting artistic movements.

Forced collectivization of independent farms leads to mass famine in Ukraine and other regions.

1933

Midat ha-din (A Measure of Strictness), written by David Bergelson, GOSET

1934

Sergei M. Kirov, a Leningrad party leader, is assassinated. Stalin uses this incident to launch a period of political repression known as the "Great Terror," in order to eliminate political opposition.

The 200 Million Gladiators, GOSET.

Socialist Realism is decreed the official artistic and sole ideology by the First All-Union Congress of Soviet Writers.

1935

Communist Party ranks are purged. Widespread arrests, show trials, deportations, and executions of alleged traitors touch virtually all segments of the population. Many citizens who attempt to emigrate are accused of treason.

King Lear, GOSET.

1936

Boytre the Bandit, GOSET.

Artists suspected of subversion are forced out of unions.

1937

Stalin's Great Terror peaks. Hundreds of thousands of people are executed or sent to labor camps.

Aleksei Granovsky dies in Paris.

Robert Falk returns to the Soviet Union.

Yekhezkel Dobrushin is arrested and deported to a Siberian labor camp.

1938

Remaining Yiddish schools are closed in the Soviet Union.

Family Ovadis, written by Peretz Markish, and *Bar Kokhba*, written by Shmuel Halkin, GOSET.

1939

Nazi Germany and the Soviet Union sign a Non-Aggression Pact. Germany invades Poland. World War II begins.

The Stalin Prize is instituted, recognizing artists whose work is considered the best embodiment of Socialist Realist art.

The last state-sponsored art exhibition featuring a Jewish section is held.

The Banquet, GOSET.

1940

Solomon Maimon, written by M. Daniel (Daniel Meyerovich), GOSET.

Isaac Babel is shot in prison.

1941

Germany invades the Soviet Union, in violation of the Non-Aggression Pact. Special killing units follow the German troops, rounding up Jews and other "undesirables."

Wandering Stars, GOSET.

Many Russian industries and war evacuees, as well as Jewish cultural institutions, among them GOSET, are relocated to Tashkent in the Uzbek Soviet Socialist Republic.

1942

The Soviet government creates five antifascist organizations, including the Jewish Anti-Fascist Committee, to mobilize support and raise funds in the West for the war effort.

Khamza and *An Eye for an Eye*, GOSET.

1943

GOSET returns to Moscow.

Solomon Mikhoels and the poet Itzik Fefer go on a seven-month tour of England and North America on behalf of the Jewish Anti-Fascist Committee.

1945

World War II ends. An estimated 26 million Soviet citizens have perished, 2.5 million of them Jews.

Freylekhs, GOSET (winner of the Stalin Prize).

(opposite) *Trouhadec,* 1927. Photograph, 18⅜ × 22⅛ in. (46.6 × 56.2 cm). Beth Hatefutsoth, Photo Archive, Tel Aviv, courtesy of Zuskin Collection

(right) *The Travels of Benjamin the Third,* 1927. Photograph, 6½ × 9½ in. (16.5 × 24.1 cm). Beth Hatefutsoth, Photo Archive, Tel Aviv, courtesy of Zuskin Collection

(below) Left to right: Solomon Mikhoels, Benjamin Zuskin, and Yekhezkel Dobrushin, Moscow, 1930. Photograph, 5½ × 8 in. (14 × 20.3 cm). Beth Hatefutsoth, Photo Archive, Tel Aviv, courtesy of Zuskin Collection

Aleksandr Tyshler, *Solomon Mikhoels as King Lear,* 1935

1946

Tumultuous Forest, GOSET.

1948

Initial support in the Soviet Union for the establishment of the State of Israel, even as alleged "Zionists" are persecuted.

Solomon Mikhoels's murder by agents of Stalin's secret police is officially announced as a car accident. He is given a sham state funeral to conceal government involvement in his death.

1949

A new campaign targets Jews as nationalists and "rootless cosmo-politans," purportedly sympathetic to the West.

The Jewish Anti-Fascist Committee is abolished, and many of its leaders are arrested.

GOSET is dissolved.

Benjamin Zuskin begins a three-year imprisonment at Lubyanka Prison.

1952

On August 12, Zuskin is shot, together with twelve other Jewish artistic, scientific, and medical figures. This "Night of the Murdered Poets" is one of the last of Stalin's purges.

1953

In January, the so-called Doctor's Plot is "uncovered." A campaign is launched against Jewish medical professionals who are accused of planning to kill Stalin and other Soviet officials.

Stalin dies on March 5.

The trial for the Doctors' Plot is canceled.

Yekhezkel Dobrushin dies in the Siberian labor camp.

GLOSSARY

AGITPROP

Contraction of the words *agitation* and *propaganda*, referring to the promotion of the ideology of the new Soviet state in the postrevolutionary period. The term is applied not only or even primarily to art (notably public and decorative art), but to all efforts to raise political consciousness and educate the masses to the party line.

BIOMECHANICS

A technique, combining acrobatics and stylized gestures, that perceived the human body as a highly trained machine. Inspired by robots and the commedia dell'arte, the technique required precise command of the body and the voice as theatrical tools.

BUND

Popular name for the General League of Jewish Workingmen of Russia, Lithuania, and Poland. The Marxist/social democratic organization of Jewish workers was first formed in the tsarist empire in 1897.

CONSTRUCTIVISM

An artistic movement, widespread in the 1920s, that initially focused on sculpture created from industrial materials, reflecting contemporary engineering and building techniques; it tended to reveal the structural elements of form and the composition of materials. Though most often associated with architecture and industrial design, Constructivism was embraced also by Russian stage designers. As a theatrical concept it manifested itself in the multifaceted and multilevel sets that occupied the entire stage.

CUBISM

An early-twentieth-century art movement developed by Pablo Picasso and Georges Braque in 1907. Drawing influence from African and Native American artistic styles, Cubism deconstructed a form into its component parts and reassembled them in such a way to suggest multiple viewpoints and perspectives.

CUBO-FUTURISM

The combination of Cubism with the basic Futurist principle of the visual representation of time. This allowed for a single image to represent several stages of movement together in a single, dynamic form.

DYBBUK

In Kabbalistic tradition, a spirit, benign or evil, that takes possession of a living person. It can be expelled by wonder-workers or Hasidic wise men who invoke the divine name.

GOLEM

A mythical creature, usually in human form, created from clay or mud by magical means and endowed with supernatural strength. The creature could perform tasks assigned to it, and even be a force for destruction. The most well-known legend of the Golem was linked to Rabbi Judah Loew of Prague, also known as the Maharal.

GOSEKT

Russian acronym for the State Yiddish Chamber Theater, 1921–24. Originally founded as the Yiddish Chamber Theater in Petrograd (1918–19) by Aleksei Granovsky, the company relocated to Moscow in November 1920. *See also GOSET.*

GOSET

Russian acronym for the State Yiddish Theater, 1924–49, which was previously known as the Yiddish Chamber Theater. There were regional branches of the State Yiddish Theater, notably in Ukraine (UkGOSET) and Belorussia (BelGOSET). *See GOSEKT.*

HABIMA

In Hebrew, "the stage." A Hebrew-language theater company founded in Bialystok in 1912 and reestablished in Moscow in 1918 by Naum Tsemakh. Evgeny Vakhtangov served as Habima's theatrical director and artistic leader, to great acclaim, until his death in 1922. In 1926, the company found it necessary to leave Moscow; the majority of the troupe members emigrated to Tel Aviv, where, eventually, Habima became the national theater of Israel.

HASKALA

An Enlightenment movement within European Jewish society from the late 1700s through the late 1800s. It promoted secular studies and occupations, and contributed to the acculturation of, among others, Russian Jews.

HEDER

A Jewish elementary school for boys.

JACK OF DIAMONDS (BUBOVNY VALET)

An avant-garde art group founded in Moscow in 1910. It was supported by many radical artists, such as Natalia Goncharova and Kazimir Malevich. The group organized regular exhibitions in Moscow and Petrograd between 1910 and 1917, some of them international in scope.

JEWISH ANTI-FASCIST COMMITTEE

A group formed by Soviet authorities after the German invasion of Russia in 1941. Its purpose was to enlist the support of the international Jewish community for the Soviet war effort.

JEWISH SOCIETY FOR THE ENCOURAGEMENT OF THE ARTS

A Jewish arts group active in Petrograd between 1915 and 1917. Branches were formed in Kiev and Kharkov.

KABBALAH

The traditional and most commonly used term for the esoteric teachings of Judaism and for Jewish mysticism.

KAMERNY

Russian for "chamber." Popular name for the Yiddish Chamber Theater founded by Aleksei Granovsky in 1918–19. Not to be confused with the Kamerny Teatr, 1914–50, the company established by Aleksandr Tairov in Moscow.

LUFTMENTSH

In Yiddish, "man of air." This archetype of shtetl culture is a dreamer, out of touch with reality, who tries and fails to achieve success through various schemes and strategies.

PALE OF SETTLEMENT

The area of tsarist Russia in Poland, Lithuania, Belorussia, Ukraine, Bessarabia, and Crimea to which Jews were confined by laws passed in 1791 and 1835. Residency outside the Pale was regulated by permits, and was an option exclusively for the wealthy and for certain highly skilled professions. The Pale was abolished in 1917.

PETROGRAD

The name officially adopted for St. Petersburg in 1914. In 1924, after Lenin's death, Petrograd became Leningrad; in 1991, with the collapse of the Soviet Union, the name reverted to the original St. Petersburg.

POGROM

A Russian word indicating an attack, tacitly or actively condoned by authorities, against a religious, ethnic, or social minority. The term most often refers to the numerous massacres of Jewish populations within the Pale of Settlement and Poland, especially from the 1880s to 1921.

NIGHT OF THE MURDERED POETS

In this purge, one of Stalin's last, thirteen prominent Jewish cultural, political, and scientific figures were executed in the basement of Lubyanka Prison in Moscow on August 12, 1952.

SHTETL

Yiddish term for a small town. Refers to the antiquated, isolated way of life of Jewish communities of Eastern Europe.

SOCIALIST REALISM

An ideology, based on a 1932 decree, enforced by the Soviet state as the official standard for art, literature, and music. The concept was officially established and defined in 1934 at the First All-Union Congress of Soviet Writers. Socialist Realism was founded on the principle that the arts should promote political and social ideals established by the state, in a readily comprehensible manner. Approved artistic styles had to reflect the utopian ideals of Soviet socialism.

SUPREMATISM

A term coined by Kazimir Malevich in 1915 to describe "the supremacy of feelings." Suprematist art relied on basic geometric figures and on contrasting colors to produce nonobjective images of natural systems.

VKhUTEMAS/VKhUTEIN

VKhUTEMAS, or the Higher Artistic and Technical Studios, was founded in 1920. It became the Higher Artistic and Technical Institute, or VKhUTEIN, in 1927.

YEVSEKTSIA (ALSO EVSEKTSIA)

The Jewish Section of the propaganda department of the Soviet Communist Party, 1918–30. It was committed to socializing Jews into the new Soviet system, often by eradicating traditional culture.

YIDDISH

A Germanic language that developed more than a thousand years ago in the Rhineland, in what is now modern Germany. It was spoken primarily by Ashkenazi Jews who lived in Central and Eastern Europe and later in countries around the world. Yiddish is written in the Hebrew alphabet. About fifteen percent of Yiddish words derive directly from Hebrew and its linguistic cousin, Aramaic. For Ashkenazi Jews, Hebrew was the language of prayer, while Yiddish was the spoken language of everyday life.

EXHIBITION CHECKLIST

This checklist is organized according to the exhibition—by company, production, and significant events.

HABIMA

Konstantin Stanislavsky, c. 1930. Photograph, 9 × 6½ in. (22.9 × 16.5 cm). Archives of the YIVO Institute for Jewish Research, New York

Evgeny Vakhtangov, 1918. Photograph, 9⅞ × 6⅛ in. (25 × 15.5 cm). Israel Goor Theater Archive and Museum, Jerusalem

Members of Habima, Moscow, 1926. Photograph, 10⅜ × 14 in. (26.3 × 35.4 cm). Collection of Eretz Israel Museum, Tel Aviv

Members of Habima in the theater lobby, Lower Kislovka, Moscow, 1926. Photograph, 10⅜ × 14 in. (26.3 × 35.4 cm). Courtesy of Vladislav Ivanov, Moscow

Habima scrapbook with photographs of company members and performances. 1920s–1950s. Book, 9 × 28 × 2 in. (22.9 × 71.1 × 5.1 cm) (open). Israel Goor Theater Archive and Museum, Jerusalem

THE DYBBUK

Natan Altman. Poster for the three-hundredth production of *The Dybbuk*, Habima, Moscow, 1926. 23 × 34 in. (58.4 × 86.4 cm). A. A. Bakhrushin State Central Theater Museum, Moscow

Program for *The Dybbuk*, Habima, Moscow, 1922. 6⅝ × 4¾ in. (17 × 12 cm). A. A. Bakhrushin State Central Theater Museum, Moscow

Hasid (Costume for The Dybbuk), 1922. Silk and cotton, height: 63 in. (160 cm). Habima National Theater of Israel, Hanna Rovina Collection Tel Aviv

Leah (Costume for Hanna Rovina in The Dybbuk), 1922. Silk and cotton, height: 63 in. (160 cm). Habima National Theater of Israel, Hanna Rovina Collection Tel Aviv

Solomon An-sky (Solomon Zainwil Rapaport), 1916. Photograph, 7¼ × 9¾ in. (18.4 × 24.8 cm). Archives of the YIVO Institute for Jewish Research, New York

Naum Tsemakh, founder of Habima, in his study with costume designs for *The Dybbuk*, Moscow, 1923. Photograph, 9 × 7½ in. (22.9 × 19.1 cm). Courtesy of Vladislav Ivanov, Moscow

Hannah Hendler as a young Hasid in *The Dybbuk*, 1922. Photograph, 9¼ × 6¾ in. (23 × 17 cm). The Jewish Museum, New York

Scenes from *The Dybbuk*. Six photographs, dimensions variable. A. A. Bakhrushin State Central Theater Museum, Moscow

Hanna Rovina as Leah in *The Dybbuk*, 1922. Photograph. Courtesy of Vladislav Ivanov, Moscow

Joel Engel. Musical score for *The Dybbuk*, 1922. Handwritten manuscript, 11 × 14 in. (27.9 × 35.6 cm). Israel Goor Theater Archive and Museum, Jerusalem

Music by Lev Pulver for *The Dybbuk* (1922). Boxed set with two long-playing records. Courtesy of the Judaica Sound Archives, Florida Atlantic University, Boca Raton

Works by Natan Altman for *The Dybbuk*

Synagogue Interior (Set Model for The Dybbuk), 1922. Reconstructed later. Wood, metal, and cloth, 11½ × 22½ × 15½ in. (29.2 × 57.2 × 39.4 cm). Israel Goor Theater Archive and Museum, Jerusalem

Synagogue Interior (Set Design for The Dybbuk), 1922. Pencil, india ink, gouache, and tempera on paper, 10⅜ × 16 in. (26.5 × 40.5 cm). Tel Aviv Museum of Art

Sender's House (Set Design for The Dybbuk), 1922. Gouache, india ink, and collage on paper, 10⅜ × 14 in. (26.3 × 35.4 cm). Collection of Eretz Israel Museum, Tel Aviv

Costume Designs for The Dybbuk, 1922. Eighteen drawings: pencil on paper or pencil and gouache on paper, dimensions variable. Israel Goor Theater Archive and Museum, Jerusalem

THE GOLEM

Poster for *The Golem, The Flood*, and *Jacob's Dream*, Habima, Moscow, 1925. 42½ × 28½ in. (108 × 72.4 cm). A. A. Bakhrushin State Central Theater Museum, Moscow

Scenes from *The Golem*, Habima, Moscow, 1925. Two photographs, dimensions variable. Courtesy of Vladislav Ivanov, Moscow

The Fifth Tower (Scene from *The Golem*), 1925. Photograph, 7⅛ × 9½ in. (18 × 24 cm). A. A. Bakhrushin State Central Theater Museum, Moscow

Sefer Raziel, Amsterdam, 1701. Book, 9¹⁄₁₆ × 7½ in. (23 × 19 cm). The Library of The Jewish Theological Seminary, New York

Works by Ignaty Nivinsky for *The Golem*

The Fifth Tower (Set Design for The Golem), 1924. Pencil, gouache, ink, and bronze paint on paper mounted on cardboard, 18 × 24⅞ in. (45.7 × 63.2 cm). A. A. Bakhrushin State Central Theater Museum, Moscow

The Fifth Tower (Set Design for The Golem), 1925. India ink and gouache on cardboard, 11.5 × 17 in. (29.4 × 44 cm). Collection of Eretz Israel Museum, Tel Aviv

Costume Designs for The Golem, 1925. Seventeen drawings: medium variable (including pencil, gouache, tempera, ink, silver paint, bronze paint, and watercolor on cardboard), dimensions variable. A. A. Bakhrushin State Central Theater Museum, Moscow

Costume Designs for The Golem, 1925. Ten drawings: pencil and watercolor on paper, dimensions variable. The Russian State Archive of Literature and Art, Moscow

MOSCOW STATE YIDDISH THEATER (GOSET)

Natan Altman. *Portrait of Mikhoels*, 1927. Oil on canvas, 41⅜ × 28⅜ in. (105 × 72 cm). A. A. Bakhrushin State Central Theater Museum, Moscow

Poster for the Yiddish Chamber (Kamerny) Theater, 1919. 32 × 24 in. (81.3 × 61 cm). The Russian State Archive of Literature and Art, Moscow

Poster for *200,000* and *Freylekhs*, GOSEKT, Moscow, 1924. 40 × 30 in. (101.6 × 76.2 cm). The Russian State Archive of Literature and Art, Moscow

Poster for *200,000* and *Three Jewish Raisins*, GOSEKT, Moscow, c. 1922–24. 40 × 30 in. (101.6 × 76.2 cm). The Russian State Archive of Literature and Art, Moscow

Members of GOSET, Moscow, c. 1924. Photograph, 5½ × 8¼ in. (14 × 21 cm). The Russian State Archive of Literature and Art, Moscow

Members of GOSET in front of their theater on Malaia Bronnaia, Moscow, 1924. Photograph, 6¾ × 8¼ in. (17 × 21 cm). The Russian State Archive of Literature and Art, Moscow

Members of GOSET, Moscow, c. 1930. Photograph. Blavatnik Collection, New York

Members of GOSET, left to right: Boris Ingster, Alexander Budeysky, Michail Steiman, Aleksei Granovsky, Lev Pulver, Benjamin Zuskin, Helena Menes, Solomon Mikhoels, Moscow, 1925. Photographic reproduction

THEATER MURALS BY MARC CHAGALL

Brochure for the exhibition of Marc Chagall's murals in the Moscow State Yiddish Chamber Theater, June 1921. Private collection, Paris

Photograph of Marc Chagall painting *Study for Introduction to the Jewish Theater*, 1920. 6¼ × 9½ in. (15.9 × 24.1 cm). Private collection, Paris

Murals by Marc Chagall

Study for Dance, 1920. Pencil and gouache on paper, 9½ × 5 in. (24.1 × 12.7 cm). Private collection, Paris

The Green Violinist (Study for Music), 1918. Pencil, gouache, and acrylic on squared brown paper, 9¾ × 5¼ in. (24.7 × 13.3 cm). Musée nationale d'arte moderne, Centre Georges Pompidou, Paris, AM 1988-22

Study for Theater, 1920. Gouache, watercolor, and pencil on squared paper, 9⅝ × 5½ in. (24.4 × 14.1 cm). Private collection, Paris

Curtain Design for the Jewish Theater, 1920. Pencil, gouache, and ink on paper, 5½ × 5⅞ in. (14 × 14.9 cm). Private collection, Paris

Study for Introduction to the Jewish Theater, 1919–20. Pencil, ink, gouache, and watercolor on paper, mounted on board, 6¾ × 19¼ in. (17.3 × 49 cm). Musée nationale d'arte moderne, Centre Georges Pompidou, Paris, AM 1988–226

Study for a Figure in Introduction to the Jewish Theater, 1920. Watercolor and gouache on paper, 14 × 6⅞ in. (35.5 × 17.4 cm). Private collection, Paris

Introduction to the Jewish Theater, Dance, Literature, Music, Theater, Wedding Feast, and Love on the Stage, 1920. Seven murals: tempera, gouache, and opaque white on canvas, dimensions variable. State Tretyakov Gallery, Moscow

AN EVENING OF SHOLEM ALEICHEM

Poster for masks by Sholem Aleichem: *Agents, It's a Lie, The Divorce Paper,* and *Mazel Tov*, GOSEKT, Moscow, 1924. 40 × 30 in. (101.6 × 76.2 cm). The Russian State Archive of Literature and Art, Moscow

Program for one-act plays by Sholem Aleichem: *Agents, The Spoiled Celebration,* and *Mazel Tov*, GOSEKT, Moscow, 1921. 8⅞ × 4⅞ in. (22.6 × 12.5 cm). A. A. Bakhrushin State Central Theater Museum, Moscow

AGENTS: A JOKE IN ONE ACT

Chaim Krashinski in *Agents*, 1921. Photograph, 5½ × 3¾ in. (14 × 9.5 cm). Beth Hatefutsoth, Photo Archive, Tel Aviv, courtesy of Zuskin Collection

Third-Class Train Car (Scene from *Agents*), 1921. Photograph, 6 × 8½ in. (15.5 × 21.5 cm). Austrian Theater Museum, Vienna, PSA 299.497

Works by Marc Chagall for *Agents*

Third-Class Train Car (Set Design for Agents), 1920. Pencil, gouache, and ink on paper, 10⅛ × 13½ in. (25.6 × 34.2 cm). Musée nationale d'arte moderne, Centre Georges Pompidou, Paris, AM 1988-253

Man (Costume Design for Agents), 1920. Pencil, ink, and gouache on paper, 10¾ × 8 in. (27.4 × 20.3 cm). Musée nationale d'arte moderne, Centre Georges Pompidou, Paris, AM 1988-254

Costume Designs for Agents, 1920. Three drawings: medium variable (including pencil, gouache, and watercolor on paper), dimensions variable. Private collection, Paris

MAZEL TOV

Marc Chagall with Solomon Mikhoels as Reb Alter in *Mazel Tov*, 1921. Photograph, 5⅛ × 3¾ in. (13 × 9.4 cm). Private collection, Paris

Solomon Mikhoels as Reb Alter and Mikhail Shteiman as Chaim (Scene from *Mazel Tov*), 1921. Photograph, 4½ × 6⅛ in. (11.5 × 15.7 cm). Beth Hatefutsoth, Photo Archive, Tel Aviv, courtesy of Zuskin Collection

Solomon Mikhoels as Reb Alter drinking tea in *Mazel Tov*, 1921. Video clip. Russian State Documentary Films and Photographs Archive, Krasnogorsk

Works by Marc Chagall for *Mazel Tov*

Kitchen (Set Design for Mazel Tov), 1920. Oil on paper mounted on board, 18⅝ × 25 in. (47.5 × 63.5 cm). Private collection, Paris

Kitchen (Set Design for Mazel Tov), 1920.
Pencil and watercolor on paper, 10 × 13½ in.
(25.5 × 34.5 cm). Private collection, Paris

Costume Designs for Mazel Tov, 1920.
Three drawings: medium variable
(including pencil, watercolor, ink, and
gouache on paper), dimensions variable.
Private collection, Paris

IT'S A LIE! DIALOGUE IN GALICIA

Benjamin Zuskin and Ely Ragaler in *It's a
Lie!*, 1921. Photograph, 4⁷⁄₁₆ × 6³⁄₁₆ in. (11.3 ×
15.7 cm). Beth Hatefutsoth, Photo Archive,
Tel Aviv, courtesy of Zuskin Collection

Works by Marc Chagall for *It's a Lie!*

Set Design for It's a Lie! 1921. Pencil and
gouache on paper, 8⅞ × 11¾ in. (22.5 ×
30 cm). Private collection, Paris

Costume Designs for It's a Lie! 1920. Four
drawings: medium variable (including
pencil, gouache, ink, red chalk, and watercolor on paper), dimensions variable.
Private collection, Paris

GOD OF VENGEANCE

Poster for *200,000: A Musical Comedy,
The Sorceress: An Eccentric Jewish Play,
God of Vengeance,* and *Three Jewish
Raisins,* GOSEKT, Moscow, 1924. 28 × 21 in.
(71 × 53.5 cm). The Russian State Archive
of Literature and Art, Moscow

Benjamin Zuskin as Shlomke in *God of
Vengeance,* 1921. Photograph, 3½ × 5½ in.
(14 × 18.9 cm). Beth Hatefutsoth, Photo
Archive, Tel Aviv, courtesy of Zuskin
Collection

Works by Isaac Rabinovich for *God of Vengeance*

*The Apartment of Yankel Tshaptshovitsh,
the Brothel Owner (Set Design for God of
Vengeance),* 1921. Pencil and oil on paper,
13 × 17¾ in. (33 × 45.2 cm). A. A. Bakhrushin
State Central Theater Museum, Moscow

Costume Designs for God of Vengeance,
1921. Three drawings: medium variable
(pencil and oil on paper mounted on cardboard, or pencil on paper), dimensions
variable. A. A. Bakhrushin State Central
Theater Museum, Moscow

URIEL ACOSTA: AN ECCENTRIC JEWISH PLAY

Poster for *The Sorceress* and *Uriel Acosta,*
GOSEKT, 1923. 28 × 40 in. (71.1 × 101.6 cm).
The Russian State Archive of Literature
and Art, Moscow

Set model for *Uriel Acosta,* based on
original design by Natan Altman. Reconstructed later. Wood and metal, 12½ × 29 ×
20¼ in. (31.8 × 73.7 × 54.4 cm). Israel Goor
Theater Archive and Museum, Jerusalem

Solomon Mikhoels, Benjamin Zuskin,
and Yekhezkel Dobrushin, Moscow, 1930.
Photograph, 5½ × 8 in. (14 × 20.3 cm).
Beth Hatefutsoth, Photo Archive, Tel Aviv,
courtesy of Zuskin Collection

Aleksei Granovsky, Natan Altman, and
Isaac Rabinovich, Moscow, c. 1922. Photo-
graph, 4⅜ × 6⅛ in. (11 × 15.5 cm). A. A.
Bakhrushin State Central Theater
Museum, Moscow

Works by Natan Altman for *Uriel Acosta*

*Library in the House of De Silva (Set Design
for Uriel Acosta),* 1922. Ink, tempera, lacquer,
and collage on cardboard, 13⅝ × 18⅞ in.
(34.6 × 48 cm). A. A. Bakhrushin State
Central Theater Museum, Moscow

*Uriel Acosta (Costume Design for Solomon
Mikhoels in the Title Role),* 1922. Ink and
opaque white on paper mounted on card-
board, 10⅞ × 8¾ in. (27.7 × 22.2 cm).
A. A. Bakhrushin State Central Theater
Museum, Moscow

THE SORCERESS: AN ECCENTRIC JEWISH PLAY

Poster for *The Sorceress,* GOSEKT, Moscow,
1922. 28 × 34 in. (71.1 × 86.4 cm). The
Russian State Archive of Literature and
Art, Moscow

Program for *The Sorceress,* GOSEKT,
Moscow, 1922. 6⅞ × 4¾ in. (17.7 × 12.4 cm).
A. A. Bakhrushin State Central Theater
Museum, Moscow

Set Model for *The Sorceress,* based on
original design by Isaak Rabinovich.
Reconstructed later. Wood, metal, and
cloth, 17 × 24 × 11 in. (42.3 × 62 × 29 cm).
Israel Goor Theater Archive and
Museum, Jerusalem

Isaac Rabinovich. *Costume Designs for
The Sorceress,* 1922. Two drawings:
medium variable (including pencil, crayon,
ink, colored pencil, and oil on paper
mounted on paper or cardboard), dimensions variable. A. A. Bakhrushin State
Central Theater Museum, Moscow

Benjamin Zuskin in the title role of
The Sorceress, 1922. Photograph, 10 ×
6½ in. (25.4 × 16.5 cm). Courtesy of Ala
Zuskin-Perelman, Or-Yehuda, Israel

Benjamin Zuskin in the title role of
The Sorceress, and Mikhail Shteiman as
Marcus, 1922. Photograph, 5½ × 4⅛ in.
(13.8 × 10.9 cm). A. A. Bakhrushin State
Central Theater Museum, Moscow

Scenes from *The Sorceress,* 1922. Two photographs. The Jewish Museum, New York

The Sorceress, 1922. Photograph. Beth
Hatefutsoth, Photo Archive, Tel Aviv, courtesy of Zuskin Collection

Scenes from *The Sorceress,* 1922. Three
photographs, dimensions variable. A. A.
Bakhrushin State Central Theater
Museum, Moscow

Music by Joseph Akhron for *The Sorceress,*
1922: "I Am the Buba Yakhna," "Come
with Me," and "Hotsmakh's Song." From
Cubo-Futurist Klezmer. Audio recording.
Courtesy of Mel Gordon

200,000: A MUSICAL COMEDY

Poster for *200,000*, GOSET, Moscow, 1935. 18 × 24¾ in. (45.7 × 62.9 cm). A. A. Bakhrushin State Central Theater Museum, Moscow

Isaac Rabichev. *Tailor Shop Workers and Rich Men (Costume Designs for 200,000)*, 1923. Pencil, crayon, ink, and watercolor on paper, 13¾ × 30 in. (34.8 × 76 cm). A. A. Bakhrushin State Central Theater Museum, Moscow

Scenes from *200,000*, including Benjamin Zuskin as Soloveitchik the Matchmaker, Solomon Mikhoels as Shimele Soroker, and four wealthy women (Eva Itskhoki, Evgenya Epstein, Rakhl Imenitova, and Esther Karchmer), and Shimele Soroker's mansion, 1923. Three photographs, dimensions variable. Beth Hatefutsoth, Photo Archive, Tel Aviv, courtesy of Zuskin Collection

Scenes from *200,000*, including Benjamin Zuskin as Soloveitchik the Matchmaker, Solomon Mikhoels as Shimele Soroker, Sara Rotbaum as Eti Meni (his wife), Ely Ragaler as Mr. Fein, Yitzhak Lurie as Solomon Fein, Shimele Soroker's tailor shop, and Mr. Fein's mansion, 1923. Four photographs, dimensions variable. A. A. Bakhrushin State Central Theater Museum, Moscow

Scenes from *200,000*, 1923. Two photographs, dimensions variable. The Jewish Museum, New York

Performance of *200,000*, 1923. Video clip. Russian State Documentary Films and Photographs Archive, Krasnogorsk

Music by Lev Pulver for *200,000* (1923): "Sher," "Not Shimele!," "Fate!" From *Cubo-Futurist Klezmer*. Audio recording. Courtesy of Mel Gordon

JEWISH LUCK

Natan Altman. Poster for *Jewish Luck*, 1925. 40 × 28 in. (100 × 71.5 cm). Collection of Merrill C. Berman, Rye, New York

Natan Altman. *Jewish Luck* (Moscow: Kinopechat, 1925). Cinema booklet, 8 pages, 12 × 9 in. (30.5 × 23 cm). Museum of Modern Art, New York

Scene from *Jewish Luck*, 1925. Film still. Courtesy of Sovkino/Photofest, New York

Jewish Luck, 1925. Film clips. The National Center for Jewish Film at Brandeis University

Works by Natan Altman for *Jewish Luck*

Costume Designs for Jewish Luck, 1925. Six drawings: pencil on paper, dimensions variable. A. A. Bakhrushin State Central Theater Museum, Moscow

Mrs. Kimbak (Costume Design for Jewish Luck), 1925. Pencil on paper, 13¾ × 8¾ in. (35 × 22.3 cm). St. Petersburg Museum of Theater and Music, St. Petersburg

AT NIGHT IN THE OLD MARKETPLACE: A TRAGIC CARNIVAL

Robert Falk. Poster for *At Night in the Old Marketplace*, GOSET, Moscow, 1925. 42 × 28 in. (106.7 × 71.1 cm). The Russian State Archive of Literature and Art, Moscow

At Night in the Old Marketplace, 1925. Photograph, 4½ × 5½ in. (10.9 × 14 cm). Beth Hatefutsoth, Photo Archive, Tel Aviv, courtesy of Zuskin Collection

Benjamin Zuskin as the second Badkhen in *At Night in the Old Marketplace*, 1925. Photograph, 5½ × 4¼ in. (14 × 10.8 cm). Beth Hatefutsoth, Photo Archive, Tel Aviv, courtesy of Zuskin Collection

Scenes from *At Night in the Old Marketplace*, 1925. Two photographs, dimensions variable. Courtesy of Vladislav Ivanov, Moscow

Benjamin Zuskin and Solomon Mikhoels as Badkhonim in *At Night in the Old Marketplace*, 1925. Photograph, 4¾ × 4⅜ in. (12.2 × 11 cm). Courtesy of Vladislav Ivanov, Moscow

Scenes from *At Night in the Old Marketplace*, 1925. Video loop. Photographs courtesy of Vladislav Ivanov, Moscow, and A. A. Bakhrushin State Central Theater Museum, Moscow

Works by Robert Falk for *At Night in the Old Marketplace*

Wedding of the Dead (Mise-en-scène for At Night in the Old Marketplace), 1925. Oil on canvas, 45⅛ × 56⅛ in. (114.5 × 142.5 cm). A. A. Bakhrushin State Central Theater Museum, Moscow

Set Designs for At Night in the Old Marketplace, 1925. Two drawings: charcoal and ink on paper, dimensions variable. A. A. Bakhrushin State Central Theater Museum, Moscow

Costume Designs for At Night in the Old Marketplace, 1925. Thirteen drawings: medium variable (including pencil, watercolor, ink, opaque white, tempera, and crayon on paper or cardboard), dimensions variable. A. A. Bakhrushin State Central Theater Museum, Moscow

THE TENTH COMMANDMENT: A PAMPHLET OPERETTA

Poster for opening night of *The Tenth Commandment*, GOSET, Moscow, 1926. 40 × 30 in. (101.6 × 76.2 cm). The Russian State Archive of Literature and Art, Moscow

Program for *The Tenth Commandment*, GOSET on tour, Voronezh, 1931. 17 × 6 in. (43.2 × 15.2 cm). A. A. Bakhrushin State Central Theater Museum, Moscow

Natan Altman. *Costume Designs for The Tenth Commandment*, 1926. Three drawings: medium variable (including pencil, gouache, and brown chalk on paper), dimensions variable. A. A. Bakhrushin State Central Theater Museum, Moscow

Members of GOSET in front of a poster for *The Tenth Commandment*, c. 1927. Photograph, 4½ × 6½ in. (11.4 × 16.5 cm). Courtesy of Ala Zuskin-Perelman, Or-Yehuda, Israel

Eda Berkovskaia as a young Hasid in *The Tenth Commandment*, 1926. Photograph, 6½ × 3½ in. (16.5 × 8.9 cm). Beth Hatefutsoth, Photo Archive, Tel Aviv, courtesy of Zuskin Collection

THE TRAVELS OF BENJAMIN THE THIRD: EPOS IN THREE ACTS

Poster for *The Travels of Benjamin the Third*, GOSET, Baku, 1927. 41 × 29 in. (104.1 × 73.7 cm). A. A. Bakhrushin State Central Theater Museum, Moscow

Program for *The Travels of Benjamin the Third*, GOSET, Moscow, 1932. 8 pages, 6¾ × 5 in. (17.5 × 12.9 cm). A. A. Bakhrushin State Central Theater Museum, Moscow

Robert Falk. *Costume Designs for The Travels of Benjamin the Third*, 1927. Seven drawings: medium variable (including pencil, watercolor, gouache, tempera, bronze paint, and opaque white on paper), dimensions variable. A. A. Bakhrushin State Central Theater Museum, Moscow

Scenes from *The Travels of Benjamin the Third*, including Moshe Goldblatt as Mendele Mokher Sforim, Gregory Lukovsky as his horse, Ya'akov Gertner as Fishke the Lame, and Moses Ney as Policeman, 1927. Five photographs, dimensions variable. Courtesy of Vladislav Ivanov, Moscow

The Dream of Benjamin and Senderl (Scene from *The Travels of Benjamin the Third*), 1927. Photograph, 5¼ × 8½ in. (13.3 × 21.6 cm). Beth Hatefutsoth, Photo Archive, Tel Aviv, courtesy of Zuskin Collection

Benjamin Zuskin as Senderl di Yidene (Senderl the Jewish Woman) and Solomon Mikhoels as Benjamin in *The Travels of Benjamin the Third*, 1927. Photograph, 7 × 4½ in. (17.8 × 11.4 cm). Courtesy of Ala Zuskin-Perelman, Or-Yehuda, Israel

Solomon Mikhoels as Benjamin and Benjamin Zuskin as Senderl in *The Travels of Benjamin the Third*, 1927. Photograph, 9 × 7 in. (22.9 × 17.8 cm). Courtesy of Ala Zuskin-Perelman, Or-Yehuda, Israel

Scenes from *The Travels of Benjamin the Third*, 1927. Three photographs, dimensions variable. Beth Hatefutsoth, Photo Archive, Tel Aviv, courtesy of Zuskin Collection

Benjamin's Dream (Scene from *The Travels of Benjamin the Third*), 1928. Photograph, 6 × 9 in. (15 × 23 cm). The Russian State Archive of Literature and Art, Moscow

Benjamin's Dream (Scene from *The Travels of Benjamin the Third*), 1928. Photograph. The Jewish Museum, New York

Music by Lev Pulver for *The Travels of Benjamin the Third* (1927): "A Banquet Dream." From *Cubo-Futurist Klezmer*. Audio recording. Courtesy of Mel Gordon

TROUHADEC: AN ECCENTRIC OPERETTA

Natan Altman. Poster for *Trouhadec*, GOSET, Moscow, 1927. 42 × 28⅜ in. (106.7 × 71.9 cm). The Russian State Archive of Literature and Art, Moscow

Natan Altman. *Costume Designs for Trouhadec*, 1927. Five drawings: medium variable (including pencil, crayon, colored pencil, and brown chalk on paper), dimensions variable. A. A. Bakhrushin State Central Theater Museum, Moscow

Scenes from *Trouhadec*, 1927. Three photographs, dimensions variable. A. A. Bakhrushin State Central Theater Museum, Moscow

Scene from *Trouhadec*, 1927. Photograph. Israel Goor Theater Museum, Israel

Scene from *Trouhadec*, 1927. Photograph, 18⅜ × 22⅛ in. (46.6 × 56.2 cm). Beth Hatefutsoth, Photo Archive, Tel Aviv, courtesy of Zuskin Collection

Scenes from *Trouhadec*, 1927. Two photographs. Courtesy of Vladislav Ivanov, Moscow

Scenes from *Trouhadec*, 1927. Two photographs. The Jewish Museum, New York

GOSET ON TOUR

Poster for *The Travels of Benjamin the Third, The Sorceress, 200,000,* and *Trouhadec,* GOSET on tour, Paris, 1928. 37½ × 25¼ in. (95.3 × 64.1 cm). A. A. Bakhrushin State Central Theater Museum, Moscow

Poster for *The Court Is in Session, 200,000, Three Jewish Raisins,* and *Grebles,* GOSET on tour, Ukraine, 1930. 40 × 30 in. (101.6 × 76.2 cm). The Russian State Archive of Literature and Art, Moscow

Members of GOSET on tour, 1928. Photograph, 6¾ × 9 in. (17 × 23 cm). The Russian State Archive of Literature and Art, Moscow

Marc Chagall with GOSET company at his villa near Paris, June 1928. Photograph, 5 × 7 in. (12.7 × 17.8 cm). Courtesy of Ala Zuskin-Perelman, Or-Yehuda, Israel

Lotte Jacobi. *Solomon Mikhoels, Alexander Granach, and Benjamin Zuskin* (top to bottom), Berlin, 1929. Photograph, 10 × 8 in. (25.4 × 20.3 cm). Lotte Jacobi Collection, University of New Hampshire

KING LEAR

Poster for *King Lear*, GOSET, Moscow Theater Festival, 1935. 36¼ × 24¼ in. (92.1 × 61.6 cm). A. A. Bakhrushin State Central Theater Museum, Moscow

Solomon Mikhoels's costume for *King Lear*, 1935. Israel Goor Theater Archive and Museum, Jerusalem

Solomon Mikhoels's wig for *King Lear*, 1935. Israel Goor Theater Archive and Museum, Jerusalem

Solomon Mikhoels as King Lear, 1935. Two photographs, each 6⅛ × 4¾ in. (15.6 × 12.1 cm). Beth Hatefutsoth, Photo Archive, Tel Aviv, courtesy of Zuskin Collection

Solomon Mikhoels as King Lear, 1935. Two photographs, each 8⅞ × 5⅞ in. (22.8 × 14.9 cm). A. A. Bakhrushin State Central Theater Museum, Moscow

King Lear (Act 1, Scene 1, the throne room of Lear's palace), 1935. Photograph, 7⅛ × 9⅜ in. (18.3 × 24 cm). A. A. Bakhrushin State Central Theater Museum, Moscow

Benjamin Zuskin as the Fool in *King Lear*, 1935. Photograph, 22⅛ × 29⁷⁄₁₆ in. (56.2 × 74.7 cm). Beth Hatefutsoth, Photo Archive, Tel Aviv, courtesy of Zuskin Collection

Performance of *King Lear;* Solomon Mikhoels putting on a wig, 1935. Video clips. Russian State Documentary Films and Photographs Archive, Krasnogorsk

Music by Lev Pulver for *King Lear* (1935): "Lear's Entry," "I Am a Jester," and "Lear's Regret." From *Cubo-Futurist Klezmer.* Audio recording. Courtesy of Mel Gordon

Works by Aleksandr Tyshler for *King Lear*

Set model for *King Lear,* 1935 (reconstructed in 1991). Gouache on cardboard and wood, 9½ × 13⅜ × 9½ in. (24 × 34 × 24 cm). A. A. Bakhrushin State Central Theater Museum, Moscow

Mise-en-scène from *King Lear,* 1935. Two drawings: medium variable (including watercolor and ink on paper), dimensions variable. A. A. Bakhrushin State Central Theater Museum, Moscow

Costume Designs for Solomon Mikhoels, 1935. Six drawings: watercolor on paper, dimensions variable. A. A. Bakhrushin State Central Theater Museum, Moscow

GOSET: THE FINAL CHAPTER

Sarah Lebedeva. *Head of Solomon Mikhoels,* 1939. Bronze, 13¾ × 10 × 9⅞ in. (35 × 25.5 × 25 cm). State Tretyakov Gallery, Moscow

Solomon Mikhoels, January 11, 1948. Photograph, 10½ × 8½ in. (26.7 × 21.6 cm). Israel Goor Theater Archive and Museum, Jerusalem

F. Kislov and G. Shirokova. *Solomon Mikhoels with a Group of Prominent Jewish Cultural Figures, Moscow,* 1941. Photograph, 3⅞ × 5½ in. (10 × 14 cm). A. A. Bakhrushin State Central Theater Museum, Moscow

Itzik Fefer, Molly Picon, Maurice Schwartz, and Solomon Mikhoels, New York, 1943. Photograph, 8 × 11 in. (20.3 × 27.9 cm). Archives of the YIVO Institute for Jewish Research, New York

Itzik Fefer, Albert Einstein, and Solomon Mikhoels, Princeton, New Jersey, June 1943. Photograph, 8 × 10 in. (20.3 × 25.4 cm). Archives of the YIVO Institute for Jewish Research, New York

Itzik Fefer and Solomon Mikhoels with Paul Robeson, Soviet Consulate, New York, summer 1943. Photograph, 8 × 11 in. (20.3 × 27.9 cm). Archives of the YIVO Institute for Jewish Research, New York

Solomon Mikhoels at Sholem Aleichem's grave, Mt. Carmel Cemetery, Brooklyn, 1943. Photograph, 10 × 8 in. (25.4 × 20.3 cm). Archives of the YIVO Institute for Jewish Research, New York

B. Z. Goldberg with Solomon Mikhoels and members of the Jewish Anti-Fascist Committee, 1945. Photograph, 6 × 9 in. (15.2 × 22.9 cm). Blatvatnik Collection, New York

Solomon Mikhoels's diary of his trip to the United States as head of the Jewish Anti-Fascist Committee, 1943. Handwritten manuscript, 18 pages, dimensions variable. The Russian State Archive of Literature and Art, Moscow

Solomon Mikhoels's speech to the Jewish Anti-Fascist Committee, Moscow, 1941. Video clip. Russian State Documentary Films and Photographs Archive, Krasnogorsk

THE FUNERAL OF SOLOMON MIKHOELS

Solomon Mikhoels with members of the Stalin Prize Committee, Moscow, 1948. Photograph, 16⅜ × 22⅛ in. (41.5 × 56.2 cm). Beth Hatefutsoth, Photo Archive, Tel Aviv, courtesy of Zuskin Collection

Solomon Mikhoels the day before his assassination, Minsk, January 1948. Photograph, 3¼ × 4¼ in. (8.3 × 10.8 cm). Archives of the YIVO Institute for Jewish Research, New York

Bier for Solomon Mikhoels's coffin, Belorussian Railroad Station, Moscow, 1948. Photographic diptych, each image 5½ × 14¾ in. (14 × 37.5 cm). Israel Goor Theater Archive and Museum, Jerusalem

Solomon Mikhoels lying in state, Moscow, 1948. Photograph, 4 × 6 in. (10.2 × 15.2 cm). Israel Goor Theater Archive and Museum, Jerusalem

Solomon Mikhoels lying in state, Moscow, 1948. Photograph, 22⅛ × 22⅛ in. (56.2 × 56.2 cm). Beth Hatefutsoth, Photo Archive, Tel Aviv, courtesy of Zuskin Collection

Benjamin Zuskin speaking at the public viewing ceremony of the late Solomon Mikhoels, 1948. Photograph, 5½ × 9 in. (14 × 22.9 cm). Courtesy of Ala Zuskin-Perelman, Or-Yehuda, Israel

Solomon Mikhoels's broken eyeglasses, 1948. Collection of Natalia Vovsi-Mikhoels, Tel Aviv

Solomon Mikhoels's funeral, 1948. Video clip. Russian State Documentary Films and Photographs Archive, Krasnogorsk

EXHIBITION FILM

Balancing Acts: A Soviet Jewish Theater, 2008. DigiBeta, 12 mins. A production of Citizen Film, Inc. Director/Producer: Sam Ball; Editor/Line Producer: Kate Stilley Steiner; Composer/Producer: William Susman; Cinematography: Sophie Constantinou

NOTES

SOVIET JEWISH THEATER IN A WORLD OF MORAL COMPROMISE

Epigraph: Ala Zuskin-Perelman, speech at Hebrew University, Jerusalem, 2007, presenting her book *Mas'ot Binyamin Zuskin* (The Travels of Benjamin Zuskin).

1. Avram Kampf, *Jewish Experience in the Art of the Twentieth Century* (South Hadley, Mass.: Bergin and Garvey, 1984), 43.

2. Quoted in J. Hoberman, *Bridge of Light: Yiddish Film Between Two Worlds* (Philadelphia: Temple University Press, 1995), 90.

3. Nahma Sandrow, *Vagabond Stars: A World History of Yiddish Theater* (New York: Harper and Row, 1977), 40–69.

4. The development of a professional theater had to wait until the emergence of the Yiddish vernacular as a literary language, a process that began in the late 1860s with the novels of Mendele Mocher Seforim (S. Y. Abramovich). His bittersweet portraits of Russian Jewish life inspired a generation of Yiddish novelists and playwrights, including Sholem Aleichem, I. L. Peretz, Sholem Asch, and Avrom Goldfadn.

5. "In 1891, the tsar had expelled Moscow's tiny Jewish community; by 1923, there were 86,000 Jews living in the city; over the next three years, the heyday of GOSET, their numbers increased by 50 percent." Hoberman, *Bridge of Light,* 90.

6. Richard G. Thorpe, "The Academic Theaters and the Fate of Soviet Artistic Pluralism, 1919–1928," *Slavic Review* 51, no. 3 (Fall 1992): 406. It was the intention of the new government to promote the party's presence in all institutions of society. Thorpe quotes Anatoly Lunacharsky, commissar of enlightenment, in a warning from March 1925: "Both the union and certain party circles are insisting energetically upon the inclusion of communists in the administration of all theaters."

7. Jeffrey Veidlinger, *The Moscow State Yiddish Theater: Jewish Culture on the Soviet Stage* (Bloomington: Indiana University Press, 2000), 30.

8. Mendel Kohansky, *The Hebrew Theatre: Its First Fifty Years* (New York: KTAV, 1969), 25.

9. Konstantin Rudnitsky, *Russian and Soviet Theatre: Tradition and the Avant-Garde,* ed. Lesley Milne, trans. Roxane Permar (London: Thames and Hudson, 1988), 53.

10. Quoted in Ruth Apter-Gabriel, ed., *Tradition and Revolution: The Jewish Renaissance in Russian Avant-Garde Art, 1912–1928* (Jerusalem: The Israel Museum, 1987), 140.

11. Rudnitsky, *Russian and Soviet Theatre,* 18.

12. The desire to develop a national Jewish culture was advanced by research in Jewish ethnography begun in St. Petersburg by S. An-sky, the author of *The Dybbuk* and a former social revolutionary. He and others conducted their search in Podolia and Volhynia, in the Ukraine, between 1911 and 1914, collecting hundreds of Jewish religious and folk objects.

13. Faina Burko, "'Habima' and the Moscow Yiddish Chamber Theater in the Early Twenties," in *Proceedings of the Ninth World Congress of Jewish Studies* (Jerusalem: World Union of Jewish Studies, 1986), 238.

14. Rudnitsky, *Russian and Soviet Theatre,* 93.

15. Quoted in Lois Adler, "Alexis Granovsky and the Jewish State Theatre of Moscow," *Drama Review* 24, no. 3 (September 1980): 37.

16. Quoted in Kohansky, *The Hebrew Theatre,* 31.

17. Jeffrey Veidlinger, "Let's Perform a Miracle: The Soviet Yiddish State Theater in the 1920s," *Slavic Review* 57, no. 2 (Summer 1998): 397.

18. Nora Levin, *The Jews in the Soviet Union Since 1917: Paradox of Survival* (New York: I. B. Tauris, 1990), 219.

19. Louis Lozowick, "Moscow Theatre, 1920s," *Russian History* 8, nos. 1–2 (1981): 142.

20. Walter Benjamin, *Moscow Diary,* ed. Gary Smith, trans. Richard Sieburth (Cambridge, Mass.: Harvard University Press, 1986), 14.

21. Thorpe, "The Academic Theaters and the Fate of Soviet Artistic Pluralism, 1919–1928," 408.

22. Zvi Gitelman, *Jewish Nationality and Soviet Politics: The Jewish Sections of the CPSU, 1917–1930* (Princeton, N.J.: Princeton University Press, 1972), 382.

23. Hoberman, *Bridge of Light,* 89.

24. Ibid., 91.

25. Veidlinger, *The Moscow State Yiddish Theater,* 53.

26. See ibid., 113, for further information on laws regarding Socialist Realism in the Soviet Union. In 1932, the passage of the resolution "On the Reconstruction of Literary and Artistic Organizations" first specified the use of Socialist Realism as the primary artistic style in the Soviet Union. Socialist Realism became the only sanctioned movement after the 1934 First Writers' Congress.

27. Sandrow, *Vagabond Stars*, 240. Sandrow cites a Central Committee Special Resolution ordering that all Russian theaters submit to a specific agenda: "Dramatic literature and the theaters must reflect in plays and performances the life of Soviet society in its incessant surge forward, and contribute fully to the further development of the best sides of Soviet Man's character."

28. Veidlinger, *The Moscow State Yiddish Theater*, 194.

29. Ibid., 211.

30. Quoted in Sandrow, *Vagabond Stars*, 241.

31. Veidlinger, *The Moscow State Yiddish Theater*, 259.

32. Arno Lustiger, *Stalin and the Jews: The Red Book: The Tragedy of the Jewish Anti-Fascist Committee and the Soviet Jews*, trans. Mary Beth Friedrich and Todd Bludeau (New York: Enigma, 2003), 329–331. Peretz Markish's poem "An Eternal Light at the Coffin (A Memorial to Solomon Mikhoels)" reads in part: "The curtain here will never fall again / In the hall, the light still burns in the chandelier / Your royal head now sleeps in an open grave / Where silhouettes, timeless, whisper your words / We say farewell to you and may you rest in peace / You carried in you the agony of a hundred years / You allowed Sholem Aleichem's tears [to] / Shine as dear as gems."

33. Hershl Hartman, "'Trial' in the Lubyanka, 1952," *Jewish Currents*, July–August 2007, 28. Hartman writes that three judges presided over the trial—theoretically based on a law passed in 1934 addressing anti-Soviet activity—in which there was no prosecutor, no defense attorneys, no spectators, no press, and no public news coverage. The defendants' guilt had been determined during interrogation.

34. Joshua Rubenstein and Vladimir P. Naumov, eds., *Stalin's Secret Pogrom: The Postwar Inquisition of the Jewish Anti-Fascist Committee* (New Haven: Yale University Press, in association with United States Holocaust Memorial Museum, 2001), 2–3. Of the individuals killed on the Night of the Murdered Poets, five were writers: the poets Peretz Markish, Leyb Kvitko, David Hofstein, and Itzik Fefer, and the novelist David Bergelson. Besides Benjamin Zuskin, the others included well-known Soviet political and medical figures, and members of the Jewish Anti-Fascist Committee.

35. A description of these "Black Years" can be found in Carol R. Saivetz and Sheila Levin Woods, eds., *August 12, 1952, the Night of the Murdered Poets* (New York: National Conference on Soviet Jewry, 1973), 8.

36. Sandrow, *Vagabond Stars*, 222.

THE POLITICAL CONTEXT OF JEWISH THEATER AND CULTURE IN THE SOVIET UNION

1. The Soviet writer Konstantin Simonov, quoted in Harold Swayze, *Political Control of Literature in the USSR, 1946–1959* (Cambridge, Mass.: Harvard University Press, 1962), 17.

2. Barukh Shpilberg, quoted in Y. Opatoshu, "Drei hebrayer," *Zamlbicher* 8 (1952), quoted in Zvi Gitelman, *Jewish Nationality and Soviet Politics: The Jewish Sections of the CPSU, 1917–1930* (Princeton, N.J.: Princeton University Press, 1972), 282. Berdichev, in Ukraine, had a reputation as the "Jewish capital" of the region; at one time, about half the town's population was Jewish.

3. Vadim Zolotarev, "Natchalnytskyi sklad NKVS USRR u seredyni 30-x pp[rr]," *Z arkhiviv VuChK-HPU-NKVD-KGB*, no. 2 (17) (2001), quoted by Timothy Snyder, *The Reconstruction of Nations: Poland, Ukraine, Lithuania, Belarus, 1569–1999* (New Haven: Yale University Press, 2003), 28n55.

4. Leon Trotsky, *Literature and Revolution* (New York: Russell and Russell, 1957), 15.

5. Anna Shternshis, *Soviet and Kosher: Jewish Popular Culture in the Soviet Union, 1923–1939* (Bloomington: Indiana University Press, 2006), 71.

6. Quoted in Arkady Vaksberg, *Stalin Against the Jews*, trans. Antonina W. Bouis (New York: Knopf, 1994), 141–142.

HABIMA AND "BIBLICAL THEATER"

1. Naum Tsemakh, "My Teacher Stanislavsky," in *Be-reyshit Ha-Bima: Nahum Zemach meyased Ha-Bima be-hazon u-ve-ma'as [The Birth of Habima: Nakhum Zemach, Founder, Habima in Vision and Practice]*, ed. Itzhak Norman (Jerusalem: Ha-Sifriya ha-Zionit [The Jewish Agency], 1966), 157.

2. Menachem Gnesin, *Darki im teatrongaivri [My Journey with the Jewish Theater]* (Tel Aviv, 1946), 111.

3. Ibid., 110.

4. Chaim Nachman Bialik, "The Journey of the Hebrew Theater," in Norman, *Be-reyshit Ha-Bima*, 20.

5. Nikolai Volkov, quoted in H. Khersonsky, *Conversations About Vakhtangov* (Moscow and Leningrad, 1940), 19.

6. Marc Chagall, *My Life* (Moscow, 1994), 165–166.

7. Natan Altman, "My Work on *The Dybbuk*," in *Evgeny Vakhtangov*, ed. L. D. Vendrovskaia and G. P. Kapterova (Moscow, 1984), 390.

8. Ibid.

9. L. D. Vendrovskaia, ed., *Evgeny Vakhtangov: Materials and Articles* (Moscow, 1959), 204.

10. Samuel Margolin, "Theater of Ecstasy: *The Dybbuk*," *Ekran* (Moscow), no. 20 (February 7–13, 1922), 5.

11. "Hotière," *L'avenir* (Paris), July 5, 1926.

12. L. Gurevich, *Art of the RSFSR* (weekly of the Petrograd State Academic Theaters), nos. 15–16 (December 24–31, 1922), 30.

13. Y. Sazonova, "Tour of Habima Theater: *The Dybbuk* by S. Ansky," *Poslednie novosti* (Paris), October 19, 1937, 2.

14. Ibid.

15. Sergei Volkonsky, "Tour of Habima Theater: *The Dybbuk*," *Poslednie novosti* (Paris), June 30, 1926, 2.

16. Gurevich, *Art of the RSFSR*, 31.

17. Nikolai Volkov, *Vakhtangov* (Moscow, 1922), 20.

18. Max Reinhardt, quoted in Norman, *Be-reyshit Ha-Bima*, 341.

19. Andrei Levinson, "Le Théâtre Habima nous donne *Le Dybouk*: Légende en trois actes de S. An-Sky," *Comœdia* (Paris), June 30, 1926.

20. Jerzy Grotowski, "He Was Not Truly Himself," *Teatralnaya zhizn* (Moscow), no. 12 (1988), 29.

21. Ibid.

22. Yuri Zavadsky, "Obsession with Creativity," in *Evgeny Vakhtangov: Materials and Articles*, 297, 296.

23. Pavel Markov, "*The Wandering Jew* in Habima," *Teatr i myzka* (Moscow), no. 26 (June 12, 1923), 881.

24. Bernhard Diebold, *Habima: Hebräisches Theater*, (Berlin: Wilmersdorf, 1928), 14 (translated by V. Kolyazin).

25. Samuel Margolin, "*The Wandering Jew*: New Production in Habima Studio," *Teatr i myzka* (Moscow), no. 26 (June 12, 1923), 905.

26. Ibid.

27. Andrei Levinson, "*Le juif errant*: Deuxième spectacle à Paris du Théâtre Habima de Moscou," *Comœdia* (Paris), July 4, 1926.

28. Margolin, "*The Wandering Jew*," 905.

29. Markov, "*The Wandering Jew* in Habima," 883.

30. Diebold, *Habima: Hebräisches Theater*, 14.

31. Ibid.

32. Ibid.

33. L. Nikulin, "*The Wandering Jew*," *Zrelishcha* (Moscow), no. 40 (1923), 7.

34. A. Volynsky, "Jewish Theater (Article 1)," *Ippokrit: Zhizn iskusstva* (Leningrad), no. 27 (July 10, 1925), 4.

35. Interview with Boris Vershilov, *Novy zritel* (Moscow), no. 8 (February 24, 1925), 4.

36. Y. Ofrosimov, "Habima," *Rul* (Berlin), no. 1785 (October 16, 1926), 4.

37. M. Zagorsky, "In the Shadow of *The Dybbuk*, *Golem*, Habima," *Novy zritel* (Moscow), no. 13 (March 31, 1925), 12.

38. Andrei Levinson, "*Le Golem*: Poème dramatique de H. Levik: Troisième spectacle du Théâtre Habima," *Comœdia* (Paris), July 1, 1926.

39. Zagorsky, "In the Shadow of *The Dybbuk*, *Golem*, Habima," 12.

40. Ibid.

41. Diebold, *Habima: Hebräisches Theater*, 12–13.

42. "Conversation with the Artist Robert Falk About His Joint Work with Konstantin S. Stanislavsky, January 28, 1944," Actor and Director Room, Research and Theory Department, All-Russian Theater Society (VTO), typescript, Russian State Archive of Literature and Art (RGALI), fund 970, inventory 18, unit 11, pp. 7, 9, 24.

43. A. V. Shchekin-Krotova, *Robert Falk and Theater* (Moscow: Khudozhnik i Zrelishche, 1990), 286.

44. "Conversation with . . . Falk . . . Stanislavsky," 7–8.

45. This and the following quotations: ibid., 4–5.

46. Ibid., 8.

47. Raikin Ben-Ari, *Habima*, trans. A. H. Gross and I. Soref (New York: T. Yoseloff, 1957), 137.

48. "Illness of K. S. Stanislavsky: From Moscow by Telephone," *Krasnaya gazeta* (Leningrad), no. 26 (October 27, 1925, evening edition), 2.

49. "Conversation with . . . Falk . . . Stanislavsky," 4–5.

50. Reinhardt, quoted in Norman, *Be-reyshit Ha-Bima*, 341.

YIDDISH CONSTRUCTIVISM: THE ART OF THE MOSCOW STATE YIDDISH THEATER

1. For more on the rivalry between Altman and Chagall, see Alina Orlov, "Natan Altman and the Problem of Jewish Art in Russia in the 1910s" (Ph.D. diss., University of Southern California, 2003), esp. 123–136.

2. Cited in Solomon Mikhoels, *Mikhoels: Stati, besedy, rechi i vospominania o Mikhoelse* [*Mikhoels: Articles, Discussions, Speeches; Memories of Mikhoels*], ed. Konstantin Rudnitsky (Moscow: Iskusstvo, 1965), 598.

3. Aleksandr Tyshler, "Maia pervaia rabota nad shekspirom" ["My first work in Shakespeare"], *Sovetskoe iskusstvo* [*Soviet Art*], February 11, 1935.

4. Karl Radek, "Bolshaia pobeda sovetskogo teatra" ["Big success of Soviet Theater"], *Izvestia,* February 27, 1935; Moyshe Litvakov, "15 yor moskver melukhisher yidisher teatr" ["15 years of the Moscow State Yiddish Theater"], *Der emes,* March 5, 1935.

5. O. Litovsky, "'Razboynike Boytre v GOSET" ["Boytre the Bandit at GOSET"], *Sovetskoe iskusstvo* [*Soviet Art*], October 17, 1936.

6. A. Anastasev, *Istoriia sovetskogo dramaticheskogo teatra,* 6 vols. (Moscow: Institute istoriia iskusstv, 1966–1971), 5:671; quoted in Jeffrey Veidlinger, *The Moscow State Yiddish Theater: Jewish Culture on the Soviet Stage* (Bloomington: Indiana University Press, 2000), 247–248.

7. V. Potapov, "Tragedia i buffonada" ["Tragedy and Buffoonery"], *Sovetskoe iskusstvo* [*Soviet Art*], August 31, 1945.

ART AND THEATER

Epigraph: Solomon Mikhoels, "In Our Studio," in *Dos Idishe kamer teatr* [*The Yiddish Chamber Theater, on Its Opening in July 1919*] (Petrograd: Jewish Theater Society, 1919). Unless noted otherwise, all translations are mine.

1. For more detailed discussions, see my books *Marc Chagall and the Lost Jewish World: The Nature of Chagall's Art and Iconography* (New York: Rizzoli, 2006), and *The Moscow Yiddish Theater: Art on Stage in the Time of Revolution* (New Haven: Yale University Press, 2007). The latter book includes memoirs, contemporary criticism of the theater, a comprehensive bibliography, and two pieces by Sholem Aleichem performed at the Moscow opening of the theater— all translated from the original languages into English.

2. Alfred Kerr, "The Moscow Yiddish Theater," October 10, 1928; repr. in Hugo Fetting, ed., *Mit Schleuder und Harfe: Theaterkritiken aus drei Jahrzehnten* (Berlin: Henschelverlag, 1981).

3. Lev Levidov, "The Jewish Theater Society and the Chamber Theater," in *Dos idishe kamer teatr.*

4. *Dos idishe kamer teatr.*

5. Mikhoels, "In Our Studio."

6. Ibid.

7. Ibid.

8. Ernst Toller, Joseph Roth, and Alfons Goldschmidt, *Das Moskauer jüdische akademische Theater* [*The Moscow Jewish Academic Theater*] (Berlin: Die Schmiede, 1928).

9. Aleksei Granovsky, "Our Theater," *Literarishe bleter* (Warsaw), 5, no. 17 (April 27, 1928).

10. P. A. [Pavel] Markov, *The Soviet Theatre* (New York: G. P. Putnam's Sons, 1935).

11. See the full text in English translation in Harshav, *The Moscow Yiddish Theater.*

12. S[olomon] Mikhoels, "Mikhoels Vofsi on the Theater" (interview), *Literarishe bleter* (Warsaw), 5, no. 17 (April 27, 1928).

13. André Van Gyseghem, *Theatre in Soviet Russia* (London: Faber and Faber, 1943).

14. David Ben-Gurion, "Diary," in Itzhak Norman, ed., *Be-reyshit Ha-Bima: Nahum Zemach meyased Ha-Bima be-hazon u-ve-ma'as* [*The Birth of Habima: Nakhum Zemach, Founder, Habima in Vision and Practice*] (Jerusalem: Ha-Sifriya ha-Zionit [The Jewish Agency], 1966).

15. Max Osborn, "Marc Chagall," *Zharptitsa* (Berlin), no. 11 (1923).

16. Ibid.

17. Faina Burko, "The Soviet Yiddish Theater in the Twenties" (Ph.D. diss., Southern Illinois University, Carbondale, 1978).

18. Abram Efros, "The Artists of Granovsky's Theater," *Iskusstvo* (Moscow), 4 (1928), books 1–2, 63–74; repr. in Felix Dektor and Roman Spektor, eds., *Kovcheg: Almanakh evreyskoy kultury* [*The Ark: Almanac of Jewish Culture*] (Moscow: Khudozhestvennaia Literatura; and Jerusalem: Tarbut, 1991).

19. Ibid.

20. Marc Chagall, *Ma vie* [*My Life*], trans. Bella Chagall (Paris: Stock, 1932).

21. Marc Chagall, "Leaves from My Notebook" (published in Yiddish in 1922), in Benjamin Harshav, ed., *Marc Chagall on Art and Culture,* texts trans. Barbara and Benjamin Harshav (Stanford, Calif.: Stanford University Press, 2004), 40.

BIBLIOGRAPHY

A. G. Tyshler: Teatr, zhivopis, grafika: Iz leningradskikh sobrany.
Exh. cat. Leningrad: Leningrad Theater Museum, 1981.

A. Tyshler: Zhivopis, grafika, skulptura. Moscow: Sovetsky
Khudozhnik, 1978.

"Abraham Goldfadn." *Encyclopaedia Judaica*, 1978,
vol. 7, 715–717.

Abramovitsh, S. Y. *Benjamin the Third.* In Dan Miron and Ken
Frieden, eds., *Tales of Mendele the Book Peddler: Fishke
the Lame and Benjamin the Third.* Trans. Ted Gorelick
and Hillel Halkin. New York: Schocken, 1996, 229–391.

Adler, Lois. "Alexis Granovsky and the Jewish State Theatre
of Moscow." *The Drama Review* 24, no. 3 (September
1980), 27–42.

Aleichem, Sholem. *See* Sholem Aleichem.

Aleksandr Tyshler 1898–1980. Exh. cat. Moscow: Sovetsky
Khudozhnik, 1983.

"Alexander Krein." *Encyclopaedia Judaica*, 1978, vol. 10,
1252–1253.

Alpatov, M. M., et al. *Trois sculpteurs soviétiques: A. S.
Goloubkina, V. I. Moukhina, S. D. Lebedeva.* Paris, Musée
Rodin, 1971.

Altshuler, Mordechai, ed. *Ha-teatron ha-yeuidi bebrit
Ha-mietsot.* Jerusalem: The Hebrew University, 1996.

Amishai-Maisels, Ziva. "Chagall's Jewish In-Jokes." *Journal
of Jewish Art* 5 (1978), 76–93.

Anski, S. [An-sky, Solomon]. *The Dybbuk.* In *Three Great
Jewish Plays.* Trans. Joseph C. Landis. New York: Applause
Theatre, 1986.

An-sky, Semyon [Solomon]. *The Jewish Artistic Heritage.* Ed.
Vasily Rakitin and Andrei Sarabianov. Trans. Alan Myers.
Moscow: RA, 1994.

Antonowa, Irina, and Jörn Merkert. *Berlin Moskau, 1900–1950.*
Exh. cat. Munich and New York: Prestel, 1995.

Apter-Gabriel, Ruth, ed. *Tradition and Revolution: The Jewish
Renaissance in Russian Avant-Garde Art, 1912–1928.*
Jerusalem: The Israel Museum, 1987.

Arbatov, Boris. *Natan Altman.* Berlin: Petropolis, 1924.

Asch, Sholem. *God of Vengeance.* In *Three Great Jewish Plays.*
Trans. Joseph C. Landis. New York: Applause Theatre, 1986.

——. *Tales of My People.* Trans. Meyer Levin. New York:
G. P. Putnam's Sons, 1948.

Azarkh-Granovskaia, Aleksandra Veniaminovna. *Vospominania: Besedy s V. D. Duvakinym.* Jerusalem: Gesharim,
and Moscow: Mosty Kultury, 2001.

Baal-Teshuva, Jacob. *Marc Chagall, 1887–1985.* New York:
Taschen, 1998.

Baer, Nancy Van Norman. *Theatre in Revolution: Russian
Avant-Garde Stage Design, 1913–1935.* Exh. cat. New York:
Thames and Hudson, and San Francisco: Fine Arts
Museums of San Francisco, 1991.

Baker, Zachary M. "Yiddish in Form and Socialist in Content:
The Observance of Sholem Aleichem's Eightieth Birthday
in the Soviet Union." *YIVO Annual* 23 (1996), 209–231.

Baron, Salo W. *The Russian Jews Under Tsars and Soviets.* 2nd
ed. New York: Schocken, 1987.

Basner, Elena. *Robert Falk: Zhivopis i grafika iz muzeev i
chastnykh sobrany.* Exh. cat. St. Petersburg: State Russian
Museum, 1992.

Belenky, Moisei, ed. *Shalom-Aleikhem—pisatel i chelovek.*
Moscow: Sovetsky Pisatel, 1984.

Ben-Ari, Raikin. *Habima.* Trans. A. H. Gross and I. Soref. New
York: T. Yoseloff, 1957.

Berkowitz, Joel. "Avrom Goldfaden and the Modern Yiddish
Theater: The Bard of Old Constantine." *Pakn Treger* 44
(Winter 2004), 10–19.

——. "The Tallis or the Cross: Reviving Goldfaden at the
Yiddish Art Theatre." *Journal of Jewish Studies* 50 (Spring
1999), 120–138.

Berkowitz, Michael. "Art in Zionist Popular Culture and
Jewish National Self-Consciousness, 1897–1914." In Ezra
Mendelsohn, ed., *Studies in Contemporary Jewry*, vol. 6,
*Art and Its Uses: The Visual Image and Modern Jewish
Society.* New York: Oxford University Press, 1990.

Besançon, Alain. "R. R. Falk (1886–1958)." *Cahiers du monde
russe et soviétique* 3, no. 4 (1962), 564–581.

Beth Hatefutsoth. *The Closed Curtain: The Moscow Yiddish
State Theater.* Exh. cat. Tel Aviv: Diaspora Museum, 1980.

Biletzky, Israel. *H. Leivik: Ha-dramaturgyah ha-hezyonit.* Tel
Aviv: Ha-kibutz Ha-meuchad: 1979.

Bober, Natalie S. *Marc Chagall: Painter of Dreams.* Philadelphia and New York: The Jewish Publication Society, 1991.

Bowlt, John E., ed. and trans. *Russian Art of the Avant-Garde:
Theory and Criticism, 1902–1934.* New York: Viking, 1976.

——. *Russian Stage Design: Scenic Innovation, 1900–1930, from
the Collection of Mr. and Mrs. Nikita D. Lobanov-Rostovsky.*
Exh. cat. Jackson: Mississippi Museum of Art, 1982.

——, and Olga Matich. *Laboratory of Dreams: The Russian
Avant-Garde and Cultural Experiment.* Stanford, Calif.:
Stanford University Press, 1996.

Bown, Matthew Cullerne. *Art Under Stalin.* New York: Holmes
and Meier, 1991.

——, and Brandon Taylor, eds. *Art of the Soviets: Painting, Sculpture, and Architecture in a One-Party State, 1917–1992.* Manchester, England, and New York: Manchester University Press, 1993.

Braun, Joachim. *Jews and Jewish Elements in Soviet Music.* Tel Aviv: Israeli Music Publications, 1978.

——. "Jews in Soviet Music." In Jack Miller, ed., *Jews in Soviet Culture.* New Brunswick, N.J.: Transaction, 1984, 65–106.

Brown, Edward. "Constructivism in the Theatre." In *Art in Revolution: Soviet Art and Design Since 1917.* Exh. cat. London: Hayward Gallery, 1971.

"Burial of a Yiddish Poet [Golfadn]." *New York Times,* January 12, 1908, 8.

Burko, Faina. "'Habima' and the Moscow Yiddish Chamber Theater in the Early Twenties." In *Proceedings of the Ninth World Congress of Jewish Studies.* Jerusalem: World Union of Jewish Studies, 1986.

Carden, Patricia. *The Art of Isaac Babel.* Ithaca, N.Y.: Cornell University Press, 1972.

Carter, Huntly. *The New Spirit in the Russian Theatre, 1917–28: And a Sketch of the Russian Kinema and Radio, 1919–28, Showing the New Communal Relationship Between the Three.* London: Brentano's, 1929.

Chagall, Marc. *Marc Chagall on Art and Culture: Including the First Book on Chagall's Art by A. Efros and Y. Tugendhold (Moscow 1918).* Ed. Benjamin Harshav. Trans. Barbara and Benjamin Harshav. Stanford, Calif.: Stanford University Press, 2003.

——. *My Life.* New York: Orion, 1960.

Chagall dans une nouvelle lumière. Exh. cat. Baden-Baden, Germany: Museum Frieder Burda, 2006.

Charyn, Jerome. *Savage Shorthand: The Life and Death of Isaac Babel.* New York: Random House, 2005.

Compton, Susan. *Chagall.* Exh. cat. London: Royal Academy of Arts, 1985.

——. *Chagall: Love and the Stage, 1914–1922.* Exh. cat. London: Royal Academy of Arts, in association with Merrell Holberton, 1998.

——. *Marc Chagall: My Life, My Dream: Berlin and Paris, 1922–1940.* Munich and New York: Prestel, 1990.

Dobert, Eitel Wolf. *Karl Gutzkow und seine Zeit.* Bern and Munich: Francke, 1968.

Dobrushin, Yekhezkel Moissevich. *Mikhoels der aktior.* Moscow: Der Emes, 1940.

Dokuchaeva, Vera. *Ignaty Ignatievich Nivinsky.* Moscow: Sovetsky Khudozhnik, 1969.

Efros, Abram. "Khudozhniki teatra Granovskogo." In Felix Dektor and Roman Spektor, eds., *Kovcheg: Almanakh evreyskoy kultury* [*The Ark: Almanac of Jewish Culture*]. Moscow: Khudozhestvennaia Literatura, and Jerusalem: Tarbut, 1991.

——. *Portret Natana Altmana.* Moscow: Shipovnik, 1922.

——. *Profili.* Moscow: Federatsia, 1930.

Ehrenburg, Ilya. *Memoirs 1921–1941.* Trans. Tatiana Shebunina. Cleveland and New York: World, 1963.

——. *People and Life: 1891–1921.* New York: Alfred A. Knopf, 1962.

——, and Vasily Grossman. *The Black Book.* New York: Holocaust Library, 1980.

Elliott, David. *New Worlds: Russian Art and Society 1900–1937.* London: Thames and Hudson, 1986.

Etkind, Mark. *Natan Altman.* Moscow: Sovetsky Khudozhnik, 1971. Rev. ed. Dresden: Verlag der Kunst, 1984.

Falen, James E. *Isaac Babel, Russian Master of the Short Story.* Knoxville: University of Tennessee Press, 1974.

Falk, R[obert] R. *Besedy ob iskusstve, pisma, vospominania o khudozhnike.* Ed. A. V. Shchekin-Krotova. Moscow: Sovetsky Khudozhnik, 1981.

Fefer, Itsik. *Lider, balades, poemes.* Moscow: Sovetsky Pisatel, 1967.

Finkel, Shimon. *Hanah Rovina: Monografiyah 'al reka' zikhronot.* Tel Aviv: Eked, 1978.

Finkel, Uri. *Sholem Aleykhem: Monografye.* Warsaw: Yidish Bukh, 1959.

Fitzpatrick, Sheila. *The Cultural Front: Power and Culture in Revolutionary Russia.* Ithaca, N.Y.: Cornell University Press, 1992.

——. *Cultural Revolution in Russia, 1928–1931.* Bloomington: Indiana University Press, 1978.

Folkovitsch, Aliah. *Mikhoels, 1890–1948.* Moscow: Der Emes, 1948.

Frieden, Ken. *Classic Yiddish Fiction: Abramovitsh, Sholem Aleichem, and Peretz.* Albany: State University of New York Press, 1995.

Frost, Matthew. "Marc Chagall and the Jewish State Chamber Theatre." *Russian History / Histoire russe* 8, nos. 1–2 (1981), 90–99.

Fülöp-Miller, René. *The Mind and Face of Bolshevism: An Examination of Cultural Life in the Soviet Union.* Trans. F. S. Flint and D. F. Tait. London: G. P. Putnam's Sons, 1927.

Gai, Karmit. *Ha-malkah nas'ah be-otobus: Rovina ve-"Habimah."* Tel Aviv: Am Oved, 1995.

Geizer, Matvei. *Mikhoels.* Moscow: Molodaia Gvardia, 2004.

——. *Mikhoels: Zhizn i smert.* Moscow: Glasnost, 1998.

Gilboa, Yehoshua A. *The Black Years of Soviet Jewry: 1939–1953.* New York: Little, Brown, 1971.

Gitelman, Zvi. *A Century of Ambivalence: The Jews of Russia and the Soviet Union, 1881 to the Present.* New York: Schocken, 1988.

——. *Jewish Nationality and Soviet Politics: The Jewish Sections of the CPSU, 1917–1930.* Princeton, N.J.: Princeton University Press, 1972.

Goldberg, A. *Unzer dramaturgie.* New York: Yiddisher Kultur Farband, 1961.

Goldenberg, Mikhail. *Zhizn i sudba Solomona Mikhoelsa: Dokumenty, stenogrammy, vsytuplenia, pisma.* Baltimore: Vestnik, 1995.

Goodman, Susan Tumarkin, ed. *Marc Chagall: Early Works from Russian Collections.* Exh. cat. New York: The Jewish Museum, 2001.

——. *Russian Jewish Artists.* Exh. cat. New York: The Jewish Museum, 1995.

Gorchakov, Nikolai A. *The Theater in Soviet Russia.* Trans. Edgar Lehman. New York: Columbia University Press, 1957.

Gordon, Mel. Liner notes for *Cubo-Futurist Klezmer: Recordings from the Moscow State Yiddish Theatre (1922–1938).* Audio recording. 2001.

——. "Granovsky's Tragic Carnival: *Night in the Old Market.*" *The Drama Review* 29, no. 4 (Winter 1985), 91–94.

Goren, B. *Di geshikhte fun yidishn teater*, 2 vols. New York: Max N. Mayzel, 1923.

Gray, Camilla. *The Great Experiment: Russian Art 1863–1922.* London: Thames and Hudson, 1962. Reissued as *The Russian Experiment in Art: 1863–1922.* London: Thames and Hudson, 1970, 1986.

György, Szegö, Judit Faludy, and Eszter Götz, eds. *Diaspora (and) Art.* Exh. cat. Trans. Magdaléna Seleanu and Vera Szabó. Budapest: Magyar Zsidó Museum, 1997.

Haftmann, Werner. *Marc Chagall.* New York: Harry N. Abrams, 1972.

Harshav, Benjamin. *Marc Chagall and His Times: A Documentary Narrative.* Trans. Benjamin and Barbara Harshav. Stanford, Calif.: Stanford University Press, 2004.

———. *Marc Chagall and the Lost Jewish World: The Nature of Chagall's Art and Iconography.* New York: Rizzoli, 2006.

———. *The Moscow Yiddish Theater: Art on Stage in the Time of Revolution.* New Haven: Yale University Press, 2007.

Hoberman, J. *Bridge of Light: Yiddish Film Between Two Worlds.* Philadelphia: Temple University Press, 1995.

———. "The Crooked Road of Jewish Luck." *Artforum* 28 (September 1989), 122–125.

Houghton, Norris. *Moscow Rehearsals: The Golden Age of Soviet Theatre.* New York: Harcourt, Brace, 1936. Reissued New York: Grove, 1962.

"Isaac Babel." *Encyclopaedia Judaica,* 1978, vol. 4, 18–22.

"Isaac Leib Peretz." *Encyclopaedia Judaica,* 1978, vol. 13, 279–283.

Ivanov, Oleg, and Kim Krivitsky. *Vakhtangov i vakhtangovtsy.* Moscow: Moskovsky Rabochy, 1984.

Ivanov, Vladislav. GOSET: *Politika i iskusstvo, 1919–1928* [*The State Jewish Theater, 1919–1928*]. Moscow: Izd-vo "GITIS," 2007.

———. "Poetika metamorfoz: Vakhtangov i Gabima." *Voprosy teatra* 13 (1993), 188–222.

———. *Russkie sezony teatra Gabima.* Moscow: Artist Rezhisser Teatr, 1999.

———. "Teatr Gabima v Moskve: Na vesakh Iova." *Znamia* 12 (1995), 168–192.

Jones, Calvin N. "Authorial Intent and Public Response to *Uriel Acosta* and *Freiheit in Krähwinkel.*" *South Atlantic Review* 47 (November 1982), 17–26.

"Jules Romains." Encyclopaedia Britannica Online. http://www.britannica.com/eb/article-9083801.

Kamensky, Alexander. *Chagall: The Russian Years, 1907–1922.* Trans. Catherine Philips. London: Thames and Hudson, and New York: Rizzoli, 1989.

Kampf, Avram. *Jewish Experience in the Art of the Twentieth Century.* South Hadley, Mass.: Bergin and Garvey, 1984.

Kasovsky, G. *Artists from Vitebsk: Yehuda Pen and His Pupils.* Trans. L. Lezhneva. Moscow: Image, 1992.

Kleberg, Lars. *Theatre as Action: Soviet Russian Avant-Garde Aesthetics.* Trans. Charles Rougle. London: Macmillan, 1993.

Klinger, Charles S. *Mendele Mocher Sforim: An Appreciation of His Contribution to Modern Yiddish Literature.* London: Yiddish Cultural Society, 1968.

Kochan, Lionel, ed. *The Jews in Soviet Russia Since 1917.* London: Oxford University Press, 1972.

Kohansky, Mendel. *The Hebrew Theatre: Its First Fifty Years.* New York: KTAV, 1969.

Kopytova, Galina. "Moissej Milner und seine Opera *Die himlen brenen.*" In Jascha Nemtsov and Ernst Kuhn, eds., *Jüdische Musik in Sowjetrussland.* Berlin: Ernst Kuhn, 2002.

Korey, William. *The Soviet Cage: Anti-Semitism in Russia.* New York: Viking, 1973.

Kostyrchenko, Gennady. *Out of the Red Shadow: Anti-Semitism in Stalin's Russia.* New York: Prometheus, 1995.

Kunin, I., ed. *Glazami sovremennika: Izbrannie staty o russkoy muzyke.* Moscow: Sovetsky Kompozitor, 1971.

Kushner, Tony, and Joachim Neugroschel. *A Dybbuk, and Other Tales of the Supernatural.* Trans. and adapted from Solomon An-sky. New York: Theatre Communications Group, 1998.

Kuthy, Sandor, and Meret Meyer. *Marc Chagall 1907–1917.* Trans. Luc Birebent. Exh. cat. Bern: Museum of Fine Arts Berne, 1995.

Leach, Robert, and Victor Borovsky, eds. *A History of Russian Theatre.* Cambridge, England: Cambridge University Press, 1999.

Lebedeva, Sarra. *Album.* Ed. M. Alpatov et al. Moscow, 1973.

Leivick, Halpern. *The Golem.* In *Three Great Jewish Plays.* Trans. Joseph C. Landis. New York: Applause Theatre, 1986.

Levin, Nora. *The Jews in the Soviet Union Since 1917: Paradox of Survival.* New York: I. B. Tauris, 1990.

Levy, Emanuel. *The Habima, Israel's National Theater, 1917–1977: A Study of Cultural Nationalism.* New York: Columbia University Press, 1979.

Liptzin, Sol. *A History of Yiddish Literature.* Middle Village, N.Y.: Jonathan David, 1972.

Liubomirsky, Ovsei [Yeshua]. *Af di lebnsvegn: Fartseykhnungen.* Moscow: Sovetsky Pisatel, 1976.

Lodder, Christine. *Russian Constructivism.* New Haven: Yale University Press, 1983.

Lozowick, Louis. "The Art of Nathan Altman." *Menorah Journal* 12 (1926), 35–36.

———. "Moscow Theatre, 1920s." *Russian History* 8, nos. 1–2 (1981).

Lustiger, Arno. *Stalin and the Jews: The Red Book: The Tragedy of the Jewish Anti-Fascist Committee and the Soviet Jews.* Trans. Mary Beth Friedrich and Todd Bludeau. New York: Enigma, 2003.

Macleod, Joseph. *The New Soviet Theatre.* London: George Allen and Unwin, 1943.

Madison, Charles A. *Yiddish Literature: Its Scope and Major Writers.* New York: Frederick Ungar, 1968.

Marc Chagall. Exh. cat. San Francisco: San Francisco Museum of Modern Art, in association with Harry N. Abrams, 2003.

Marc Chagall: Les années russes, 1907–1922. Paris: Musée d'Art Moderne de la Ville de Paris, 1995.

Marc Chagall: Meisterwerke 1908–1922. Exh. cat. Berlin: BA-CA Kunstforum, 2006.

Marc Chagall: Oeuvres sur papier. Exh. cat. Paris: Centre Georges Pompidou, 1984.

Marc Chagall and the Jewish Theater. Exh. cat. New York: Solomon R. Guggenheim Museum, 1992.

Marcade, Jean-Claude. "Le contexte russe de l'oeuvre de Chagall." *Marc Chagall.* Paris: Centre Georges Pompidou, 1984.

Marshall, Herbert. *The Pictorial History of the Russian Theatre.* New York: Crown, 1977.

Mayzel, Nachman. *Dos yidishe shafn un der yidisher shrayber in Sovetnfarband.* New York: Yiddisher Kultur Farband, 1959.

"Mendele Mokher Seforim." *Encyclopaedia Judaica,* 1978, vol. 11, 1317–1323.

Mestel, Yakov. *70 yor teater repertuar.* New York: Yiddisher Kultur Farband, 1954.

Meyer, Franz. *Marc Chagall: Life and Work.* Trans. Robert Allen. New York: Harry N. Abrams, 1964.

Mikhoels, Solomon. *Mikhoels: Stati, besedy, rechi i vospominania o Mikhoelse.* Ed. Konstantin Rudnitsky. Moscow: Iskusstvo, 1965.

———. "Sholem Aleikhem: Aiinokters." Moscow: Der Emes, 1940.

Miller, Jack. *Jews in Soviet Culture.* New Brunswick, N.J.: Transaction, 1984.

Misler, Nicoletta, ed. *Marc Chagall: Gli anni russi 1908–1922.* Exh. cat. Florence: Palazzo Medici Riccardi, 1993.

Mlotek, Eleanor. *S. Ansky (Shloyme-Zanvl Rappoport), 1863–1920: His Life and Works.* New York: YIVO Institute for Jewish Research, 1980.

Moddel, Philip. *Joseph Achron.* Tel Aviv: Israeli Music Publications, 1966.

Morse, Mitchell J. "Karl Gutzkow and the Modern Novel." *Journal of General Education* 15 (October 1963), 175–189.

"Moses Michael Milner." *Encyclopaedia Judaica,* 1978, vol. 11, 1586.

"Moshe Litvakov." *Encyclopaedia Judaica,* 1978, vol. 11, 404–405.

"Nahum Zemach." *Encyclopaedia Judaica,* 1978, vol. 16, 981–982.

Nakhimovsky, Alice Stone. *Russian-Jewish Literature and Identity.* Baltimore and London: The Johns Hopkins University Press, 1992.

Niger, Samuel. *H. Leyvik.* Toronto: H. Leyvik Yoyvl-Komitet, 1951.

The Night of the Murdered Poets. New York: National Conference on Soviet Jewry, 2002.

"Noted Jewish Bard [Goldfadn] Dead." *New York Times,* January 10, 1908, 7.

Old Voices—New Faces: Soviet Jewish Artists from the 1920s–1990s. Exh. cat. Washington, D.C.: B'nai B'rith Klutznick National Jewish Museum, 1992.

Paris–Moscou 1900–1930. Exh. cat. Moscow: Ministère de la Culture de l'USSR, and Paris: Centre Georges Pompidou, 1979.

Peretz, I. L. *Night in the Old Market.* Adapted by Aleksei Granovsky. *Drama Review* 29, no. 4 (Winter 1985), 95–122.

Perlmutter, Sholem. *Yidishe dramaturgn un teater kompozitors.* Ed. Yakov Mestel. New York: Yiddisher Kultur Farband, 1952.

Picon-Vallin, Béatrice. *Le théâtre juif soviétique pendant les années vingt.* Lausanne: La Cité/L'Age d'Homme, 1973.

Rabinovich, Israel. *Of Jewish Music, Ancient and Modern.* Trans. A. M. Klein. Montreal: Book Center, 1952.

Rajner, Miriam. "The Awakening of Jewish National Art in Russia." *Jewish Art* 16–17 (1990–91), 98–121.

Ravina, Menashe. *Yo'el Engel ve ha-musikah ha-yehudit.* Tel Aviv: Ha-mosad Le-musikah Ba-am, 1947.

Redlich, Shimon. *Propaganda and Nationalism in Wartime Russia: The Jewish Antifascist Committee in the USSR, 1941–1948.* Boulder, Colo.: East European Quarterly, 1982.

Ro'i, Yaacov, ed. *Jews and Jewish Life in Russia and the Soviet Union.* New York: Routledge, 1995.

———, and Avi Bekar, eds. *Jewish Culture and Identity in the Soviet Union.* New York: New York University Press, 1991.

Rokem, Freddie. "Hebrew Theater from 1899 to 1947." In Linda Ben-Zvi, ed., *Theater in Israel.* Ann Arbor: University of Michigan Press, 1996.

Romains, Jules. *Le mariage de Le Trouhadec.* Paris: Gallimard, 1959.

Roose-Evans, James. *Experimental Theater from Stanislavsky to Peter Brook.* London: Routledge, 1970.

Rosenberg, Marvin. *The Masks of King Lear.* Berkeley: University of California Press, 1972.

Rubinstein, Joshua, and Vladimir P. Naumov, eds. *Stalin's Secret Pogrom: The Postwar Inquisition of the Jewish Anti-Fascist Committee.* Trans. Laura Esther Wolfson. New Haven: Yale University Press, in association with United States Holocaust Memorial Museum, 2001.

Rudnitsky, Konstantin. *Russian and Soviet Theatre: Tradition and the Avant-Garde.* Ed. Lesley Milne. Trans. Roxane Permar. London: Thames and Hudson, 1988.

Russian Painters and the Stage 1884–1965. Exh. cat. Austin: University Art Museum, The University of Texas at Austin, 1977.

"S. An-Ski." *Encyclopaedia Judaica,* 1978, vol. 3, 34–35.

Safran, Gabriella, and Steven J. Zipperstein, eds. *The Worlds of S. An-sky: A Russian Jewish Intellectual at the Turn of the Century.* Stanford, Calif.: Stanford University Press, 2006.

Samuel, Maurice. *The World of Sholem Aleichem.* New York: Alfred A. Knopf, 1943.

Sandrow, Nahma. *Vagabond Stars: A World History of Yiddish Theater.* New York: Harper and Row, 1977.

Sarabyanov, Dmitry Vladimirovich. *Mark Shagal.* Moscow: Izobrazitelnoe Iskusstvo, 1992.

———. *Robert Falk.* Ed. A. W. Shchekin-Krotova. Trans. Helmut Barth. Dresden: VEB Verlag der Kunst, 1974.

"75,000 at Poet's [Goldfadn] Funeral." *New York Times,* January 11, 1908, 1.

Shaffer, Harry G. *The Soviet Treatment of Jews.* New York: Praeger, 1974.

"Shalom Aleichem." *Encyclopaedia Judaica,* 1978, vol. 14, 1272–1286.

Shatskikh, Aleksandra. *Vitebsk: Life of Art.* New Haven: Yale University Press, 2007.

Shatsky, Yakov, ed. *Hunderd yor Goldfadn.* New York: YIVO Institute for Jewish Research, 1940.

Shchedrin, Vasily. *Uravnenie GOSETA: Problemy istory evreyskogo teatra v SSSR.* Moscow: Jewish Heritage Society, 1997.

Shehori-Rubin, Zippora. "Habimah in Russia—Theater with a National-Zionist Mission, 1918–1926." *Shevut: Studies in Russian and East European Jewish History and Culture* 6, no. 22 (1997), 79–103.

Shmeruk, Khone. *Peretzes yeush-vizie: Interpretatsie fun Y. L. Peretzes "Bay nakht oyfn altn mark": Un kritishe oysgabe fun der drame.* New York: YIVO Institute for Jewish Research, 1971.

Sholem Aleichem. *The Adventures of Menahem-Mendl.* Trans. Tamara Kahana. New York: G. P. Putnam's Sons, 1979.

———. *Ale verk fun Sholem Aleychem.* New York: Farvert, 1942.

———. *The Bewitched Tailor.* Moscow: Foreign Languages, 1960.

———. *The Letters of Menakhem-Mendl and Sheyne-Sheyndl, and Motl, the Cantor's Son.* Trans. Hillel Halkin. New Haven: Yale University Press, 2002.

"Sholem Asch." *Encyclopaedia Judaica*, 1978, vol. 3, 684–687.

"Sholem Asch Reconsidered." Conference at Yale University, May 13–15, 2000. http://www.library.yale.edu/judaica/asch/index.html.

Shtudyes in Leyvik: Forshungen vegn zayn lebn un shafn geleyent oyf dem simpozyum in Bar-Ilan Universitet tsum dikhters hundertyorikn geboyrntog. Ramat Gan, Israel: Bar Ilan University, 1992.

Sidney, Alexander. *Marc Chagall.* London: Cassell, 1978.

Simonov, Ruben. *Stanislavsky's Protégé: Eugene Vakhtangov.* Ed. Helen Choat. Trans. Miriam Goldina. New York: DBS, 1969.

Slonim, Marc. *Russian Theater from the Empire to the Soviets.* New York: Collier, 1961.

Soroker, Yakov. *Rossiiskie muzykanty yevrei* [*Russian Jewish Musicians*]. Jerusalem, 1992.

Sosnovskaya, Alla. "Was Habima a Jewish Theater or a Russian Theater in Hebrew?" In Yisrael Elliot Cohen and Michael Beizer, eds., *Jews in Eastern Europe.* Jerusalem: The Hebrew University, 1993.

Stahl, Nanette. *Sholem Asch Reconsidered.* New Haven, Conn.: Beinecke Rare Book and Manuscript Library, 2004.

Steinberg, Theodore L. *Mendele Mocher Seforim.* Boston: Twayne, 1977.

Steinecke, Hartmut. "Gutzkow, die Juden und das Judentum." In Hans Otto Horch and Horst Denkler, eds., *Conditio judaica: Judentum, Antisemitismus und deutschsprachige Literatur vom 18. Jahrhundert bis zum Ersten Weltkrieg,* vol. 2. Tübingen, Germany: M. Niemeyer, 1988.

Syrkina, Flora Yakovlevna. *Aleksandr G. Tyshler.* Moscow: Sovetsky Khudozhnik, 1987.

Ternovets, Boris. *Sarah Lebedeva.* Moscow: Iskusstvo, 1940.

Thorpe, Richard G. "The Academic Theaters and the Fate of Soviet Artistic Pluralism, 1919–1928." *Slavic Review* 51, no. 3 (Fall 1992), 389–410.

Tradition and Vanguard: Jewish Culture in the Russian Revolutionary Era. Exh. cat. San Diego: Founders Gallery, University of San Diego, 1994.

Vaksberg, Arkady. *Stalin Against the Jews.* Trans. Antonia W. Bouis. New York: Alfred A. Knopf, 1994.

van Voolen, Edward. *Marc Chagall en het Joods Theater.* Exh. cat. Amsterdam: Joods Historisch Museum, 2002.

Varneke, Boris. *History of Russian Theatre, Seventeenth Through Nineteenth Century.* New York: Macmillan, 1951.

Veidlinger, Jeffrey. "Let's Perform a Miracle: The Soviet Yiddish State Theater in the 1920s." *Slavic Review* 57, no. 2 (Summer 1998), 372–397.

———. *The Moscow State Yiddish Theater: Jewish Culture on the Soviet Stage.* Bloomington: Indiana University Press, 2000.

Vendrovskaia, Liubov, and Galina Kaptereva, eds. *Vakhtangov, Evgeny, 1883–1922.* Moscow: Progress, 1982.

Vitali, Christoph, ed. *Die Grosse Utopie: Die russische Avantgarde 1915–1932.* Exh. cat. Frankfurt: Schirn Kuntshalle, 1992. Published in English as *The Great Utopia: The Russian and Soviet Avant-Garde, 1915–1932.* New York: Solomon R. Guggenheim Museum, 1992.

———. *Marc Chagall: The Russian Years 1906–1922.* Exh. cat. Frankfurt: Schirn Kunsthalle, 1991.

Vovsi-Mikhoels, Natalia. *Moi otets Solomon Mikhoels.* Tel Aviv: Ha-kibutz Ha-meuchad, 1982–83; Montricher, Switzerland: Noir sur Blanc, 1990; and Moscow: Vozvrashchenie, 1997.

Waife-Goldberg, Marie. *My Father, Sholom Aleichem.* Sholom Aleichem Family Publications, 1999.

Waldman, Mosheh, ed. *H. Leivik, poète yiddish: Hommages et textes choisis.* Paris: Gopa, 1967.

Warnke, Nina. "Theater as Educational Institution: Jewish Immigrant Intellectuals and Yiddish Theater Reform." In Barbara Kirshenblatt-Gimblett and Jonathan Karp, eds., *The Art of Being Jewish in Modern Times.* Philadelphia: University of Pennsylvania Press, 2008, 23–41.

Weinberg, Jacob. "Joel Engel: A Pioneer in Jewish Musical Renaissance." *Jewish Music Forum* 7 (1946–1947), 33.

Weisser, Albert. *The Modern Renaissance of Jewish Music, Events, and Figures, Eastern Europe and America.* New York: Bloch, 1954.

Weitzner, Jacob. *Sholem Aleichem in the Theater.* Northwood, England: Symposium, and Madison, N.J.: Fairleigh Dickinson University Press, 1994.

Wilson, Jonathan. *Marc Chagall.* New York: Nextbook-Schocken, 2007.

Wisse, Ruth R. *I. L. Peretz and the Making of the Modern Jewish Culture.* Seattle: University of Washington Press, 1991.

Worrall, Nick. *Modernism to Realism on the Soviet Stage: Tairov–Vakhtangov–Okhlopkov.* Cambridge, England, and New York: Cambridge University Press, 1989.

Yablonskaya, M. N. *Women Artists of Russia's New Age 1900–1935.* New York: Rizzoli, 1990.

"Yekhezkel Dobrushin." *Encyclopaedia Judaica*, 1978, vol. 6, 144.

Di yidishe drame fun 20stn yorhundert: Jacob Gordin, Shalom-Aleichim, David Pinsky, Leon Kobrin, vol. 1. New York: Yiddisher Kultur Farband, 1977.

Yudel, Mark. *I. L. Peretz, 1852–1915: His Life and Works.* New York: Educational Department of the Workmen's Circle, 1952.

Zohn, Hershel. *The Story of Yiddish Theater.* Las Cruces, N.M.: Yucca Tree, 1979.

Zuskin-Perelman, Ala. *Mas'ot Binyamin Zuskin.* Jerusalem: Carmel, 2006.

———. *Puteshestvie Veniamina: Razmyshlenia o zhizni, tvorchestve i sudbe evreyskogo aktera Veniamina Zuskina.* Moscow: Mosty Kultury, and Jerusalem: Gesharim, 2002.

Zylbercweig, Zalmen. *Hantbukh fun yidishn teater: A shtudirbukh.* Mexico City: YIVO Institute for Jewish Research in Los Angeles, 1970.

SUSAN TUMARKIN GOODMAN is Senior Curator at The Jewish Museum, where she has organized numerous exhibitions and written and edited many catalogues. Her exhibition catalogues on Russian art include *Marc Chagall: Early Works from Russian Collections* (2001), *A Witness to History: Yevgeny Khaldei, Soviet Photojournalist* (1997), and *Russian Jewish Artists in a Century of Change, 1890–1990* (1995). Among her other publications are *Dateline Israel: New Photography and Video Art* (2007), *The Emergence of Jewish Artists in Nineteenth-Century Europe* (2001), *After Rabin: New Art from Israel* (1998), and *From the Inside Out: Eight Contemporary Artists* (1993).

ZVI GITELMAN is Professor of Political Science and Preston R. Tisch Professor of Judaic Studies at the University of Michigan. He is the author or editor of fourteen books, including *A Century of Ambivalence: The Jews of Russia and the Soviet Union, 1881 to the Present* (second edition, 2001). Professor Gitelman's research focuses on the management of multiethnic societies, particularly in the former Soviet Union. He is completing a study on ethnic identities among Jews in Russia and Ukraine, and is researching the Holocaust in the USSR.

BENJAMIN HARSHAV is Professor of Comparative Literature, J. and H. Blaustein Professor of Hebrew Language and Literature, and Professor of Slavic Languages and Literatures at Yale University. He is the author of *The Moscow Yiddish Theater: Art on Stage in the Time of Revolution* (2008), *Marc Chagall and the Lost Jewish World: The Nature of His Art and Iconography* (2006), *Marc Chagall and His Times: A Documentary Narrative* (2003), which won the Koret Jewish Book Award. Among his other books are *The Polyphony of Jewish Culture* (2007), *Explorations in Poetics* (2007), *Sing, Stranger: A Century of American Yiddish Poetry* (2006, with Barbara Harshav), *Language in Time of Revolution* (1993), *The Meaning of Yiddish* (1986), and six volumes of his selected writings in Hebrew. In 2005, he was awarded the EMET Prize for achievements in art, science, and culture by the Prime Minister of Israel.

VLADISLAV IVANOV is Chairman of the Theater Department at the Gosudarstvennyi Institute Iskusstvoznania, State Institute of Studies of the Arts, Moscow, and the author of two books on Soviet Jewish theater, GOSET: *Politika i iskusstvo, 1919–1928* (2007) and *Russkie sezony teatra Gabima* (1999). He was also editor in chief of the almanac *Mnemosyna: Documenty i facty iz istorii otechestvennogo teatra XX veka* (issues 1–4), and the author of numerous articles and publications on the art of Evgeny Vakhtangov, Sergei Eisenstein, Alexander Tairov, Mikhail Chekhov, Nikolai Evreinov, Vasilij Sakhnovskij, and others.

JEFFREY VEIDLINGER is Associate Director of the Robert A. and Sandra S. Borns Jewish Studies Program, Alvin H. Rosenfeld Chair in Jewish Studies, and Associate Professor in the Department of History at Indiana University, Bloomington. His first book, *The Moscow State Yiddish Theater: Jewish Culture on the Soviet Stage* (2000), won a National Jewish Book Award, the Barnard Hewitt Award for Outstanding Research in Theatre History, and was named an Outstanding Academic Title by *Choice* magazine. His second book, *Jewish Public Culture in the Late Russian Empire*, is forthcoming from Indiana University Press. In 2006, he was named a Top Young Historian by History News Network.

INDEX

Note: Page numbers in *italics* refer to illustrations. Captions are indexed as text.

Boldface numerals refer to page numbers.

Abbreviations

AAB A. A. Bakhrushin State Central Theater Museum, Moscow

ARS © 2007 Artists Rights Society (ARS), New York/ADAGP, Paris

AT Art © Estate of Aleksandr Tyshler/ RAO, Moscow/VAGA, New York

AZP Courtesy of Ala Zuskin-Perelman, Or-Yehuda, Israel

BH Beth Hatefutsoth, Photo Archive, Tel Aviv, courtesy of Zuskin Collection

BOH *Be-reyshit Ha-Bima: Nahum Zemach meyased Ha-Bima be-hazon u-vema'as* [*The Birth of Habima: Nakhum Zemach, Founder, Habima in Vision and Practice*], ed. Itzhak Norman (Jerusalem: Ha-Sifriya ha-Zionit [The Jewish Agency], 1966)

CGP Musée nationale d'art moderne, Centre Georges Pompidou, Paris

IGT Israel Goor Theater Archive and Museum, Jerusalem

NA Art © Estate of Natan Altman/RAO, Moscow/VAGA, New York

ORT Valery Dymshits, Alexander Ivanov, et al., *The Hope and the Illusion: The Search for a Russian Jewish Homeland: A Remarkable Period in the History of ORT, 1921–1938* (London: World ORT, 2006)

RF Art © Estate of Robert Falk/RAO, Moscow/VAGA, New York

RSA The Russian State Archive of Literature and Art, Moscow

STG State Tretyakov Gallery, Moscow

VI Courtesy of Vladislav Ivanov, Moscow

YIVO Archives of the YIVO Institute for Jewish Research, New York

Cover: STG/ARS/ Photograph © Volker Naumann
Frontispiece: AAB/NA

Goodman essay: **Frontispiece** AAB. **2** RSA. **3** VI. **4** AAB (left), Vladislav Ivanov, *GOSET: Politika i iskusstvo, 1919–1928* [*The State Jewish Theater. 1919–1928*] (Moscow: Izd-vo "GITIS," 2007) (right). **5** VI (top), IGT/NA (bottom). **6** © St. Petersburg State Museum of Theater and Music/NA. **8** AAB. **9** AZP. **10** AZP (left), BH (right). **11** AAB/AT. **12** YIVO (top). **12–13** IGT.

Gitelman essay: **Frontispiece** Collection of Merrill C. Berman, Rye, New York/NA. **15** Photo by Laski Diffusion/Getty Images. **17** ORT, fig. 105 (top), YIVO (bottom). **18** ORT, fig. 84. **19** American Jewish Joint Distribution Committee (JDC) Archives, New York. **20** American Jewish Joint Distribution Committee (JDC) Archives, New York (left), ORT, fig. 72 (right). **21** ORT, fig. 27. **22** ORT, fig. 109. **23** American Jewish Joint Distribution Committee (JDC) Archives, New York. **24** AZP. **25** Joshua Rubinstein and Vladimir P. Naumov, eds., *Stalin's Secret Pogrom: The Postwar Inquisition of the Jewish Anti-Fascist Committee*, trans. Laura Esther Wolfson (New Haven: Yale University Press, in association with United States Holocaust Memorial Museum, 2001).

Ivanov essay: **Frontispiece** AAB. **28** YIVO (left), BOH, p. 47 (right). **29** Tel Aviv Museum of Art/NA. **30–34** IGT/NA. **35** IGT/NA (left), Bernhard Diebold, *Habima: Hebräisches Theater* (Berlin-Wilmersdorf: H. Keller, 1928), fig. 7 (right). **36** IGT/NA. **37** IGT/NA (left), The Jewish Museum, New York (right). **38** AAB. **39** BOH, p. 297 (left), BOH, p. 43 (right). **40** AAB. **41–42** RSA. **43** RSA (left), AAB (right). **44–45** RSA. **46** BOH, p. 343. **47** BOH, p. 315.

Veidlinger essay: **Frontispiece** AAB. **50** STG. **51** AAB. **53** AAB. **55** AAB. **56** AAB/RF. **57** AAB/RF (left), BH (right). **58–59** AAB/NA. **60** AAB/NA (top), AAB (bottom). **61** AAB/RF. **62** AAB. **63–65** AAB/AT. **67** AAB/AT.

Harshav essay: **Frontispiece** ARS. **70** RSA. **73** Vladislav Ivanov, *GOSET: Politika i iskusstvo, 1919–1928* [*The State Jewish Theater. 1919–1928*] (Moscow: Izd-vo "GITIS," 2007). **74–75** BH. **76** CGP/ARS. **77–79** ARS. **80** ARS (left), BH (right). **81–82** BH. **84–85** CGP/ARS. **86–87** ARS.

Habima and GOSET: An Illustrated Chronicle: **Frontispiece** ARS. **90** IGT/NA. **91** Collection of Eretz Israel Museum, Tel Aviv/NA. **92** AAB/NA. **93** IGT/NA. **94** IGT/ NA (left), Collection of Eretz Israel Museum, Tel Aviv (right). **95** AAB (top),

Habima National Theater of Israel, Hanna Rovina Collection, Tel Aviv/NA (bottom). **97–101** AAB. **102** RSA. **103** AAB (top left, bottom left), RSA (right). **104–105** AAB. **108–115** STG/ARS/ Photographs © Volker Naumann. **117** RSA. **118** Austrian Theater Museum, Vienna. **119** CGP/ARS. **120–121** ARS. **122** Courtesy of Jacob Baal-Teshuva, New York. **123** ARS. **124** BH. **125–127** ARS. **128** RSA. **129** AAB. **130** IGT. **131** RSA. **132–133** AAB/NA. **135** RSA (top), IGT (bottom). **136–138** AAB. **139** AZP. **141** AAB. **142** AAB (top), BH (bottom). **143** BH. **144** Collection of Merrill C. Berman, Rye, New York/NA. **145** Sovkino/ Photofest, New York. **146** AAB/NA. **147** © St. Petersburg State Museum of Theater and Music/NA. **148** RSA/RF. **149** VI. **150–153** AAB/RF. **155** RSA. **156** AAB/NA (left), BH (right). **157** AAB/NA (left), © St. Petersburg State Museum of Theater and Music/NA. **159–160** AAB. **161** BH. **162–163** AAB/RF. **164** RSA/NA. **165–167** AAB/NA. **168** AAB. **169** RSA. **170** AAB. **171** AAB/AT. **172** AAB/AT. **172–173** BH. **174** AAB/AT (top left, top right), IGT (bottom). **175** AAB. **177** AAB. **178** RSA. **179** YIVO. **180** YIVO (left), IGT (right). **181** STG/Art © Sarah Lebedeva/ RAO, Moscow/VAGA, New York.

Artist Biographies: **183** *Russische Avantgarde, 1910–1930: Sammlung Ludwig Köln* (Munich: Prestel-Verlag, 1986), p. 18. **185** Christoph Vitali, ed., *Marc Chagall: The Russian Years, 1906–1922* (Frankfurt: Schirn Kunsthalle, 1991), p. 2. **186–187** VI. **190** IGT. **191–192** VI. **193** The Jewish Museum, New York (left), BOH, p. 38 (middle), VI (right). **194** BOH, p. 178. **195** AZP.

Timeline: **196** Mendel Kohansky, *The Hebrew Theatre: Its First Fifty Years* (New York: KTAV, 1969), p. 21 (left), RSA (right). **197** BH (left). **198** The Jewish Museum, New York (top), RSA (bottom). **199** VI (left), The Museum of Modern Art, New York/NA (right). **200** BH. **201** BH (top, middle), IGT/ AT (bottom).